LB3051
.S583
cop. 2

Smith, Fred M.

Educational measurement for
the classroom teacher.

177721

DEMCO

EDUCATIONAL MEASUREMENT
FOR THE CLASSROOM TEACHER

FRED M. SMITH   SECOND EDITION

SAM ADAMS

Louisiana State University

HARPER & ROW, PUBLISHERS
New York   Evanston   San Francisco   London

EDUCATIONAL MEASUREMENT FOR
THE CLASSROOM TEACHER, *Second Edition*

Copyright © *1966, 1972 by Fred M. Smith and Sam Adams*

Printed in the United States of America. All rights reserved. No part of this book may be used or reproduced in any manner whatsoever without written permission except in the case of brief quotations embodied in critical articles and reviews. For information address Harper & Row, Publishers, Inc., 49 East 33rd Street, New York, N.Y. 10016.

Standard Book Number: 06-046303-1

Library of Congress Catalog Card Number: 72-174530

To our wives and daughters

LB 3051
.S583
cop. 2

CONTENTS

LIST OF FIGURES

LIST OF TABLES

PREFACE

Like many textbooks, this is the outgrowth of the teaching experience of the authors. We have long felt that the classroom teacher, the central figure in the educative process, should have a somewhat specialized type of background in educational measurement. He is only indirectly involved in certain administrative phases of testing, and research is not generally regarded as his major interest. He is "on the firing line," however, when it comes to testing his own students. The use of teacher-made and standardized tests as tools of instruction is therefore of major interest to him. And it is he who has the thorny task of assigning marks at the end of the grading period. Consequently, we have attempted to concentrate our treatment on those phases of measurement that are of specific interest to in-service or prospective classroom teachers.

The annotated reading lists at the end of each chapter are designed to be timely and applicable rather than extensive. The "Questions and Activities" sections should be noted. Many of the questions in them are based on actual situations that have arisen during our teaching careers in elementary and secondary schools, colleges, and universities. Some of these questions are much easier to ask than to answer.

PREFACE TO THE SECOND EDITION

In the rapidly changing field of educational measurement, published materials, including textbooks, require almost continuous revision. Furthermore, as a text undergoes the test of actual classroom usage, the users constantly find ways to improve presentations. The combined influence of both of these factors led to the revision of this text.

Numerous topics of current importance have been added. Among these are treatments of behavioral objectives and of criterion referenced measurements. Also, each topic has been critically reviewed in the light of its contribution to the achievement of our basic goals. However, these goals have *not* changed. It is our hope for this edition, as it was for the earlier one, that it puts the emphasis on problems of concern for the classroom teachers, both pre- and in-service.

F.M.S.
S.A.

I

INTRODUCTION AND PERSPECTIVE

One of the classics in educational literature, Rousseau's *Emile,* is based on the teaching that occurred when a teacher devoted his entire effort to the instruction of a single student. Probably under such conditions there would be little need for testing; the teacher would be able to appraise the student's achievement on the basis of personal contact. Also, many other aspects of the educative process would be greatly simplified.

Why is education concerned with measuring achievement? For one thing, the "education as a science" movement requires measurement. Also, many phases of the work of a teacher—diagnosing, marking and reporting, passing or failing—would be vastly complicated without measurement. Thus, measurement has become an integral part of education.

Part I of this text is devoted to some basic aspects of educational measurement as it functions in the modern American school and assesses the fundamental nature of measurement, measurement in education, some basic statistical operations, and features of a desirable measuring instrument.

1

FUNDAMENTAL NATURE
OF MEASUREMENT

The dictionary gives several meanings of the term *measure*. However, a basic concept shows through in all of them. This concept is essentially that, when we compare a known quantity with an unknown quantity, we gain information about the unknown quantity. For example, in measuring the length of a pencil, we compare the unknown length (the pencil) with a known length (a ruler or a yardstick). From this we learn that the pencil is, for example, 5 inches long. The number (5) alone does not serve as an adequate description; neither does the unit (inches) alone suffice.

It is only when the pencil is described in terms of a number *and* a unit that information is conveyed.

Measurement in the educational sense is somewhat more complex than is physical measurement. What we are attempting to measure is far more complex than the length of a pencil, and the usual measuring instruments (tests, examinations, and others) are less exact than a ruler. However, educational measurement has the same general goal as physical measurement, namely, the gaining of information about a subject of interest.

IMPORTANCE OF MEASUREMENT IN CONTEMPORARY LIFE

The use of measurement in our lives is so much a part of us that we frequently are not conscious of it. As illustration, consider a family on a vacation trip. Before leaving home, the family plans a route and the distances between stops. Usually these distances are envisioned in terms of hours of travel. This, in turn, requires consideration of the rate of travel, a somewhat more complex measurement involving distance and time. Usually the family will be concerned with the cost of the trip; fuel consumption is estimated, based on the dual concept of distance and gasoline mileage of the car. Planning the daily schedule is based on measurements. Their own rate of speed is constantly compared with speed limits; gasoline prices are noted in various areas; sight-seeing stops frequently involve prices of admission; meal stops confront the family with prices on menus; highway markers frequently indicate distances in miles or fractions of a mile; even the billboards sometimes cite sizes, prices, population, dates, rates of interest, or distances—all of which are forms of measurement. Many of the measurements described lead to evaluations or decisions. Shall we try to go that far today? Can we afford to visit this tourist attraction? What kind of mileage would we get if we used less expensive gasoline? Many such evaluations involve measurements accompanied by judgments.

The physical sciences, such as chemistry and physics, are generally considered to have reached a high degree of development. For example, in the simple case of a free-falling body, extremely accurate measurements are possible. As a result, one can predict with little likelihood of error the pattern by which a body will fall. In such areas as the fundamental particles, measurements have been made with so much precision as to serve as a source of confusion to the layman. Space ventures involve an accuracy of measurement that would have been considered impossible a few decades ago.

In the biological sciences, such as zoology and botany, many areas of study do not lend themselves to exact measurements. Consider the difficulty one would encounter in trying to measure the pattern of movement of a goldfish. Such patterns are extremely complex. Further, because measurements are difficult, predictions of anticipated movements would be highly unreliable. By way of contrast, consider the two types of motion mentioned: the falling body and the swimming fish. In one case, measurements are quite accurate and predictions generally valid; in the other, measurements are very difficult to obtain, and predictions are generally unreliable.

The social sciences are concerned primarily with the most complex of subjects—people. Accurate behavior measurements of an individual or a group are extremely difficult to obtain. As a result, the social sciences, *as sciences*, have not achieved a very high degree of development.

It is apparent that the degree of advancement of a science is largely determined by the accuracy of measurement in the field. To some degree, this explains why a great deal of work still remains to be done to improve measuring instruments in the social sciences.

Measurement in education

A student told his mother that he had made 95 on a test. She was highly pleased. But, as a measurement, what was lacking? Did this mean 95 correct answers? Did the test contain 100 questions? 200 questions? Was the 95 a percent? Was it the highest score in the class? The lowest score? Obviously, this information was incomplete, because the student cited merely a pure number without any means of interpretation. A certain amount of so-called educational measurement has been of this type—a number or letter that actually told little about the subject being measured.

The forward movement in education could not have occurred until progress had been made in the area of educational measurement. For example, suppose one wanted to compare the effectiveness of two teaching methods. This comparison, of course, would be possible only if measuring instruments were available to indicate the amount of progress associated with each method.

A basic point in educational measurement is that such measures cannot occur in the abstract. Thus, a test is not given just to measure generally. It must be designed to measure certain desired outcomes or objectives. Consider, for example, an earlier era when the oral test was widely used. A student might know the subject matter to perfection but might become excited over the type of test and fail completely. Regardless of the objectives of teaching, such a test is essentially a measure of poise, which probably was not one of the objectives at all.

Similarly, during a later period, the essay test was used almost exclusively in educational measurement. This type of test gave a decided advantage to the student who could organize well and write well. These are very important attributes but might not be among the immediate goals for a particular unit of work.

A modern testing program would be likely to use both oral and essay tests, along with a wide variety of other types. The type of test for a particular unit should be determined largely by the nature of the desired learning outcomes.

Progress in testing has been basic to progress in teaching, because some sort of measurement is essential to scientific development. A major forward step has been the realization that testing is a vital part of teaching, rather than a separate operation. Concurrently, the realization has grown that our goals in testing should be identical with those in teaching. This has made it necessary to develop a wide variety of testing techniques, each with its own unique contributions to the measurement process. One of the marks of a good test is that the teacher has used types of items that can measure the degree of progress of each student toward the specific goals of the learning experience. Much more work is needed on this problem of fitting particular test items to specific teaching-learning goals.

MEANING OF MEASUREMENT

As indicated earlier, the term *measure* is used in daily life to describe a variety of activities and outcomes. When a term is used frequently, its meaning often becomes confused. It is necessary, then, to clarify its basic meaning before a discussion of it can proceed very far.

Definition of measurement

Measurement in its broadest sense is essentially the systematic collection and orderly arrangement of information. It implies both the *process* of collecting and ordering the information and the *result* of this process. It may be used either as a verb, *to measure*, or as a noun, *a measure*. It may refer to the unit of measurement or to the instrument used. It may refer to a variety of things measured, such as the height of a door, the size of a woman's foot, a volume of gas, or the social adjustment of a child.

Types of measuring scales

Man attempts to measure many different things and employs many different procedures, devices, and units. Obviously he is not able to measure all things with the same degree of accuracy. Although measurement scales may appear to be precise quantifications, this is not the case. Different kinds of measuring scales are used with different degrees of preciseness. Numerals are used with most scales, but they do not always indicate the accustomed quantitative relationships between 1, 2, 3, and 4. The four most commonly used measuring scales are discussed next in the order of their degree of preciseness.

Nominal scale.   Some targets for the collection of objective information lend themselves to no more than a classification of similar-dissimilar. Such traits as male-female, plant-animal-mineral, left-handed–right-handed-ambidextrous, probationary status-nonprobationary status can be treated only in this manner. The numerals used to indicate classes in this scale have no quantitative meaning. When classifying people on the basis of sex, the numeral 1 may be assigned to males and 2 assigned to females, but this is designed only to indicate a mutually exclusive class.

Ordinal scale.   A more precise degree of measurement is reached when we are able to arrange objects in order of greater-lesser. Many qualitative traits can be arranged in this manner. Girls in a beauty contest are usually ranked in order of those possessing greater or lesser degrees of beauty. The students in a class may be arranged in order of the number of words they can spell correctly, the variety of arithmetic problems they can solve, or the number of questions they answer correctly on an intelligence test.

It should be understood that the numerals used in the ordinal scale indicate only a rank or standing in a group. They do not maintain precise quantitative relationships, nor do they indicate the absolute amount of a trait possessed by any individual in the group. Because this scale is used extensively in education, we should explore its implications further.

Let us suppose that 32 students are ranked on the basis of the number of items answered correctly on an intelligence test. To the student who answers the most items correctly we assign the numeral 1. The next student is assigned the numeral 2, and so on until the student who answers the least number of items correctly is assigned the numeral 32.

What does this scale tell us? What can we say about Student 16, for example? Can we assume that he is half as brilliant as

Student 8 and twice as brilliant as Student 32? The number 16 is twice 8, and 32 is twice 16; but we cannot make either of these assumptions on the basis of this scale. One reason for our inability lies in the nature of the units of the scale. First, they are only rankings, rather than units of intelligence. Second, intervals between ranks are not necessarily equal. If our intelligence test consisted of 75 items, Student 1 may have answered 72 correctly; Student 2 may have answered 70 correctly; Student 3, 69; Student 4, 66; Student 5, 64; Student 6, 60; and so on.

On the basis of this scale, we can say only that Student 16 is more intelligent than Student 17 (if our test is reliable) and less intelligent than Student 15. Because the intervals are not necessarily equal, we cannot even say that he has the same degree of superiority over Student 17 that Student 15 has over him.

In education and psychology special problems in measurement are frequently confronted. We cannot depend on having equal units on a scale, and a meaningful zero is seldom encountered. As a result, a comparison between the achievement of an individual and that of a reference (norm) group is often relied on. For example, on a certain test, a student's percentile rank is computed. This merely compares his achievement with that of a reference group. A rank of 80 tells the student in question that he scored better than did 80 percent of the norm group.

Interval scale.   It can now be seen that a scale with equal intervals would be a distinct advantage over a scale that merely ranked things; the interval scale has this advantage. The amount of difference between adjacent intervals on the scale is the same. A common example is the calendar. Days on the calendar represent equal amounts of time. Equal amounts of time separate 4, 6, and 8 days. This kind of relationship is not true of the ordinal scale.

However, we still cannot make such statements as, "The world is twice as old on the twentieth day of the month as it was on the tenth." The reason for our inability to make such statements is obvious—the world did not begin on the first day of the month. Because zero on the interval scale does not represent an absolute lack of what is being measured, the ratios among the numerals do not hold true.

Ratio scale.   The most precise scale of measurement is the ratio scale. Numerals used in this scale have all the characteristic meanings and relationships of true numbers. This scale has equal intervals, and zero on the scale represents the complete absence of that which is being measured.

Measures of length, weight, and loudness are examples of ratio scales. We can determine, with a great deal of precision, the absolute length of something. Furthermore, we know that an object 4 feet long is twice the length of a thing that is 2 feet long. Unfortunately, as yet we have found no way to apply a ratio scale to the measurement of human characteristics. As has been pointed out, this lack of precise measurements is, in part, accountable for the social sciences' developmental lag behind the physical and biological sciences.

Differences between measurement and evaluation

The terms *measurement* and *evaluation* are often used interchangeably. Though they are closely associated, they are not synonymous. This confused use of the terms can lead to confused practices and result both in poor measurement and poor evaluation. The essential differences between measurement and evaluation, therefore, need to be clarified.

Measurement, the science of collecting and ordering information, should be objective and impersonal. Evaluation involves the *use* of information collected by the process of measurement. If we use a ruler and determine that a desk is 5 feet long and 3 feet wide, this is measurement. If we then say that the desk is too large to go through an 18-inch door, this is evaluation. Tests given in school are attempts to *measure* the achievement of students. Grades assigned on the basis of test results are *evaluations* of students' achievement. Evaluation involves values and purposes. These may vary among individuals and societies. If an evaluation is to be true and honest, it should be based on the most accurate and valid measurement possible. For measurement to be accurate and valid, it must be objective. We might conclude that measurement is scientific in nature, while evaluation is philosophical. Evaluation may involve subjective judgments, but it should be based on clearly defined purposes and objectively collected information.

Educational evaluation is an almost endless task. In addition to grading students, teachers are frequently called upon to evaluate them in such situations as: (1) Should Student A be advanced to a higher grade level? (2) Should B be invited to join an accelerated (or remedial) class? (3) Should I recommend that C be admitted to a particularly difficult college curriculum?

ACCURACY OF MEASUREMENT

In growing up, we come in contact with measures that vary widely in degree of accuracy. Small children find such comparative terms as younger and older, taller and shorter, to be sufficient for their needs. Later, the reading of time to the nearest hour is mastered. Distance measurements usually are very inexact when carried out by small children. A part of the normal growth pattern is improvement in the accuracy of measurements.

An important point, however, is that we never achieve absolute accuracy in measures. Regardless of the exactness we try to achieve, we are, at best, making estimates of quantities. The better the estimate, the more closely it approaches the true value, but we never reach the point at which exactness can be claimed. A measurement that is accurate to seven decimals can always be carried to the eighth or ninth decimal. Acceptance of this principle, however, does not serve as a deterrent in our efforts to improve the accuracy of measures.

Factors affecting accuracy

Several factors influence the accuracy of a measurement. For example, the nature of that which is to be measured is of major importance. Distance is a simple concept and can be measured with a high degree of exactness. But how could you measure your resistance to colds? Would you determine the time between colds? If so, would you measure from the time they began or ended? Would you consider a minor cold in the same way that you would consider a severe one? Would you be concerned with the influence of medication? Obviously, this somewhat more complex type of measurement involves a multitude of problems.

Even more complex types of measures are encountered in the fields of education and psychology. Indeed, we sometimes find it difficult even to define what we are seeking to measure. Preciseness of concepts used is a second factor necessary for accurate measurement. Consider, for example, the measurement of intelligence. If this highly desirable attribute were somehow related to head circumference, length of foot, weight, height, or some other readily measurable characteristic, life would be much simpler for those who try to measure intelligence. However, in the absence of such relationships, it is necessary to resort to indirect measurements, using such techniques as confronting the subject with a problem and observing his success or failure in solving it.

In the earlier attempts to measure intelligence, it was assumed that a single factor was involved. The problem has become even more difficult, however, with the wide acceptance of the theory that there are numerous factors in intelligence. This view is almost inescapable: Teachers and parents constantly observe that some people read well but have trouble with mathematics, draw well but verbalize poorly, reason well but have trouble with reading. There is little room to doubt that the concept of intelligence is a multifaceted one.

A third factor influencing the accuracy of measurement is the nature of the available instruments. Cartoonists occasionally depict the bewildered housewife explaining to the rug salesman that her living room is as long as a couch and two chairs—a classic use of a poor measuring instrument. A dime-store ruler would normally be less accurate than a carpenter's square. The accuracy of chemist's balances varies widely and is generally in direct relation to their cost. It is axiomatic that a set of measures cannot be more accurate than is the instrument used.

Still another factor affecting accuracy is the skill of the person using the instrument. Even the most accurate yardstick is of little value when it is used carelessly or with a lack of understanding. The very *best* of classroom tests will measure poorly if the teacher permits cheating or disorder. A standardized test can be used to yield unreliable results if the teacher fails to observe time limitations. The teacher who is a pacer, a key-jangler, or a knuckle-cracker may destroy the effectiveness of a good test if he drives his class to distraction while they are being tested. The scorer who uses a Form A key to score a Form B test can ruin the results of the best test administered in the most proper manner. Further, even the most accurate measures can be useless if the measurer does not know how to interpret his results.

The inexactness of educational measurements

Measurement is less accurate in education than in many other fields. All the factors affecting the accuracy of measurement contribute to this problem.

Man, the subject of educational measurement, is perhaps the most complex creature on earth. He is so complex, and his qualities are so interdependent, that they cannot be isolated for study. For example, we have not been able completely to isolate hereditary influences from environmental influences. We are not always sure whether we are measuring capacity to learn or desire to learn, nor are we sure of the extent to which each has contributed to our measurement. Furthermore, most of the qualities of people we are interested in measuring for educational purposes cannot be measured directly. We can observe such things as height, length, and weight directly; but such things as intelligence and achievement can only be inferred. All we can do is ask a person to perform under more or less structured conditions and then infer that he possesses more or less intelligence from our observation of his performance.

Another problem that one encounters in using man as a subject of measurement is that of change. A person is continually changing. Each day he is somewhat different from what he was the day before. A desk or table does not change in size or structure from day to day; and if some change does occur in the size of the desk, we can see it and measure the extent of the change. The changes in a person, however, may be so subtle and varied that we cannot see them or know how they may influence our measurement. A person is changed even by the process of being measured.

The concepts of human qualities that we attempt to measure for educational purposes are often so nebulous that they add to the difficulties of measurement. There is often little understanding and agreement among educators as to the meaning and behavioral manifestations of such common concepts as achievement, ability, intelligence, knowledge, and aptitude. There is a genuine need for more precise definitions of concepts used in education, and these definitions should include the behavioral manifestations of the concepts.

The instruments used in educational measurement are not nearly as accurate as those used in fields such as chemistry, physics, or biology. Paper-and-pencil tests usually yield only ordinal scales in the form of percentile units. The limitations of ordinal scales have already been discussed, but those based on test scores have a further limitation. A test is only a small sample of a person's knowledge, skill, or aptitude in a given field. It is probable that a person may score lower than another merely because he does not know the particular items in the sample and not because his general level of knowledge, skill, or aptitude is lower. This is called sampling error. Because of this, a person who scores 66 on a test might actually know more than a person who scores 70. The problem is further complicated by the fact that the items of a test, unlike degrees on a thermometer, do not necessarily measure equal units of knowledge, skill, or aptitude. Because of these limitations, we must conclude that no educational test has yet been developed which is as accurate as a 10-cent ruler.

What of the training and ability of persons who use educational measurements? Again it must be stated that much improvement is needed. Evidence of misused test results may be found almost anywhere tests are used extensively. Many who have taken a course in measurement feel that they do not have enough time to put into practice the principles of test construction and interpretation they have learned.

Educational measurement is a difficult process. All four factors that influence accuracy appear to work against it. At best, measurements in education are only observations of behavior samples from which we attempt to make inferences concerning the relative amounts of a quality possessed by different individuals.

The difficulties discussed here should not lead you to conclude, however, that educational measurement is impossible. Indeed, much improvement has been made during the twentieth century, and great strides in research and development are being made at present. Not much can be done about the complex nature of man, but we can simplify our concepts and make them more concrete. We can improve our measuring instruments, and above all we can learn more about the proper construction and use of tests. This last task is the chief contribution teachers can make toward better educational measurements and fairer evaluations based on them.

QUESTIONS AND ACTIVITIES

1. A teacher's statement that "no measurement is exact" was challenged by a student who asked, "What could be more exact than a dozen apples?" How would you reply?

2. List ten types of measures you use in daily life. Which do you consider to be most exact? Why?

3. In this chapter, the statement is made that "a person is changed by the process of being measured." Do you agree? Disagree? Explain your position.

4. A scientist, parent of one of your students, asks, "If I can measure the weight of an atom, why can't you measure my son's achievement in English?" How would you answer?

5. What do you see as the greatest single deficiency in the field of educational measurement today? Explain.

6. A statement was made in this chapter to the effect that we have not yet been able to adapt the ratio scale to the measurement of human characteristics. What type of scale is obtained with a teacher-made achievement test? How much more would we know about a student's achievement if we could use a ratio scale in its measurement?

SUGGESTED READINGS

Cronbach, Lee J., *Essentials of Psychological Testing* (3rd ed.), Harper & Row, 1970.
    Chapters 1 and 2 in this book present an excellent, easy-to-read overview of test development and use.

Kerlinger, Fred N., *Foundations of Behavioral Research*, Holt, Rinehart & Winston, 1964.
    A sophisticated, yet understandable and interesting, introduction to the scientific approach is to be found in chapter 1. A similar introduction to measurement is presented in chapter 23.

Mehrens, William, and Robert Ebel (eds.), *Principles of Educational and Psychological Testing: A Book of Selected Readings*, Rand McNally, 1967.
    Unit One of this book presents seven articles on measurement theory and scaling which are excellent for the student who wishes to pursue this area in depth.

Thorndike, Robert L., and Elizabeth Hagen, *Measurement and Evaluation in Psychology and Education* (3rd ed.), Wiley, 1969.

An interesting and informative introduction to measurement is presented in chapters 1 and 2.

2

MEASUREMENT IN EDUCATION

The concept of measurement as an integral and vital part of teaching is comparatively new. Educators have had more difficulty in finding the proper role for tests than for any other phase of teaching. Although there has been some progress, much still remains to be done.

HISTORICAL PERSPECTIVE

The classic beginning point for examinations is described in the Old Testament. A test, administered to the Ephesians by the

Gideonites, consisted of a single item: The subject was asked to pronounce the word *shibboleth.* Anyone failing to pronounce it properly was immediately slain. As a measuring instrument, this certainly left much to be desired.

Before the beginning of the Christian era, China used a system of examinations as a means of selecting public officials. This system was beset with weaknesses but seems to have had a stabilizing effect on the Chinese nation. Specifically, it helped preserve unity within the empire by keeping the Chinese language as a standard and by keeping before the people the ancient traditions and customs of their civilization.

Educational measurement before the twentieth century

Testing, as associated with teaching, cannot be said to have started on a particular date. However, it is accepted that Socrates subjected his students to continuous questioning as a means of teaching. Religious groups have used the catechistic, or question-and-answer, method of instruction for many centuries. Informal instruction in the home has relied on this procedure over the years.

In higher education, examinations have been used for several centuries. The examination system was well established in European universities and was adopted by the new institutions established in America. The orations, disputations, and other such activities usually held at commencement exercises served the general purpose of final examinations. Also, extensive use was made of the oral examination. One can sympathize with the college students in early America who were faced with an oral examination held in the presence of up to 20 people. When we add to this the fact that most of the questioning was done by a visiting committee and that the examination might last up to 6 hours, we can imagine the unhappy plight of these students.

Written examinations were introduced in British universities around 1760, but their use in American universities apparently did not begin until about 1830. These early tests were used to evaluate not only a student's progress but also the type of instruction he had received and, to some extent, the proficiency of the instructor.

At the lower levels of education, extensive use was made of oral testing. Also, the copy book, the sampler, and other such devices were used as teaching-testing devices. A formal system of testing was used in the schools of Boston. The school committee's annual inspection of the schools included an oral examination of each pupil. As enrollments grew, oral examinations became unfeasible. Eventually, around 1845, the task of examining students was assigned to a subcommittee, which evolved a series of written tests. These tests were administered by members of the committee (*not* teachers in the schools) during the course of the school year, without advance announcement, and each phase lasted for 1 hour.

Early written tests

When one considers the amount of time and effort required in oral testing, he can understand that the development of the written test was a major forward step in testing. Universities steadily increased their use of written examinations; however, secondary and elementary schools were slower to change. The pioneering work of the Boston group in 1845 did not gain wide acceptance, though it did make a profound impression on some educators. Among these was Horace Mann, who listed the following advantages of the written test over the oral test: (1) It is impartial. (2) It is fair. (3) It is thorough. (4) It prevents favoritism. (5) It prevents interference by the teacher. (6) It makes the results available to all. (7) It reveals the ease or difficulty of the questions.

The growth of enrollments in the schools made adoption of written examinations inevitable. These tests were exclusively of the essay type for many years; but, early in the twentieth century, a series of studies began to cast doubt on the reliability of such examinations. The classic case was the study made by Starch and Elliott, in which 116 high school teachers graded the same geometry test paper. The grades ranged from 28 to 92. Similar studies, made in a variety of subject areas, also revealed a startling lack of consistency. It was shown, for example, that the same teacher, regrading the same paper after a period of several weeks, could not agree with himself. Such studies indicated a definite need for further research and development in testing.

Objective tests

Around the turn of the century, several educational leaders were giving major attention to the development of standardized achievement tests. Most of them made use of various forms of short-answer, or objective, test items. With the publication of research results indicating the unreliability of essay tests, educators tended more and more to switch to the new testing techniques with which they were coming in contact through their use of standardized tests. This led to some rather strange practices for a while, especially in those schools that did not own duplicating equipment. For example, a teacher might stand before his class and read off a seemingly endless list of true-false questions. Since then, as facilities have become available and as our knowledge of tests and testing practice has increased, the short-answer test has become a valuable tool for the teacher.

Some contributors to the testing movement

The list of those who have worked in the testing movement is legion. In addition to the pioneers already mentioned, several others should be singled out for their conspicuous contributions. One such man was Joseph M. Rice, an American physician who, in 1894, produced a list of spelling words as a testing instrument. While it probably would not be accurate to call this a standardized test, Rice used it as though it were. Having devised the list, he conducted an experiment to ascertain the ideal length of a spelling period in school. In a study involving around 100,000 students, he found that a short spelling period (10 to 15 minutes) seemed to be as effective as a much longer one. As you can imagine, these results were greeted with much skepticism.

LIBRARY
L.S.U. IN SHREVEPORT

Another American, E. L. Thorndike, contributed in so many ways to the testing movement that it would be difficult to list the one most outstanding contribution of this man, sometimes referred to as "the father of the testing movement." Thorndike and his students were responsible for many of the early standardized tests and rating scales. In 1908, they produced the Stone Arithmetic Test; the following year, the Thorndike Handwriting Scale. Other tests followed in rapid sequence. Thorndike published material on statistical procedures that were useful in interpreting test results. Through articles, books, contributions to yearbooks, and in other ways, Thorndike did a great deal to further the testing movement in American education.

Reference has been made to the fact that several investigations pointed up the basic limitations of the essay test. One investigator in this area was Robert Ashburn. In 1937, he conducted a study of the consistency with which university lecturers in the general humanities course at West Virginia University graded examination essays. He found a general lack of consistency among the lecturers and a lack of consistency in grades assigned by the same lecturer when the papers were regraded two weeks later. Ashburn's concluding statement is a classic in the field. He says, ". . . The passing or failing . . . of about 40 percent depends not on what they know or do not know, but on *who* reads the papers. . . . The passing or failing of about 10 percent depends, not on what they know or do not know, but on *when* the papers are read."[1]

Tyler and the eight-year study

With the wide acceptance of the objective test as a measuring instrument, educators showed a pronounced tendency to measure factual knowledge alone. There was the ever present danger that isolated facts and minute details might receive undue emphasis in testing, not because they were significant, but solely because they were easy to test. One of those who recognized this danger and

[1] R. R. Ashburn, "An Experiment in the Essay-Type Question," *Journal of Experimental Education,* September, 1938, pp. 1-13.

tried to combat it was Ralph W. Tyler. He insisted that a test was effective only if it measured progress toward achievement of *all* teaching goals. Thus, testing must be linked to the broader and deeper outcomes of learning.

Tyler helped to design the Eight-Year Study, comparing the effectiveness of "progressive" and "traditional" schools by means of a specially devised testing program. He developed a series of tests that went beyond the mere quantification of the number of facts a student could memorize, instead trying to measure the student's ability to comprehend and apply his knowledge. In the procedure used by Tyler's group, no tests were constructed until the group agreed on the objectives of instruction. This approach was, and still is, of crucial importance in testing, since there is always the temptation for a teacher to test students on factual knowledge alone, just because this is a relatively easy type of test to prepare.

Developments since World War II

Under the impetus of World War I, one development of vital importance to testing was the construction and use of the first group intelligence tests, the Army Alpha and the Army Beta. World War II also brought about considerable change in the testing movement, although no innovations comparable to Army Alpha and Army Beta. One important change resulting from World War II was the rapid expansion in the use of multiple-aptitude tests. Another was an increase in the types of aptitude and achievement tests available for use.

The problem of processing, classifying, and assigning millions of service men and women demanded that more appropriate testing procedures be devised. Then elaborate machinery was developed to speed up the classification and interpretation of test data. New counseling and guidance procedures were used to cope with large numbers of people. Perhaps the greatest single advance in testing to come out of World War II was in the area of interpretation and use of test results.

A major development since World War II has been the growing realization that testing is not an end in itself but rather an integral part of teaching. Various leaders have constantly emphasized that we do not have separate objectives in teaching and testing. They have helped effect a change in attitude toward certain types of test items. For example, the true-false test, highly popular a few decades ago, is now much less so because teachers have realized that it is very difficult to test the higher levels of learning with this type of item. Further, despite the previously cited weaknesses of the essay test, it is now widely accepted that many of the goals of instruction (ability to organize and ability to write, for example) can best be tested with this type of item.

In addition to innovations in types of tests, a considerable change has occurred in the use of tests. Despite the fact that no test can serve as a perfect predictor of academic achievement, standardized tests have come to serve a major role in college admissions. And after admission, many college students take tests as part of the placement program within the institution.

Another trend is the growing use of nationwide testing programs. Considerable amounts of testing have been done by Selective Service. Admission to professional schools, such as medicine and law, is frequently influenced by test results. The National Merit testing program, designed to help locate students of outstanding ability who might be in need of scholarship assistance, has become a very large-scale operation. There are many other tests of this sort currently in use.

One of the most recent trends has been the emphasis on testing of observable behavior rather than innate psychological qualities. Many major testing programs do not include an "intelligence test" as such. Aptitude batteries are used instead, because aptitude is a more behaviorally defined concept. This point will be discussed more fully in Chapter 16.

Another aspect of testing on a national scale is in the National Assessment of Educational Progress project. This program tests carefully selected samples in certain subject areas in order to evaluate the educational status of the American population, both student and young adult.

PURPOSES OF MEASUREMENT IN EDUCATION

We have just seen that improved educational practices of the twentieth century have coincided with the development of improved measuring instruments. In many cases, improvement in educational practice has been directly dependent on improved ability to measure educational results. Since an exhaustive treatment of uses of measurement in education would go beyond the scope of this text, we will mention only a few of the more fundamental and general purposes of educational measurement as it may be used by the teacher, the administrator, and the guidance counselor.

The teacher uses information obtained through measurement as the basis for preparation and presentation of learning experiences. Information about students' abilities and past achievements enables the teacher to start at the level of his students and adapt the presentation to their particular capacities. During the learning experience, such information enables the teacher to check on the progress of his students and modify his teaching accordingly. At the end of a unit or learning experience, information gained through measurement aids him to evaluate student achievement and forms the basis for assigning the marks which are such an integral part of education today. Such information gives the teacher not only a basis for evaluating students' achievement but also a standard to gauge his own effectiveness. Is there a particular concept or skill that nearly the whole class failed to develop properly? The trouble may well be some inadequacy in the teacher's presentation. As you can see, this same information furnishes the basis for preparing the next learning experience, and the cycle begins anew.

The school administrator is faced with a large number of problems, many of which can be solved better if he possesses adequate quantitative information about students. Shall the school inaugurate a new remedial or advanced course next year? Do we need ability grouping in the school? How shall students be selected for various ability groups? All these questions pertaining to the curriculum can be answered if the principal has objectively collected quantitative information to guide him. At the district and state level, the relative effectiveness of schools, curricula, and teaching methods can be determined only with aid of objectively collected and properly used quantitative information.

Two basic functions of *the guidance counselor* may be aided by the use of educational measurement: (1) promoting self-understanding and (2) helping students make wise decisions about their future. Quantitative information about a student's specific and general abilities, interests, and past achievements may properly form the basic starting point for both these functions. The information a counselor gains through educational and psychological measurements may also help him make student referrals to agencies better equipped than he is to aid a student with special problems.

This discussion of the purposes of educational measurement has touched only a few of the general uses. The teacher will find innumerable problems arising out of specific situations in which information gained through educational measurement will aid him in finding a solution.

ROLE OF MEASUREMENT IN THE PROMOTION OF LEARNING

Testing has a greater influence on learning than many teachers realize. The type of tests a teacher gives determines the type of studying his students will do and the kinds of learning they will achieve. A teacher may have lofty goals, such as broad perspectives and deep understanding, but if he tests for the ability to recall numerous unrelated facts, this is what his students will study for and learn. If a teacher tests for the ability to apply knowledge, students will go beyond superficial memorizing and study for implications and applications. For the student, at least, testing goals dominate teaching goals.

Another way that measurement influences the learning process is by providing knowledge of results. The results of measurement enable both the teacher and the learner to know if the latter is moving efficiently toward the goals of the course. Is he developing the knowledge and skills desired, or is he developing bad habits or missing significant aspects of knowledge? Frequent measurement can make the learning process more efficient.

Frequent measurement can also sustain the learning process by providing positive reinforcement. Thorndike's *Law of Effect*, paraphrased briefly, states that we tend to repeat those behaviors which result in satisfaction and avoid those behaviors which result in dissatisfaction. Contemporary psychologists refer to those results which are satisfying as positive reinforcement, and those which are dissatisfying as negative reinforcement. A person will tend to continue to engage in behavior which is positively reinforced and avoid behavior which is negatively reinforced. To most students, knowledge of a task well done, good grades and subsequent praise are positively reinforcing results. If test scores and grades are high, learning behavior is positively reinforced, and the student is likely to continue such behavior. If test scores and grades are low, regardless of the amount of effort expended, the student is likely to begin to search for other activities through which he may gain satisfaction.

The implication of these points is that frequent checks on student progress can be more important in promoting learning than midterm or final examinations. This is especially true if the teacher uses these frequent measurements to provide *immediate* knowledge of results, that is, if he grades the papers (tests, homework, reports) promptly and returns them to the students. Time spent in class reviewing returned test papers can be time well spent when the student is able to see and discuss his mistakes.

METHODS OF EDUCATIONAL MEASUREMENT

There are three basic methods of measuring those aspects of human behavior, such as achievement and aptitude, that are of primary concern to teachers. Each method is peculiarly adapted to measuring particular kinds of achievement or aptitude.

The most widely used method is the *paper-and-pencil* test. Verbal, numerical, or spatial symbols are employed in tests to create situations in which the student is to respond. The situations may be highly structured, as in the case of matching or multiple-choice items, or somewhat unstructured, as with the essay item. The paper-and-pencil test is most useful in indicating the possession of knowledge or the development of such mental skills as interpretation, translation, and analysis.

There are many situations in such classes as speech, physical education, and home economics where the ability to perform properly is a primary objective. *Knowledge* of the technique may be determined by a paper-and-pencil test, but knowledge does not assure the *ability to exhibit* the technique. It is one thing to memorize the rules of public speaking but quite another to deliver a speech effectively before an audience. In courses where ability to exhibit a technique under realistic conditions is an important objective, *observation of performance* is the most effective method of measurement. Observation of performance is made more systematic and objective when some kind of rating scale or check list is used.

Rating scales also improve the use of the third method of measurement in education—*production of a sample.* In many courses, the student's ability to use his knowledge and skill to produce a finished product is an important objective. Academic courses such as English stress the ability to use the language to write a theme or report. Classes in woodworking, art, and home economics all stress ability to produce well-constructed products. The most effective way to measure this ability is to ask the students to produce a sample product, i.e., write a theme, paint a picture, bake a cake, or, in the case of student teachers, construct a test.

This text will deal primarily with the proper construction and use of paper-and-pencil tests, because these are used most widely in educational measurement. A special chapter is devoted to the use of the other two methods, however. Educational objectives that they can measure most effectively are quite important, and should be used with the same care and objectivity as the most highly sophisticated paper-and-pencil test.

CRITERION REFERENCED MEASUREMENT

As teachers read the professional literature in education, they are likely to encounter the term *criterion referenced measurement* with increasing frequency. A criterion referenced test is one designed to determine whether or not the student has learned to perform a particular function at a specified level of quality. For example, our criterion might be that after 12 weeks in a typing class the student should be able to type 30 words per minute with four or fewer errors. Our test then would be designed to find out if the student could perform this specific task. Another example of a criterion referenced approach might be the following: We decide that after several weeks of practice, the student should be able to recall the scores of the 100 addition combinations, a maximum of ten errors being allowable. We would then, on test day, present him with the addition combinations and see how many of the scores he could supply correctly.

This is quite different from the traditional or "norm referenced" approach. You may have encountered norm referencing in the standardized tests you have used. You will recall that these tests indicate the level of a student's performance in terms of such things as percentiles and standard scores. Through use of a standardized test, you find out how well a student performs in relation to some group called the "norm group." For example we discover that Johnny, who took an arithmetic achievement test designed for grades 5 and 6 and who made a percentile rank of 65 on that test, did better than 65 percent of the children in the norm group. This approach to measurement is designed to compare a student's performance with that of other students.

Criterion referenced and norm referenced test compared

The basic difference between the criterion referenced and the norm referenced approach to measurement is in the way we look at the results. In the norm referenced approach, we are interested in how Johnny compares with other people, whereas, in the criterion referenced approach, we are interested in how well Johnny can perform a specified function. A very important prerequisite to the use of criterion referenced approach to measurement is that one must state very clearly and specifically just what the criterion is. This involves the use of specific behavioral objectives as discussed in Chapter 6.

The actual *construction* of criterion referenced and norm referenced tests is very similar. The same methods are used; the same types of items are used. The same rules for item writing are applicable. The only difference is in the *purpose* for which items are designed and selected. In the criterion referenced approach, the teacher is primarily concerned with whether or not the items truly reflect the criterion. In the norm referenced approach, the items are designed and selected to reflect the objectives and content of the course and also to give as much *spread* or dispersion, to the scores as possible. Hence, on a norm referenced test, items are selected at about the middle range of difficulty, since these yield widely dispersed scores. The item analysis procedures described in Chapter 12 were developed for use with norm referenced tests.

It should be pointed out that neither approach is inherently superior to the other. There are situations in which one approach may be more *appropriate* than the other. For example, if a guidance counselor is trying to help a student decide which college he should attend, it is helpful to know how the student performs in relationship to the competition which he would meet at different colleges. On the other hand, in situations where specific knowledges and skills can be identified as being necessary for further learning, we need to know the extent to which the student has acquired these knowledges and skills.

Implications for grading

The criterion referenced approach and the norm referenced approach require different procedures when used for assigning grades. The principal purpose in the norm referenced approach to measurement is to spread the scores according to different levels of achievement. Grades are then assigned according to these different levels as revealed by the test. In the criterion referenced approach, the basic purpose of the test is to determine whether the student can perform the stated criterion. His grade is assigned on the basis of the extent to which he can perform the criterion.

We may illustrate this procedure using the original example given in this section. In that instance we used a common criterion in typing: The student should be able to type 30 words per minute with four or fewer errors. The teacher may decide that successful accomplishment of the criterion on a typing test would merit an A, then give B, C, D, or F grades as speed decreased and/or errors increased.

There are two limitations to the criterion referenced approach which must be considered carefully when the teacher contemplates using it in testing situations for which grades will be given. First, it can be used only when it is possible to state a specific behavioral task worthy of separate attention. In some subjects, such as social studies and science, there may be so many small tasks related to general achievement that it would not be feasible to concentrate on the separate teaching and testing of each one. The second limitation is encountered with students who can perform *better* than the criterion. If an A is given for accomplishing the criterion, the incentive to do one's best is reduced for those who can exceed this level of performance. If the teacher sets the criterion high enough to challenge the best students, then it may be unrealistic for the majority of the class. The teacher might set different criteria for different students. However, giving A's for different qualities of performance raises difficult problems, also.

In concluding this section we should point out that the person who is being introduced to the field of educational measurement need not become overly concerned with whether a given test is criterion referenced or norm referenced. To the present time this is more of an issue for specialists in the field. Hence, in keeping with the basic purpose of this text, no attempt is made to treat the topic of criterion referenced measurement in an exhaustive manner.

QUESTIONS AND ACTIVITIES

1. Why do teachers give tests?

2. A teacher recently remarked that if he gave a test, but subsequently taught his class as if the test had not been given, then he should not have given the test at all. Do you agree? Disagree? Explain.

3. The Army Beta test was an interesting innovation. Prepare a class report on the unique features of this test.

4. Teachers are sometimes accused of overtesting. In your own educational experience, have you encountered such teachers? Explain.

5. For your own teaching area, list outcomes that could *not* be tested with (a) oral tests, (b) essay tests, (c) short-answer tests.

SUGGESTED READINGS

Ahman, J. Stanley, and Marvin D. Glock, *Evaluating Pupil Growth* (3rd ed.), Allyn & Bacon, 1967.
     An excellent overview of the place of measurement and evaluation in the school program is presented in chapter 1.

Chauncey, Henry, and John Dobbin, *Testing: Its Place in Education Today,* Harper & Row, 1963.
     This is one of the most understandable general treatments of educational measurement currently available. Every teacher and school administrator could profit from reading it.

Ebel, Robert L., "Improving the Competence of Teachers in Educational Measurement," *The Clearing House,* October, 1961, pp. 67-71.
This article presents the most common faults in teachers' use of tests, with suggestions on how to overcome them.

Ebel, Robert L., "Measurement in Education," *Encyclopedia of Educational Research* (4th ed.), Robert L. Ebel (ed.), Macmillan, 1969.
In an explicit style, this article covers the basic rationale for educational measurement, its development, and its current issues.

Hornacks, John E. and Thelma Schoonover, *Measurement for Teachers*, Merrill, 1968.
This easily read book presents an excellent introduction to the role of measurement in education in chapters 1 and 2.

Karmel, Louis J. *Measurement and Evaluation in the Schools*, Macmillan, 1970.
Chapter 1 of this book presents an overview of the role of tests in education; chapter 2 discusses the principal issues and problems in educational measurement.

Lien, Arnold J., *Measurement and Evaluation of Learning*, Brown, 1967.
Although not treated in depth, the role of measurement and evaluation is presented in a very explicit and meaningful way in chapter 1.

Moughamian, Henry, "General Overview of Trends in Testing," in W. B. Michael (ed.), *Review of Educational Research: Educational and Psychological Testing*, February, 1965.
Chapter 1 should give the teacher a perspective of current developments in the field of educational measurement.

Popham, James W. and T. R. Husek, "Implications of Criterion Referenced Measurement," *Journal of Educational Measurement* 6:1-10, Spring, 1969.

This article is an insightful treatment of the differences between norm referenced and criterion referenced tests, it also considers the different kinds of thinking necessary for interpreting and evaluating criterion referenced tests.

3

SOME BASIC STATISTICAL OPERATIONS

Were you ever confronted with the task of extracting information from a mass of data? It can be a very frustrating experience.

A student teacher had given her class the first test of the school year. Having scored the papers, she recorded the results in her class roll book, in which students were listed alphabetically. The next day, she reported to her supervisor that she had "sat and looked at them for two hours, but they didn't make a bit of sense." This same expression could apply to any person who is confronted with data that requires some sort of "processing."

Essentially, the field of statistics is concerned with procedures for the treatment of data. When properly applied, these procedures permit us to summarize data in a meaningful manner and to draw justifiable conclusions. We will deal here with several basic statistical procedures frequently encountered by classroom teachers.

This treatment of elementary statistics is designed so that, if need be, it can be studied in a purely descriptive way. If, however, there is interest in the computational procedures related to some or all of the statistical measures presented, then the appropriate illustrative material should be studied quite carefully. As a third alternative, if the student is expected to build up some degree of proficiency in these computations, it will be essential that he do some practice work. Problems for this purpose should be drawn from local sources.

USES OF STATISTICS IN EDUCATION

Statistical methods are being used in many areas other than education. Since we are primarily concerned with the classroom teacher, however, this discussion will be limited to those uses that could have application in the classroom.

Assigning marks

Did you ever have a teacher who "graded on the curve"? Many teachers who profess to use this procedure actually do not use it. Some teachers, for example, will list test scores in order from high to low, set up letter-grade brackets on the basis of breaks in the distribution, and assign marks accordingly.

In many situations, this method has yielded results that were satisfactory. Although we recommend a variation of it as a grading procedure, it is an open question whether this could be called "curve grading" in the technical sense. The data have been processed; that is, the scores were arranged in a particular order. Hence, this could be considered a statistical procedure. Yet true curve grading, which we will discuss after a survey of required processes, involves a more sophisticated treatment.

Interpreting standardized test scores

The preliminary work on standardized tests is quite statistical. One of the merits of the standardized test is that so much of this type of work is done for the teacher. A basic knowledge of statistics is necessary, however, if the teacher is to give meaningful interpretation to those items of information which he reads out of the test manual. For example, Johnny's score places him in the top quartile. How can this mean anything to the teacher if he does not know what a quartile is? In short, even the best test manual will be of little value to a teacher whose statistical background is deficient.

Determining the homogeneity of a group

A teacher is often interested in the degree of variability within a class or other group. He might be satisfied with a simple inspection of a set of test scores, after they have been arranged in some type of pattern. Just a comparison of the high score and the low score might suffice for certain purposes. But for many applications, he must use more exact procedures in order to reach any valid conclusions as to the degree of homogeneity of a group.

Comparing performances

Imagine yourself in the position of trying two teaching methods in your classroom. You set up an experimental group and a control group which, as far as you can tell, are equal in ability. You use one method in one group, another in the second group. At the end of the experiment, you use a measuring instrument that is designed to provide the scores you need in order to evaluate the two methods. Again, it would be possible for you to gaze at the scores for hours without seeing the relative merits of the two methods. Would a comparison of the top scores in each group be sufficient for a judgment? or of the low scores? Statistical procedures must, of course, be employed to (1) arrive at a single figure that represents the achievement of each group, (2) compare the two groups in order to see how they differ, and (3) interpret the differences to see if they indicate a significant degree of superiority of one method over the other.

Selecting individuals for specialized treatment

Some high schools are making extensive use of "opportunity classes" for high-ability students. Frequently, one of the criteria for selecting a student is his achievement on certain standardized tests. Sometimes national or regional norms are considered adequate; however, school officials are often more interested in the student's rank on the basis of local norms. Some relatively simple statistical procedures are necessary in order to use this approach. The same general method could be applied in other types of situations in which individuals are selected for some sort of specialized treatment.

For years, colleges and universities have used test batteries, interpreted on the basis of local norms, as a device in counseling new students. For example, students who scored above certain prescribed levels might complete freshman English in one semester instead of two or more.

More recently, colleges have been using achievement test scores for advanced placement, so that a student who shows outstanding proficiency may get credit for courses which he does not take. This, too, usually requires some sort of statistical analysis.

Understanding the literature

Any professional person who fails to keep in contact with the literature in his field is faced with immediate obsolescence. This is as true for a teacher as it is for a doctor or a lawyer. Even a casual examination of major educational journals will illustrate the need for some background in statistics. A tremendous amount of experimentation is under way, and published reports of such experiments are frequently incomprehensible to the person who is deficient in statistical background. Hence, statistics is a necessary tool for the classroom teacher who wants to understand the professional literature in his own field.

THE FREQUENCY DISTRIBUTION

In the processing of scores for purposes of interpretation, one of the most fundamental procedures is that of grouping the scores into a *frequency distribution.* This method consists essentially of setting up a series of *intervals,* each with established limits, then tabulating each score into the appropriate interval.

There is nothing particularly theoretical about a frequency distribution. It is a simple grouping device; however, there are two major advantages in using this method in working with large numbers of scores: (1) it is much more convenient to work with 10 or 15 intervals, each with its designated number of scores, than it is to work with a large number of individual scores and (2) the use of the frequency distribution contributes to accuracy, in that an individual is far less likely to make errors of calculation when he works with the relatively simple structure of a frequency distribution than with a large number of scores.

Constructing the frequency distribution

The construction of a frequency distribution is a straight-forward operation consisting of a few well-defined steps.

1. Determine the range.   In a set of scores, the range is a measure of the "spread" between the highest score and the lowest score. For example, if the top score is 100 and the lowest score is 50, the range is 51. Can you see why the range is 51 instead of 50? In usual applications, we would think of the scores as ranging from 50 *to* 100. But someone actually scored 50 and someone scored 100. So our terminology would be 50 *through* 100, yielding a range of 51. Thus the range is found by adding one to the difference between the high score and low score.

Let us consider a set of scores representing the achievement of a group of high-school seniors on a test of listening comprehension. The scores are: 113, 126, 131, 131, 123, 107, 109, 121, 118, 118, 118, 118, 116, 116, 115, 114, 113, 112, 111, 110, 110, 109, 108, 105, 101, 96, 94, 94, 139, 137, 97, 103, 104, 102, 128, 129, 129, 124, 120, 119, 117, 116, 114, 114, 112, 109, 105, 131, 122, 121. In this group, the lowest score is 94 and the highest score is 139. (139 – 94) + 1 = 45 + 1 = 46, which is the range.

2. Determine the width of the interval to be used.   The range is to be broken down into categories called intervals, which, in turn, will serve as devices for grouping scores. For our purposes, let us establish as a working condition that we should have not fewer than 10 and not more than 15 intervals. If we divide the range, 46, by 10, we find that we could use an interval width of 5 to cover the range in 10 intervals. If we divide 46 by 15, we find that a width as low as 3 could be used. Hence, we could use an interval width of 3, 4, or 5. In our illustration, we have used the latter.

3. Set up the frequency distribution.   The distribution is essentially a set of intervals, so arranged as to include all scores. Having determined an appropriate interval width, we set up the bottom interval to include the lowest score. In our case, the lowest score is 94. Hence, our bottom interval could be 90-94, 91-95, 92-96, 93-97, or 94-98. Any of these would be acceptable, though as a matter of convenience, we use 90-94. Incidentally, this is read "90 through 94" and hence has a width of 5. If in doubt, a bit of finger counting should provide the proof. Having established the bottom interval, we work upward as shown, continuing until provision is made for all scores. Technically, the 90-94 interval begins at 89.5 and ends at 94.5. In some processes, this must be considered, but we usually write the intervals using whole numbers as shown in Table 1.

Table 1
The frequency distribution

Interval	Scores	Frequency
135-139	11	2
130-134	111	3
125-129	1111	4
120-124	1111 1	6
115-119	1111 1111	10
110-114	1111 1111	10
105-109	1111 11	7
100-104	1111	4
95-99	11	2
90-94	11	2
		$n = 50$

4. Tabulate the scores.   Having set up the frequency distribution, we take each score and place it within the proper interval. Then we set up the "frequency" column as shown.

It should be mentioned that grouping scores into a frequency distribution does involve certain risks. For example, the fact that Betty scored 112 or John scored 114 cannot be read from the distribution. All that we can tell is that 10 people scored in the 110-114 interval. Further, we cannot tell from the distribution how the scores are dispersed within the interval. For example, it is not inconceivable that all 10 scores in the 110-114 interval were 110 (or 114). Now that the scores have lost their identity, our best "educated guess" for any one of these scores is 112, the midpoint of the interval. Nevertheless, for many statistical processes, we must use the frequency distribution as a starting point, despite the risks described.

MEASURES OF CENTRAL TENDENCY

One of the most useful types of measures in statistical work is that of central tendency. As the term implies, this is a measure of the tendency of scores to center around a particular point. The prime purpose of central-tendency computation is to arrive at a number that best represents all of the numbers in a group. In this context, you will immediately associate central tendency measures with the more familiar term *average*. When a student says he has an 85 average in a particular course, isn't he saying that this number represents a group of measures in the course? As applied to a classroom situation, measures of central tendency are valuable in (1) helping a student see how his achievement compares with that of a group and (2) comparing the achievement of two groups, or of the same group on two sets of scores. Three measures of central tendency are the mean, median, and mode.

The mean

When a teacher refers to an average, he is very likely to be referring to the mean. In a set of ungrouped scores—that is, scores that have not been tabulated into a frequency distribution—we arrive at the mean simply by adding the scores and dividing by the number of scores. For example, the set of listening comprehension scores cited in our example totals 5749. If we divide this by 50 (the number of scores), we arrive at a mean of 114.98 for this set of scores.

Computing the mean.   The procedure for computing the mean from ungrouped scores is very simple in principle, though it can become quite laborious if we are dealing with a large number of scores. Consider, for example, the endless opportunities for error in adding a large number of scores. As a result, the so-called short method of computing the mean from scores that have been tabulated in a frequency distribution is widely used. This is essentially a three-part operation: (1) we assume a mean, (2) we compute a correction for the assumed mean, and (3) we correct the assumed mean to arrive at the true mean. This procedure is illustrated in Table 2.

The steps that are carried out in this illustration follow:

Table 2

Computing a mean from a frequency distribution

Interval	Frequency	Deviation (x')	Weighted (fx') Deviation
135-139	2	+5	+10
130-134	3	+4	+12
125-129	4	+3	+12
120-124	6	+2	+12
115-119	10	+1	+10
110-114	10	0	+56
105-109	7	-1	-7
100-104	4	-2	-8
95-99	2	-3	-6
90-94	2	-4	-8
	50		-29
			Sum = +27

Assumed mean (midpoint of 110-114 interval) = 112

Algebraic sum of fx' column $(\Sigma fx') = +27$

Correction in intervals units $(c) = \dfrac{+27}{50} = +.54$ of an interval

Correction in score units $(ci) = +.54 \times 5$ (interval width) $= +2.70$

Assumed mean (AM) + correction $(ci) = 112 + 2.70 = 114.70 =$ true mean

1. Assume a mean. Since the assumed mean (AM) is to be corrected, it can be placed in any of the intervals. However, the closer the AM is to the true mean (TM), the simpler is the process of correction. After you select an interval within which you are placing your AM, it is further assumed that the numerical value of the AM is the midpoint of this particular interval.

2. Set up the deviation pattern $(x'$ column). The only reference point is the AM. Consequently, deviations are measured from this point. You will note that the deviation is measured in interval units. For example, the 125-129 interval is removed from the AM

interval by 3 intervals. Positive deviation figures are assigned to intervals above the *AM*, and negative values are used for those below the *AM*. Hence, the −3 assigned to the 95-99 interval simply means that it is 3 intervals below the *AM*.

3. Multiply each interval deviation by the number of scores in this interval. This is a device by which we "weight" deviations to allow for the fact that we have varying frequencies as we go from one interval to another. To illustrate, the 10 scores in the 115-119 interval influence the outcome exactly in the same way as do the 2 scores in the 135-139 interval. The *weighted deviation, fx'*, reflects the combined influence of numbers of scores and deviations from the *AM*.

4. Sum the *fx'* column algebraically. This normally means that we get two subtotals, one for the positive values and one for negative values. The sign of the algebraic sum indicates the direction of the error made in locating the *AM*. A negative value of this sum (abbreviated $\Sigma fx'$) means that our *AM* is too high, so that a subtractive correction will be necessary. The opposite would apply to a positive value of $\Sigma fx'$.

5. Divide $\Sigma fx'$ by the number of scores. In our illustration, a $\Sigma fx'$ of +27 for a distribution involving 50 scores indicated that our *AM* was removed from the *TM* by 27/50 or .54 of an interval.

6. Multiply the correction by the interval width ($c \times i$, or ci). One of the merits of this procedure is that, to this point, our measures have been in interval units rather than score units. This permits us to do most of the computations with relatively small numbers. Now, however, in order to arrive at a *TM* in terms of scores, we convert the correction from interval to score units by multiplying c by interval width.

7. Get the algebraic sum of *AM* and *ci*. In our illustration, we had a positive *ci* product, so we added this to the *AM*. Of course, if we had a negative *ci* product, we would subtract this value from the *AM*.

You will note that our value of the mean, based on un-grouped scores (sum of scores divided by number of scores), was 114.98, while that based upon the *AM* method was 114.70. This is a relatively close check. However, the two differ enough to illustrate the fact that the two methods seldom yield identical results. Can you explain why this might happen?

Some features of the mean.   The mean is widely used in educational work. It is basic to certain other statistical procedures and is relatively easy to comprehend and to explain. But the mean can be very misleading when extreme scores are involved. You have probably heard about the man who drowned in a pool the mean depth of which was only 2 feet. But he drowned in the 10-foot part. As applied to scores, consider five students who, on a 100-point test, had scores of 100, 100, 95, 95, and 10. The mean score is 80, despite the fact that two had perfect and two had near-perfect achievement. Despite this weakness, however, the mean is a valuable measure in many types of school situations.

The median

The median is that point within a set of scores that divides the set in half. In other words, it is the point above which (or below which) half of the scores lie. Sometimes this is an actual score—for example, if we had raw scores of 85, 84, 82, 80, and 75, the score 82 would be the median. But if we had 85, 84, 82, 80, 75, and 70, the median would be 81, midway between the third score and the fourth score.

Computing the median.   Once the scores have been tabulated in a frequency distribution, the approach necessary to compute the median differs from that used to obtain the mean. This process is illustrated in Table 3.

1. Calculate $n/2$. Since we have 50 scores in the distribution, the problem is to locate the point below which 50/2 or 25 scores lie. If we had an odd number of scores, such as 55, the median would still be the point below which half the scores (55/2 or 27.5) lie.

2. Locate the interval within which the median lies. Adding upward, we find that by going through the 100-114 interval, or by

Table 3

Computing a median from a frequency distribution

Interval	Frequency
135-139	2
130-134	3
125-129	4
120-124	7
115-119	11
110-114	9
105-109	6
100-104	4
95-99	2
90-94	2
	$n = 50$

Half the scores $(n/2) = 25$

going to the point 114.5, we have included 23 scores. Obviously, the median lies in the 115-119 interval.

3. Locate the median within the appropriate interval. We need to go far enough into the 115-119 interval to include 2 scores. In order to do this, we make another assumption, namely, that scores are uniformly distributed *within* an interval. As specifically applied here, we assume that the 11 scores are uniformly spaced between the limits 114.5 and 119.5. Hence, we need to move up into this interval far enough to include 2 scores. This means we would go 2/11 or .18 of the way through the 115-119 interval. Note that this is a fractional part of an interval.

4. Convert to score units. Since 5 is the interval width, .18 of the interval (.18 × 5) is .9. This means that the median is located .9 above the lower limit of the interval in question.

5. Locate the median. We do this by adding the .9 to 114.5, the exact lower limit of the 115-119 interval. Hence, the median is 115.4.

In this computation, we have consistently worked upward from the bottom, using the line of reasoning that the median is the point *below* which half of the scores lie. Obviously, we should arrive at the same result if we worked downward from the top of the distribution, interpreting the median as the point *above* which half of the scores lie. Some people use one method to check the other.

Some features of the median.   As another measure of central tendency, the median can be used for some of the same purposes as the mean, such as comparisons between groups or comparisons of an individual's performance to that of a group. The median is sometimes a better indicator of central tendency than the mean, especially in cases where extreme scores are involved. For example, in the illustrative set of scores—100, 100, 95, 95, and 10—we found a mean of 80. The median of 95 is a better indicator of the achievement of the group, though this very same feature can, under certain circumstances, be considered a weakness. Since the median is arrived at solely by *counting* scores, the *sizes* of scores do not affect it; hence wide individual variations can occur within a set of scores without changing the median at all. For example, consider a set of scores in which Student A made 100, Student B made 90, Student C made 80, Student D made 70, and Student E made 60. The median is 80. But if Student A had made 120, Student B had made 100, and Student E had made 10, the median would still be 80. We can see that there are certain situations in which the median is too stable to be an effective indicator of central tendency.

The mode

The least useful of the measures of central tendency is the mode. As applied to raw scores, the mode is simply the most frequently recurring score. After scores have been tabulated in a frequency distribution, the mode is the midpoint of the most populous interval.

Some features of the mode.   Probably the only real strength of the mode is that it is easily obtained; therefore it has been used where crude measures were adequate. For example, some teachers have used the mode as a starting point in what they called "curve grading." Yet, even this simple procedure is not free of possible complications. What happens if the distribution has two modes? or three? Such an event is not unusual at all. Probably the greatest weakness of the mode is its instability. As an example, let us take a small class with these test scores: 98, 96, 94, 92, 90, 90, 87, 83, and 80. What is the mode? What would the mode be if *one* of the students scoring 90 found an error in grading so that his score went to 96?   Such instability drastically curtails the value of the mode as a measure of central tendency.

MEASURES OF VARIABILITY

The measures of central tendency, discussed earlier, perform a vital function in statistical treatment. But meaningful interpretations of data are possible only when measures of central tendency are accompanied by measures of variability.

What and why?   A term that crops up constantly in educational circles is *individual differences.* Although persons who have not taught may think that this term is overused, experienced teachers testify that the one thing you can be sure of in a classroom is variability. Consequently, measures of variability are helpful in working with data.

To illustrate the importance of variability measurement, let us assume that test scores in Group A were 100, 90, 80, 70, and 60. In Group B, the scores were 82, 81, 80, 79, and 78. In each case, the mean is 80. Hence, if we used this measure of central tendency by itself, we would assume that Groups A and B were very similar. Yet, obviously, this is not true. The key difference is in the variability of the two sets of scores.

The range

The simplest measure of variability is the range. This is simply the difference between the highest score and the lowest score, increased by one. In Set A, the range is (100 - 60) + 1 or 41. For Set B, it is (82 - 78) + 1 = 5. In describing these sets of scores, we can now use two measures: "a mean of 80 and a range of 41" and "a mean of 80 and a range of 5."

We have used the range earlier in setting up a frequency distribution. Although the range is sometimes useful as a crude indicator of "spread" or variability, it is not generally a very reliable measure. A particular objection is its instability. For example, if we had a range of 50 in a set of 1000 scores, and we raised the top score by 20 points, the range would increase to 70, despite the fact that 999 scores remained unchanged.

Another difficulty with the range is that there is no basic point of reference. The zero has no particular significance, unless some student actually scores zero. The range takes no cognizance of any measure of central tendency. Rather, it is a number which measures variability—but "variability from what" is difficult to say. This weakness has led to the development of other variability measures that measure deviation patterns around some central reference point.

Standard deviation (σ)

One might wonder why variability could not be measured by an averaging process. For example, with scores of 80, 70, and 60, deviation from the mean of 70 can be shown as follows:

Score	Deviation from Mean
80	+10
70	0
60	-10
	Sum = 0

Despite the obvious fact that two of the scores do deviate from the mean, the algebraic sum of the deviations is zero.

One way around that difficulty is to add the deviations, disregarding signs. Indeed, this type of measure is occasionally used. Another approach is to deal with *squared* deviations. Since squaring either a positive or negative number yields a positive quantity, this procedure yields measures of variability all of which are positive. It is the basic principle in computing the standard deviation (σ).

Computing the standard deviation.   The procedure for computing the standard deviation is illustrated in Table 4.

Table 4

Computing the standard deviation from a frequency distribution

Interval	Frequency (f)	Deviation (x')	Weighted Deviation (fx')	Frequency X Squared Deviation (fx'²)
135-139	2	+5	+10	50
130-134	3	+4	+12	48
125-129	4	+3	+12	36
120-124	6	+2	+12	24
115-119	10	+1	+10	10
110-114	10	0	0	0
105-109	7	−1	−7	7
100-104	4	−2	−8	16
95-99	2	−3	−6	18
90-94	2	−4	−8	32
$N = 50$		$\Sigma fx' = +27$		$\Sigma fx'^2 = 241$

$$c = \frac{+27}{50} = .54$$

$$\sigma = i \sqrt{\frac{\Sigma fx'^2}{N} - c^2}$$

$$\sigma = 5 \sqrt{\frac{241}{50} - (.54)^2}$$

$$\sigma = 5\sqrt{4.53}$$

$$\sigma = 10.65$$

In the computation, N is the number of scores, c is the correction used in converting the assumed mean to the true mean, i is the interval width, and $\Sigma fx'^2$ is the total of the fifth column. The basic formula is

$$\sigma = i \sqrt{\frac{\Sigma fx'^2}{N} - c^2}$$

The standard deviation is frequently associated with the mean. As you will note in Table 4, only the fx'^2 column has been added to Table 2, which was used in computing the mean. Also note in that column only the x' quantity is squared. As mentioned earlier, the basic logic is to process the data so as to measure deviation in positive quantities. It would serve no purpose, for example, to square f, since you cannot have a negative frequency; that is, you cannot have fewer than no scores in an interval. In effect, for each interval, we obtain the entry for column 5 by multiplying the entries in columns 3 and 4; thus x' multiplied by fx' is fx'^2.

It is now possible to add another item of information to that previously known regarding one set of 50 scores: The standard deviation is 10.65. When associated with the mean, we can describe the set of scores as having a mean of 114.70 (central tendency measure), and a standard deviation of 10.65 (variability measure).

An application. One of the most useful applications of σ is in work with the "normal curve." This curve is basically mathematical in its origin. For our purposes, however, it is sufficient to envision the curve as the type of figure that would result if a graph were made of certain types of data.

Let us assume, for example, that height measurements have been made for a very large number of fifth-grade boys. This sample should represent a wide diversity, since members were *not* selected because they were unusually tall or unusually short. These height measures are tabulated into a frequency distribution. Then a graph is made by locating on the x axis the midpoints of intervals, with the frequency of each interval represented by distance along the y axis. Such a graph should approximate the bell-shaped curve shown in Figure 1.

It is easy to think of situations in which we would not be able to assume normality. For example, if we had limited our sample of fifth-grade boys to those who were exceptionally tall or exceptionally short, our distribution would not be normal in that the peak of the curve would be shifted to the left or right. Would you get a normal curve of test scores if you gave a tenth-grade class a test designed for third grade? or if you gave the third grade class a test designed for tenth grade? Generally, we can assume normality if the measure in question is well suited to the factor being measured.

The normal curve has been studied intensively by mathematicians. A few features are of interest in educational work. For example, if we establish limits at Mean $+1\sigma$ and Mean -1σ, we will have included 68 percent of the area under the curve. As applied to scores, this means that approximately 2/3 of a normally distributed set of scores will lie within the range Mean $\pm 1\sigma$. About 95 percent lie within the range Mean $\pm 2\sigma$, and for all practical purposes, all of them lie within Mean $\pm 3\sigma$.

A specific application of these concepts is in the oft-mentioned but seldom understood process of curve grading.

Let us assume that a set of scores is approximately "normal." Since the range of Mean -3σ to Mean $+3\sigma$ includes essentially all the scores, we can think of a 6σ distance between these two limits. Since the usual letter-grade system includes five categories (A, B, C, D, F), each grade would be assigned a width of 1.2σ (a 6σ distance divided into 5 equal parts). We establish the mean as the midpoint of the C range (Figure 2), the n measure .6 of a σ (half of 1.2) above and .6σ below the mean. The limits thus established determine the range of scores to be assigned C marks. Scores lying above the C range up to $+1.8\sigma$ are assigned B marks. Scores above 1.8σ are A's. Scores below C and down to Mean -1.8σ are D's. Those below the D limit are F's. In a normal set of scores, this procedure yields 3.5 percent A's and F's, 23.8 percent D's and B's, and 45 percent C's. As you can see, if you were to

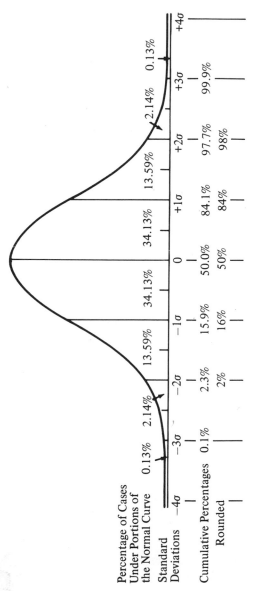

Figure 1.
The normal curve.

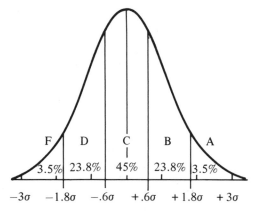

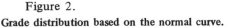

Figure 2.
Grade distribution based on the normal curve.

use curve grading you would start out by computing the mean and standard deviation for your set of scores.

A word of caution is necessary about the use of curve grading. As a point of departure, we assume that we have a normal distribution. As the group involved becomes smaller, this assumption becomes more and more difficult to justify. Consequently, grading strictly on the basis of the normal curve is of limited use in classes of ordinary size, but it is frequently useful where large groups are involved, such as college freshman classes of 200 to 300 members.

MEASUREMENT OF RELATIONSHIPS

There are occasions when it is important to know whether or not any relationships exist between two sets of measures. This type of measurement is called *correlation*, the inference being "co-relation" or mutual relationship. Types of measures that we would expect to demonstrate some degree of correlation include age and height, weight and height, age and weight. But it is seldom satisfactory simply to conclude that a relationship exists, without ascertaining its degree. Consequently, a more exact approach is needed.

Since quantitative measures essentially involve numbers, systems have been devised to measure relationships numerically. The *coefficient of correlation* represents such a measure. Let us consider, for example, the relationship between the diameters and the circumferences of circles. If you list a group of identifiable circles in the order of increasing diameters, then prepare a similar list for circumferences, the two lists will be identical, since without exception, larger diameters are associated with larger circumferences. This would constitute a perfect positive correlation, the coefficient being +1.0. The sign merely signifies that the two measures vary in the same direction. On the other hand, suppose you apply varying pressures to an enclosed volume of a gas. As the pressure increases, the volume correspondingly decreases. This, too, would constitute a perfect correlation in that there are no exceptions; however, in this case, increasing pressure results in decreasing volume. Hence, the coefficient of correlation would be −1.0. If we are concerned with two sets of measures that are totally unrelated, we would expect a coefficient of zero. In practice, we seldom encounter any such extreme cases. Far more commonly, we deal with intermediate coefficients: +.35, −.52, −.28, or others of this type. While the formal interpretation of such coefficients is beyond the scope of this book, many of these measures indicate that there is a real relationship but that it is by no means perfect; that is, there are exceptions to the relationship pattern.

Computation.   A very useful method of computing a coefficient of correlation is that developed by Karl Pearson. Sometimes this coefficient is referred to as a *Pearson r.*

To illustrate this operation, let us consider the group of 50 students whose results on a test of listening comprehension we have used earlier. We also know each student's grade average, based upon a 4-point scale. These results are shown in Table 5.

In order to compute the coefficient of correlation, or, in effect, to compute the degree of relationship between listening

Table 5

Grade averages and listening comprehension scores of 50 students

Student Number	Listening Comprehension	Grade Average
1	126	3.27
2	131	4.00
3	131	3.87
4	123	3.06
5	107	3.24
6	109	3.09
7	121	3.45
8	118	2.98
9	118	2.73
10	118	2.77
11	118	3.29
12	116	2.81
13	116	3.36
14	115	2.84
15	114	2.71
16	113	2.51
17	113	2.67
18	112	2.91
19	111	2.25
20	110	3.51
21	110	2.41
22	109	2.36
23	108	2.81
24	105	2.29
25	101	2.21
26	96	1.98
27	94	1.57
28	94	1.73
29	139	4.00
30	137	3.81
31	97	1.79
32	103	2.19

Table 5 (Continued)

Student Number	Listening Comprehension	Grade Average
33	104	2.15
34	102	2.03
35	128	2.76
36	129	3.76
37	129	3.10
38	124	3.64
39	120	3.31
40	119	3.07
41	117	2.97
42	116	3.19
43	114	2.77
44	114	2.69
45	112	2.55
46	109	3.21
47	105	2.37
48	131	3.74
49	122	2.67
50	121	2.79

comprehension and grade averages, we use a *scatter diagram* (sometimes abbreviated as *scattergram*), in which we show one frequency distribution along the horizontal axis and the other along the vertical axis. Such a computation is shown in Table 6.

The computation of the coefficient of correlation is carried out in a series of operations, as shown in the following steps based on the listening comprehension-grade average problem.

Operation 1.   Prepare the scatter diagram. You will note that, by arranging the grade-average distribution along the horizontal axis and the listening comprehension scores along the vertical axis, we have established a large number of cells. When we tabulate an individual's data in a cell, we are classifying him on both

Table 6
Scattergram based on listening comprehension scores and grade averages (50 students)

	Grade Averages															
	1.50-1.74	1.75-1.99	2.00-2.24	2.25-2.49	2.50-2.74	2.75-2.99	3.00-3.24	3.25-3.49	3.50-3.74	3.75-3.99	4.00-4.24	fy	y'	fy'	fy'^2	$\Sigma x'y'$
135-139										(20) 1 20	(25) 1 25	2	+5	+10	50	45
130-134									(12) 1 12	(16) 1 16	(20) 1 20	3	+4	+12	48	48
125-129						1	(3) 1 3	(6) 1 6		(12) 1 12		4	+3	+12	36	21
120-124					(-2) 1 -2	1	(2) 1 2	(4) 2 8	(6) 1 6			6	+2	+12	24	14
115-119					(-1) 1 -1	5	(1) 2 2	(2) 2 4				12	+1	+10 / +56	10	5
110-114				2	5	2			1			10	0	0	0	0
105-109				(2) 3 6		1	(-1) 3 -3					7	-1	-7	7	3
100-104			(6) 4 24									4	-2	-8	16	24
95-99		(12) 2 24										2	-3	-6	18	24
90-94	(20) 2 40											2	-4	-8 / -29	32	40
fx	2	2	4	5	7	10	7	5	3	3	2	$\Sigma=50$		$\Sigma fy'=+27$	$\Sigma=241$	$\Sigma=224$
x'	-5	-4	-3	-2	-1	0	+1	+2	+3	+4	+5					
fx'	-10	-8	-12	-10	-7	0	+7	+10	+9	+12	+10					
fx'^2	50	32	36	20	7	0	7	20	27	48	50	$\Sigma=50$	$\Sigma=+1$	$\Sigma=297$	$\Sigma=224$	
$\Sigma x'y'$	40	24	24	6	-3	0	4	18	18	48	45					

Computations based on the scattergram in Table 6

Listening Comprehension (x axis)

Correction $(c_x) = \dfrac{1}{50} = .02$

Standard Deviation $(\sigma'x) = \sqrt{\dfrac{297}{50} \; -(.02)^2}$

$$= \sqrt{5.94}$$

$$= 2.44$$

Grade Averages (y axis)

Correction $(c_y) = \dfrac{27}{50} = .54$

Standard Deviation $(\sigma'y) = \sqrt{\dfrac{241}{50} \; -(.54)^2}$

$$= \sqrt{4.53}$$

$$= 2.13$$

Correlation Coefficient $(r) = \dfrac{\dfrac{\Sigma x'y'}{N} \; -c_x c_y}{\sigma'_y \sigma'_x}$

$$= \dfrac{\dfrac{224}{50} \; -(.02)\;(.54)}{(2.44)\;(2.13)}$$

$$= \dfrac{4.47}{5.20}$$

$$= .86$$

---

sets of measures. For example, if we place a tally in the upper left-hand cell, we are classifying a person as having a listening comprehension in the 135-139 interval and a grade average in the 1.50-1.74 interval. This process is continued until each individual's data is tabulated.

Operation 2.   Assume a mean for each distribution. In our illustration, we assume the mean for listening comprehension as the midpoint of the 110-114 interval. For grade average, we assume the mean as the midpoint of the 2.75-2.99 interval. For convenience, we mark the assumed mean intervals with heavy lines.

Operation 3.   Set up each distribution as we did in computing mean and σ. For example, for listening comprehension scores, we set up columns y', fy', and fy'^2. Identical procedures are carried out for grade averages, as shown in the rows below the scatter diagram.

Operation 4.   For each set of data, compute c and σ as shown. For purposes of simplification, we leave both c and σ in interval units, that is, in neither case do we multiply by interval width.

Operation 5.   For each cell containing scores, establish a product deviation. This is the quantity shown in parentheses in the upper right-hand corner of the cell. To illustrate this, the upper right-hand cell deviates from the assumed mean 2.75-2.99 by five intervals. Also, it deviates from the assumed mean 110-114 by five intervals. Hence, the product deviation for this cell is 25. This is repeated for each cell. You will note that some of the product deviations are negative. As you probably recall, this type of graph is divided into four quadrants,

$$x \; \frac{2 \quad | \quad 1}{3 \quad | \quad 4}$$
$$-\; y$$

In quadrant 1 both x and y are plus; in quadrant 2, x is minus and y is plus; in quadrant 3, both x and y are negative; in quadrant 4, x is plus and y is minus. Consequently, when xy products are used, they are plus for quadrants 1 and 3, and minus for quadrants 2 and 4.

Operation 6.   For each cell containing scores, compute a weighted product deviation. This appears in the lower left-hand corners of cells. It is obtained by multiplying the product deviation of each cell by the number of scores in that cell.

Operation 7.   Compute $\Sigma x'y'$ for columns and rows. For the listening comprehension scores, the entry in the $\Sigma x'y'$ column for each interval is simply the algebraic sum of the weighted product deviations for that interval. For example, in the 120-124 interval, the $\Sigma x'y'$ entry is $6 + 8 + 2 - 2$, or 14. This operation is repeated for each column (shown below the scatter diagram) and each row (shown to the right of the scatter diagram).

Operation 8.   Having computed the $\Sigma x'y'$ entry for all rows, we total the column ($\Sigma x'y' = 224$ in the illustration). This is repeated for the columns, and our total is again 224. This serves as a check, since failure to achieve the same $\Sigma x'y'$ total for columns and rows indicates that an error has been made.

Operation 9.   Compute r. The formula is

$$r = \frac{\dfrac{\Sigma x'y'}{N} - c_x c_y}{\sigma'_x \sigma'_y}$$

It should be repeated that, as shown in the illustration, c_x, c_y, the σ_x and σ_y are all in interval units. They have not been multiplied by interval width. Our substitution is

$$r = \frac{\dfrac{224}{50} - (.02)(.54)}{(2.44)(2.13)} = .86$$

In view of the size of the sample (50), there is every reason to believe that a coefficient of correlation of .86 indicates the existence of a true relationship between the two sets of measures.

Uses.   The coefficient of correlation is a valuable tool in educational research, test development, and many other aspects of school work; however, it is not as extensively used by classroom teachers as are some of the other statistical operations considered here.

Some of the major uses of the coefficient of correlation are the following:

1. The simple determination of relationships of the type used in the illustration. It is not unusual, for example, to have a faculty study group in a particular school make use of this device in answering their own questions.

2. Determination of test reliability and validity. For example, in a test-retest procedure for checking reliability, you would have two scores for each student. A correlational procedure would indicate the degree to which the test agreed with itself in the two sets of scores. In validating one test against another, a similar technique could be used. Here, the coefficient of correlation would indicate the degree to which one test measured what the other measured. This is discussed further in Chapter 4.

3. Prediction of future performance. If it has been ascertained that a relationship exists between two sets of measures; but if for some subjects, only one set of measures is available, it can serve as a basis of prediction for the other set. In our original illustration, the existence of an *r* of .86 between listening comprehension and grade averages means that if for some other members of our group we knew only grade averages, we would have some basis for predicting the scores they would make on the test of listening comprehension and vice versa.

Probably, to a classroom teacher the chief value of some background knowledge regarding the coefficient of correlation is that it contributes to his ability to keep abreast of research in his own field. Published reports of statistical research appear constantly in professional journals. Many of these studies involve correlational procedures. In reading them, the teacher can benefit only if his own background permits him to follow the report with a fair degree of understanding.

QUESTIONS AND ACTIVITIES

1. A student asks you why curve grading is not more widely used. How would you explain?

2. Would you consider it to be an indication of good teaching if there is a high coefficient of correlation between intelligence quotients and the grades received by students in your class? Explain.

3. How would you interpret a negative coefficient of correlation between intelligence quotients and grades received by students in your class?

4. Would it be possible for the mean salary of teachers and administrators in a school to be higher than the salaries of most of the teachers? Explain.

5. It has been said, "Half the people in the United States are below average." Do you agree? Explain your position.

6. Would you expect a greater standard deviation among a randomly selected group of adults or among a group of college seniors? Explain.

SUGGESTED READINGS

Adkins, Dorothy C., *Statistics: An Introduction for Students in the Behavioral Sciences,* Merrill, 1964.

The teacher interested in learning more about statistics should find this book very helpful. It thoroughly, yet understandably, covers the concepts used most frequently in education. The "self-testing" feature should prove a valuable aid.

Bartz, Albert C., *Elementary Statistical Methods for Educational Measurements,* Burgess, 1963.

This is a practical introduction to basic statistical procedures commonly used with tests.

Bradley, Jack I., and James N. McClelland, *Basic Statistical Concepts,* Scott, Foresman, 1963.

This little book is designed to be used as a self-teaching device in learning the basic statistical concepts and computations.

Diederich, Paul B., *Short-Cut Statistics for Teacher-Made Tests,* Evaluation and Advisory Service Series No. 5, Educational Testing Service, 1960.

As its title indicates, this bulletin presents some simplified techniques involving statistical procedures of use to teachers. It is available free from ETS.

Downie, N. M., and R. W. Heath, *Basic Statistical Methods* (2nd ed.), Harper & Row, 1965.
This is a good introductory text in the field. It thoroughly covers the fundamental concepts and procedures.

Franzblau, Abraham N., *A Primer of Statistics for Non-Statisticians,* Harcourt Brace Jovanovich, 1958.
This is an excellent overview of the meaning and computation of the measures of central tendency, variability, and correlation. The average teacher should be able to understand it with little difficulty.

Smith, G. Milton, *A Simplified Guide to Statistics for Psychology and Education* (4th ed.), Holt, Rinehart & Winston, 1970.
This is an easy-to-follow presentation of basic concepts and procedures.

FEATURES OF A DESIRABLE
MEASURING INSTRUMENT

A major purpose of this work is to help the teacher construct good tests for use in his class. We will be discussing proper techniques of writing objectives, writing items, administering tests, and scoring them. You may reasonably wonder, "What characteristics are we trying to build into a test through the application of all these techniques?" In this chapter we hope to clarify this question by presenting the basic criteria by which a test may be evaluated.

What is a good test? A test may be said to be good or poor depending on the extent to which an affirmative answer can be given to the following question: "How well does the test measure what it is intended to measure?" The first part of that question, "How well does the test measure . . ." involves the concept of test *reliability*. The second part of the question ". . . what it is intended to measure," involves the concept of test *validity*.

RELIABILITY

Reliability may be defined as the degree to which a measurement indicates the true amount of the thing measured. In this context reliability, accuracy, and consistency are all similar terms. Let us consider the meaning of the concept further through the use of a few concrete examples. If you placed this book on a set of scales that indicated its weight as 8 pounds, you might doubt that this was an accurate indication of its weight. Similarly, if the best student in your class made the lowest score on an achievement test, you might doubt that this was an accurate indication of his achievement. In both these examples you would not be entirely willing to *rely* on the measurement as an accurate quantification of the thing measured.

Reliability is a fairly simple concept to understand in the measurement of physical characteristics such as height and weight. Envision if you will a co-ed whose weight is usually 105 pounds. One morning she steps on the bathroom scales and they show her weight as 130 pounds. She may immediately doubt the accuracy of the scales. She is not willing to *rely* on this reading as an accurate measure of her true weight. If, however, repeated measures of her weight, even with different sets of scales, continue to show 130 pounds, she would probably have to conclude that her weight had increased and that she really did weigh 130 pounds. When we get *consistent* results over many repetitions of a measurement, we are usually willing to *rely* on the results as being *accurate* indications of the thing measured.

When we move into the realm of human behavior, however, the approach to reliability becomes a little more complicated. Suppose someone were to ask you, "What is your bowling ability?" How would you reply? Would you say something like, "My bowling ability is exactly 172 pins per game"? or "Every time I bowl a game I knock down 172 pins"? You probably could not be this definite. A behavioral concept, like bowling ability, is not nearly as definite, nor as stable, as a physical concept such as the weight of something.

To determine your bowling ability, you could bowl a large number of games, determine your average score per game and the standard deviation of your scores. Let us assume that you have found your average score per game to be 160 pins and the standard deviation of your scores to be 5. Now if someone asks about your bowling ability, you can say something like, "My average game is 160 and about 2 games in 3 I will bowl between 155 and 165." In this statement you have presented a much more realistic and *reliable* estimate of your bowling ability than would be the case if you cited a figure based on your performance during a single game.

Now let us move into the realm of behavior measured by most educational tests. How confident can we be that a student's score on a single achievement test accurately reflects his true achievement? To check on the reliability of a person's bowling score, we can ask him to bowl a large number of games and obtain a mean and standard deviation. But it would not be feasible to ask him to take the same test over and over again. How can we estimate the reliability of a single test? Well, if we cannot ask one student to take the test a great many times, we can ask a large number of students to take the test twice. We then note the consistency of the students' scores on the two administrations. To the degree that each score on the second administration is about the same as his score on the first, the test is reliable.

If you remember the discussions in the previous chapter, you may recall that the statistical technique used to determine the relationship between two sets of scores is correlation. This is the principal procedure (but not the only one) used by standardized test publishers to determine the reliability of their tests.

Methods of determining test reliability

Although correlating two sets of scores obtained on the same students with the same test is the principal *statistical* procedure used by test publishers to indicate reliability, slightly different procedures may be used to obtain the scores. The selection of the procedure to be used is influenced by the type of test being investigated and the purposes for which it will be used. The different approaches should be understood by test users.

Test-retest.   When the same test is administered to the same group of persons on two separate occasions, this is referred to as the test-retest method. The greater the degree of correlation between the two sets of scores thus obtained, the greater is the reliability of the test. If the correlation coefficient is high, we are willing to rely on the test as a fairly accurate indication of the thing measured.

The test-retest method is of particular significance when the stability of scores over a period of time must be considered. If, for example, the test is to be used to help high school students plan their vocational or college careers, we need some indication that the information obtained today about the students will not be drastically different from that which might be yielded two or three years from today.

This method has the disadvantage of repeating the same questions to the same individuals. One of the undesirable outcomes of this is the *practice effect,* the general improvement of scores as a result of taking the same test a second time. Because the practice effect helps some persons more than others, it complicates the procedure and the interpretation of results. Furthermore, since the two administrations are usually only a few days apart, some persons remember the way they answered the questions the first time.   Others have looked up answers to questions they did not know. If a longer period of time is allowed to elapse between the two administrations—several months, for example—then the persons may have changed so much that we would not expect them to score the same. This is quite certain to be the case in achievement testing. Therefore, other procedures may be more appropriate.

Equivalent forms.   The equivalent-forms method is used to overcome some of the problems associated with the practice effect. In this method two equivalent forms of the same test are given to the same group of persons, and their scores on the two forms are correlated. The period of time between administration of the two forms may be considerably shorter than that necessary with the test-retest method. In some cases both forms may be administered on the same day, or if the test is not too long and the persons are mature enough, both forms may be administered at the same sitting.

This method is used to determine the degree to which two different forms of the same test yield the same scores. Form A and Form B of the same test are supposed to measure the same thing. The items supposedly cover the same material and behaviors at the same level of difficulty. If we wish to measure the growth of the group of students over a period of time, we may test them at the beginning of the period with Form A and the end with Form B. If the two forms are not equivalent, however, a determination of growth is not possible. Therefore, when two forms of a test are available, information concerning their equivalency is necessary.

Use of the method is limited, however, because equivalent forms of a test are not always available, hence it is not always feasible to undertake two administrations. Because of the limitations of both the test-retest and the equivalent-forms method, a third procedure is widely used by test publishers. This is called the split-half method.

Split-half.   In the split-half method the test is administered to a group of persons only once. The test is then divided into two equal parts and each part is scored as if it were a separate test. The split is usually made on the basis of odd-numbered versus even-numbered items. The coefficient of correlation between the two sets of scores is then determined. The higher the correlation coefficient, the greater is the reliability of the test.

A statistical technique used with the split-half method is the Spearman-Brown formula. This formula is used to compensate for the fact that reliability is reduced as test length is reduced. When the test is split into two halves, each is only half as long as the total test. The Spearman-Brown formula indicates how much higher the reliability coefficient would be if it were based on the total test, rather than on two parts which are only half as long.

Caution should be used when interpreting reliability coefficients based on the split-half method, since it has certain special limitations. It cannot be used with speed tests or with tests that measure different kinds of ability or knowledge. It is less meaningful than the other two methods when evidence of score stability is important. Aptitude tests are used in schools to predict future performance of individuals. In such cases it is more useful to have an indication of the stability of test scores over a period of time than to know only that both halves of the test are consistent with each other. Finally, the split-half method usually results in higher coefficients of reliability than either of the other two methods.

Kuder-Richardson method.   When studying the reliability of a standardized test as reported in the examiner's manual, you may come across a statement such as this: "All reliability coefficients were determined by using Kuder-Richardson formula 21." The Kuder-Richardson formulas are statistical techniques for determining the reliability of a test from one administration, as in the case of split-half reliability.

Also similar to the split-half method, this procedure reveals only the extent to which a test is internally consistent. It does not indicate the stability of scores, nor the equivalency of forms. The Kuder-Richardson method *differs* from each of the other methods in the statistical technique employed. Each of the others uses correlation. The Kuder-Richardson formulas are themselves statistical procedures. However, the reliability coefficients yielded are interpreted in the same general manner as are those obtained by other methods. The higher the coefficient the greater is the accuracy of the test.

Factors affecting reliability

At this point you may well ask, "What determines the reliability of a test?" Generally, these five factors affect it: (1) clarity of test directions and items, (2) conditions of testing, (3) length of the test, (4) range of ability of persons tested, and (5) accuracy of scoring.

If the directions and questions of a test are unclear, then obviously students will not know what knowledge or ability they are supposed to demonstrate nor how they are supposed to demonstrate it. We could not expect a test to yield high reliability coefficients if its directions and items were subject to different interpretations by the persons taking it. Nor would we be willing to rely on the results of such an instrument.

Perhaps you have taken tests at times when conditions of testing were so distracting that you were unable to work effectively. Such things as heat, light, and noise can operate to cause the best-prepared student to do poorly. The emotional and physical state of the student taking the test can also aid or hinder his efforts. The test administrator should strive to be aware of all conditions that may operate for or against students during testing.

If two tests are equal in all other respects, the one that is longer will be more reliable. However, there are limits beyond which this statement will not hold true. Clearly, if a test were lengthened indefinitely, a point would be reached where any increased reliability due to increased length would be offset by a decrease caused by fatigue of the student.

Due to the nature of the statistical technique involved in calculating reliability (correlation), the greater the range of ability of the persons tested, the higher will be the reliability coefficient.

The best-constructed tests will yield low reliability if not accurately scored. Scoring is not too great a problem with short-answer tests that may be objectively scored by hand or machine.

Scoring problems are encountered most often with essay tests, and certain personality and performance measures where the examiner must make judgments about the quality of a student's response. Low scorer reliability is one of the most serious problems encountered with essay tests.

Reliability and the teacher-made test

Reliability discussed as an abstract concept may be of little value to the college student or in-service teacher seeking to improve his own test. Such a person may well ask, "Now which of these methods can I use to establish the reliability of the tests I construct for my classes?" Surely a teacher's test ought to be reliable. Yet, the methods of establishing reliability discussed above are hardly feasible for a teacher with little statistical background and even less time for such investigations. What can the classroom teacher do?

The teacher should give careful consideration to the factors that affect reliability. He can be sure that the items and the directions are simple, direct, and clear. He can maintain testing conditions that are optimum for concentration. He should make the test sufficiently long to allow the student to demonstrate the full extent of his knowledge and skill. After the test has been given, he can score it carefully and accurately. At the lower grades, he can test frequently and reserve judgment until sufficient data have been collected.

A teacher can actually check the reliability of his own tests by a simple procedure of ranking. Suppose that a teacher plans to give four tests on a unit of material, with all tests covering similar objectives. He may logically expect his best students to be at the top on all four tests, his average students to be in the middle, and his poorest students to be at the bottom. If, after ranking the students on each test, the teacher finds that on each test the rankings are similar, then he may assume that he has obtained consistent and reliable results.

Table 7
Rankings on three tests

Name	Test 1	Test 2	Test 3
Bob	1	3	21
Carol	2	1	2
Fran	3	1	2
Abbie	4	4	1
Madge	4	6	6
Jack	6	9	5
Dan	7	6	4
Jane	8	5	8
Adam	8	10	9
Sal	10	14	7
Zeke	1	10	18
Jim	11	19	10
Sue	11	8	12
Cal	14	12	10
Ann	15	12	13
Norma	15	15	14
Janet	17	16	14
Sarah	18	20	20
Sam	19	18	16
Fred	20	21	19
Peter	21	17	17

Table 7 portrays the actual rankings on three tests given to a class in educational measurement. Note small individual changes in rank and one large shift. Bob, who ranked first and third on Tests 1 and 2, fell to last place on Test 3. (Subsequent investigation revealed that he was ill during Test 3.) Some individual variations may be expected. However, you may note that generally the top quarter remains in the top on all three tests, the bottom quarter remains there, and the average group is in the middle on all three tests.

This procedure is probably followed by many teachers. If the results on a test are inconsistent with those which the teacher has come to expect from a class, such results are usually viewed with a great deal of skepticism. However, actual rankings on similar tests make the procedure purposeful and concrete. Such a procedure can only be used when tests cover similar material and similar objectives. It would not be logical, for reliability purposes, to compare a literature test with a grammar test, for example.

Before leaving the concept of reliability, consider its influence in the grading process. Since no test yields completely precise results, any attempt to assign a grade based on one test is an extremely hazardous procedure. Many teachers assume that a difference of only one score on one test represents an actual difference in achievement. This is rarely true. The situation is even worse when an essay examination is used. Essay tests have several desirable features, but high reliability is not one of them. In the primary grades, tests must be rather short due to the limited attention span of young children. This tends to make test results at the primary level even less reliable than at other levels. At all levels it is best to reserve judgment until a sufficient number of test scores are available to indicate student achievement. Even when data based on several tests are used, the teacher should be conscious of the lack of complete reliability and should look for score differences large enough to represent actual differences in achievement. Procedures for assigning grades are discussed in detail in Chapter 13.

VALIDITY

What does the test measure? Does it measure what I want to measure? Does it measure what I teach? All these questions pertain to validity.

If we again use an analogy from the physical sciences, validity is a relatively simple concept. The assumption that a yardstick measures length or that a quart container measures liquid volume is rarely questioned. Such things as length, or volume of a liquid can be seen and measured directly. Therefore we can be pretty certain of just what we are measuring.

In the area of social sciences, however, you may remember that many personal characteristics of interest to teachers can neither be seen nor measured directly. Did you ever see a person's knowledge, understanding, or intelligence? The only thing you can see is a person's behavior. You can see him responding in various ways to different kinds of questions and directions. From a person's behavior (which *can* be seen) we *infer* certain characteristics (which *cannot* be seen). The question of validity then becomes: "What kinds of behavior will allow me to infer which characteristics?" For example, if I ask a pupil to list five individual rights guaranteed in the first ten amendments of the United States Constitution, will this allow me to infer that he "understands" the implications of these rights for his daily life? About all you can actually infer from such a behavior is that the pupil had memorized five items. This problem of having to make inferences from observed behavior to unobserved characteristics means that we must define in behavioral terms each concept that we would have our pupils learn. Having done this, we are in position to evaluate the validity of teacher-made tests.

Furthermore, tests only *sample* a student's proficiency or knowledge. From this sample we generalize about his degree of proficiency in the whole field. Sometimes our samples (tests) accurately represent the unit of study as we have tried to teach it. When this is the case, our test is a valid one, and our evaluations based on it are well founded. When a test does not accurately reflect what we have tried to teach, and when other factors, such as writing ability or poise, are allowed to influence the student's test score, then the test is not valid.

Finally, it should be noted that the same test can be valid for some purposes but quite invalid for others. Hence, validity is not only concerned with the test itself; it also deals with the question of proposed usage—the question of "valid for what?"

Types of validity

Because tests are constructed and given for different purposes, the actual approach to validity may differ slightly, depending on the purposes of the test. However, the basic concept remains the same. Let us look briefly at the major approaches to test validity.

Face validity.   This is determined by examination of the title and appearance of the test. A test may be said to have face validity if it appears to measure what its author says it measures.

This is obviously a rather superficial approach to validity. There have been tests that did not measure what they appeared to measure at all. A thorough examination of the test, often involving various statistical procedures, is necessary to determine what it actually measures. However, face validity can be a significant feature in the public relations of testing. If we inform our pupils that they are to take an arithmetic test, they probably will imagine problems involving numerals. If we then give them a test of arithmetical reasoning with no numerals, they may feel that we have not been entirely honest with them and become suspicious of our motives and our tests. Such suspicions could put our entire testing program in a negative and undesirable light. Furthermore, if the pupil is suspicious, anxious, and even hostile, reliability of the test results will be adversely affected. Generally speaking, the pupil should know why he is asked to take a test and on what he is being tested.

Content validity.   This is one of the most important features of testing for the classroom teacher. The reason for this is that content validity is an essential feature of achievement tests, and these are the kinds of tests teachers themselves construct. An achievement test is valid if it actually measures those things the teacher tried to teach. All teachers do not teach alike, nor do they all emphasize the same objectives. A test may be valid for one teacher and not valid for another.

There are actually two dimensions to content validity. These are (1) the actual content, or *subject matter,* covered by the test and (2) the *behavior* required of the student in responding to the items of the test. For example, 80 items of an American history test might be distributed according to subject matter with 20 items each: colonial period, American Revolution to Civil War, Civil War to World War I, and World War I to present. Using such information, a teacher could determine if the subject-matter emphasis was similar to his own. However, he could not determine completely the validity of the test, since no information is given concerning the behavior required in responding to the test items. Must the pupil only recall facts he has memorized about each historical period, or must he demonstrate higher mental skills? This question is just as important in establishing the validity of an achievement test as is the question of the subject matter covered by the test.

Of course, when a teacher is constructing his own tests he should build validity into it. This can be done if he knows not only what content his pupils were supposed to have learned, but also what they were supposed to be able to do with the content.

As the teacher writes items for his test, he should know from which area of subject matter each item is drawn and what behavior is required in responding to it. Obviously a teacher can construct valid tests only if he knows explicitly what his pupils are supposed to accomplish. He must know what *behaviors* they are supposed to develop, not just what content they are supposed to cover. Clear statements of behavioral objectives are so essential to the testing process, as well as the teaching-learning process, that Chapter 6 is devoted entirely to their construction.

Concurrent and predictive validity.   Predictive validity is an important feature of aptitude and intelligence tests because these types of tests are usually given in schools for the purpose of prediction. We often assign pupils to advanced, average, and remedial classes on the basis of scores made on an aptitude test. In so doing, we are predicting that those who score high on the test will learn quickly and easily and that those who score low will have more difficulty in learning. High aptitude for a given endeavor is usually defined as the ability to learn quickly and to perform well in the area.

When a test is used for this purpose, the question of validity becomes specifically, "Do persons who make high scores on this test really learn more readily than do persons who make low scores?" To state the question technically we might ask, "To what extent do scores on this test correlate with grades (or some other index of performance) in this course?" The higher the correlation coefficient between scores on the test and grades in the course, the more confidence we have that it is a valid predictor of performance. It should be noted here that a test might be a valid predictor of performance in one school and not in another. Therefore, it is a good practice to validate a test at the local level before too much faith is placed in it.

Concurrent validity is estimated by the same procedure that is used with predictive validity, that is, correlation of test scores with grades or some other criterion of performance. The only difference in the two procedures involves the time at which the test scores and grades are obtained. In predictive validity, the test scores are obtained at one time (usually the beginning of the school term) and the grades are obtained at another (usually the end of the school term). In concurrent validity the test scores and grades are obtained at the same time—*concurrently*. Concurrent validity is used at any time we may wish to obtain some kind of empirical evidence of validity such as a correlation coefficient.

It is fairly easy to see that if we wish to check the validity of an English or a mathematics aptitude test, we can correlate it with grades obtained in the course. If we wish to validate a general scholastic aptitude test, we can correlate it with grade-point averages. Suppose we have an intelligence test, however. With what could we correlate scores on an intelligence test to prove that it really did measure intelligence? Would we use school grades? Some people might not accept the definition of intelligence which this would imply, that intelligence is the ability to make an A in school. How about correlating scores on this test with scores on an older intelligence test whose validity has already been established? This is sometimes done. The problem that immediately rises from this practice is, "How do we know that the *older* test is valid?" If it was validated by yet an older test, and that one validated by another even older test, then we may ask, "How was the original one validated?" Obviously it is difficult to prove that a test which attempts to measure some innate or internal quality like intelligence really does measure that which it purports to measure. Some other approach to validity is needed—perhaps more of a rational than an empirical approach. This is embodied in the last type discussed: construct validity.

Construct validity.   This approach is of greater concern to educational researchers than to teachers, since it is used more often in the experimental study of innate qualities, such as personality and intelligence, rather than with tests of direct concern to teachers. Let us explore its meaning and application with two concrete examples.

Suppose we have developed a test designed to screen out neurotic applicants from an important training program. We might assume that the test should agree with the diagnosis of a competent psychiartist. On the basis of this assumption, we would have the psychiatrist conduct a diagnostic interview with each person in a group seeking psychiatric aid and rank them according to their degree of neurosis. We would then give our test to this same group of persons and correlate the "neurosis scores" yielded by the test with those obtained by the psychiatrist. If we found that there was a positive relationship between the diagnosis of the test and that of the psychiatrist, then we would conclude that our test was valid, at least to the extent of the relationship.

In studying a new test of general intelligence, we might assume that general intelligence would increase rapidly in young children, less rapidly in adolescents and level off at maturity. We then could give the test to groups of people who varied in age from 3 to 30 years and plot the average scores of each age group on a line graph. If the resulting curve confirmed our hypothesis, we conclude that we have evidence of the test's validity.

These two examples, it is hoped, indicate enough of the nature and role of construct validity to enable the classroom teacher to read and understand the ordinary test manual. Those wishing to do research into innate psychological qualities will need a more sophisticated course than that for which this text is designed.

USABILITY

A third major feature to be considered in determining the quality of a test is its usability or practicality. A test may be highly reliable and valid, yet not be practical for use in a school testing program. Such is the case with the individually administered intelligence tests, such as the Stanford-Binet and the Wechsler scales. These tests possess high reliability and validity but are impractical for schoolwide testing programs for several reasons: (1) They can be administered properly only by a person trained in the process; (2) they can be administered to only one person at a time; and (3) they require from 1 to 1-1/2 hours to administer. These tests are used, therefore, only in special cases where the need for the information is believed to justify the time and expense required to collect it. The aspects of practicality implied in this example include administration, interpretation of scores, scoring, and cost.

Administration.   A test that is to be used in a schoolwide testing program should be sufficiently simple so that any teacher who is willing to study the directions can administer it. If an instrument requires a graduate psychologist or psychometrist to administer it, then it will naturally have limited use in a school.

Interpretation of scores.   To be used in a schoolwide testing program, a test should not require a graduate psychologist to interpret it. Certain personality measures usually require interpretation by persons specially trained in their use, but most aptitude and achievement tests yield scores that the average teacher can understand if he is willing to study the test manual. (Test score interpretation is never a simple matter, regardless of the test. Teachers should be cautious about using a test with various "gimmicks" that tend to oversimplify the meaning of the scores.)

Scoring.   A test should be easily scored if it is to be useful in a schoolwide testing program. Some individually administered intelligence tests and personality assessments require expert judgments to be made in scoring. Most group tests use some form of answer sheet that can be easily scored, either by hand or machine. In the primary grades, answer sheets cannot be used very effectively, and the scoring of tests at this level may take a little longer than at other levels, but it can still be done objectively.

Cost.   Cost must be considered in any educational program. It is a factor in purchasing tests, but it should be considered *only after* the other important features have been investigated. If two tests are equally reliable, valid, and simple to administer, interpret, and score, then obviously we should choose the one that costs less. It is certainly not sound economy, however, to buy a test of low reliability and validity merely because it does cost less than a better one.

QUESTIONS AND ACTIVITIES

1. Describe tests you have taken that, in your opinion, had low reliability.

2. What are some specific steps you could take in preparing a test for your class so as to assure a valid test?

3. Examine the manuals for several standardized tests and prepare a report on the methods used in establishing reliability.

4. The statement was made in this chapter that "... psychological qualities of interest to teachers are measured neither *directly* nor *absolutely.*" What does this statement mean?

5. Why is content validity of much greater importance in achievement tests than in aptitude tests? What type of validity is of primary importance in aptitude tests? Why?

SUGGESTED READINGS

Brown, Frederick G., *Principles of Educational and Psychological Testing,* Dryden, 1970.
> Chapters 3 through 7 treat the concepts of reliability and validity in a considerable degree of depth. However, the student wishing to pursue the topics should be able to follow the discussions with a minimum statistical background.

French, John W. and William B. Michael (co-chairman), *Standards for Educational and Psychological Tests and Manuals,* American Psychological Association, Inc., 1966.
> This pamphlet was prepared by a joint committee of the American Psychological Association, the American Educational Research Association, and the National Council on Measurement in Education. As its title indicates, it presents specific standards for the guidance of test publishers and users.

Green, John A., *Teacher-Made Tests,* Harper & Row, 1963.
> Reliability, validity, and usability are discussed in chapter 7 in terms the teacher can understand easily.

Lyman, Howard B., *Tests Scores and What They Mean,* Prentice-Hall, 1963.
> Some specific aspects of validity and reliability are discussed in chapter 3 in terminology that teachers can readily understand.

Mehrens, William A., and Robert Ebel, *Principles of Educational and Psychological Measurement,* Rand McNally, 1967.
> Units Three and Four present reprints of seventeen articles on reliability and validity. The student wishing to read in more depth will find these to be excellent references.

Thorndike, Robert L., and Elizabeth Hagen, *Measurement and Evaluation in Psychology and Education* (2nd ed.), Wiley, 1961.

A thorough discussion of validity, reliability, and practicality is presented in chapter 7.

USING TEACHER-MADE TESTS

By far the greatest portion of a teacher's testing activity centers around tests he constructs himself. Standardized tests are usually administered once or twice a year, while teacher-made tests may be administered several times a week. The proper use of teacher-made tests is essential to effective teaching. Part II, the longest section of our book, is intended to help the new teacher perform this important function well.

It should be evident that teacher-made tests are designed to measure achievement, rather than intelligence or other personal and social qualities. In Chapter 4, the measurement of achievement was discussed in general terms to give the prospective teacher a perspective of this function. Each chapter in Part II discusses one of the major steps in measuring achievement or in using a specific type of test item.

These five steps should be followed in the proper measurement of achievement:

1. Determine the objectives of instruction.
2. Construct an instrument to measure achievement toward these objectives.
3. Administer the instrument.
4. Interpret the data.
5. Evaluate the instrument.

Chapter 5 deals with procedures; Chapter 6 deals with objectives; Chapters 7-11 deal with the construction of instruments; Chapter 12 deals with evaluating the instrument; Chapter 13 deals with interpreting the data.

5

PROCEDURES IN ACHIEVEMENT TESTING

According to theory, there are two essentials for good measurement: An accurate instrument must be available; this instrument must be used with the requisite skill. In measuring achievement, however, there is at least one other requirement: The measurer must be clear about what he is trying to measure. Frequently, this last requirement is not met in teacher-made measures of achievement.

Achievement may be defined as a change in behavior in a desired direction. Learning, or, in the educational sense, achieving, results in changed responses to certain types of stimuli. The development of new ways of behaving—the modification of earlier modes of behavior—is so closely associated with learning that the term *learning outcomes* is sometimes applied to such behavioral changes.

Achievement can occur in a variety of ways and at a variety of levels. Some illustrations are (1) improving physical skills, such as handwriting, playing tennis, and sewing; (2) increasing knowledge, such as learning the members of the President's Cabinet or the operations necessary to enact a law; (3) increasing understanding, such as the prediction of outcomes under a given set of conditions; (4) increasing one's appreciation for good music, art, or literature; and (5) developing new and broadened interests. Obviously, some types of learning outcomes (such as an increase in knowledge) are fairly easy to measure, while others (such as music appreciation) are considerably more difficult to measure.

This chapter is designed to present an overview of the principal procedures that should be followed in measuring achievement with teacher-made tests.

DETERMINE THE OBJECTIVES OF INSTRUCTION

Objectives usable in test construction must, in some ways, be different from those with which many teachers have been familiar in the past. First, they must be stated in terms of observable student behavior. It is the student who achieves, and it is he who will take the test to demonstrate this achievement. An objective, therefore, must be stated in terms of behavior that you will ask the student to demonstrate.

Second, the objective must be specific. Good citizenship, for example, is a highly desirable objective; but it is much too broad to use in test construction. Only after it has been broken down into the component aspects of good citizenship could it be used in test construction. Furthermore, we would expect such a broad objective to be accomplished during the total school program, rather than in any one grade, course, or unit of instruction.

PLAN AND CONSTRUCT AN INSTRUMENT

As was mentioned earlier, the first step in measuring achievement is to establish a clear statement of objectives. When this has been completed, the teacher is ready to proceed with construction of a test to measure achievement of these objectives; however, a basic plan of approach needs to be developed before the actual construction of test items begins. Some features of such a plan are described next.

Test all desired outcomes of instruction.   It is easy to allow a statement of objectives to become meaninglessly abstract. If a statement says that a major goal has been to teach an understanding of the principles of operation of a lift pump, then it is incumbent upon the teacher that he test for *understanding,* rather than a memorized sequence of steps. In view of the fact that certain outcomes of instruction are easier to test than others, there is always the tendency to test achievement on these easier levels— not because they are more important, but solely because they are easy. All of the desired instructional outcomes should be reflected in the test.

It is inherent in the testing process that different objectives call for different testing devices. For example, would you attempt to measure skill in sentence construction with a true-false test? Would you attempt to cover a wide diversity of topics with a time-consuming essay test? In cases where a number of outcomes are to be measured, you will find that different types of test items are needed to measure effectively the different types of achievement. Hence, many teacher-made achievement tests incorporate a variety of types of test items.

Testing emphases should parallel teaching emphases.   Probably few practices in test making are more obnoxious to students than to be tested on trivia that did not appear in instruction. Teachers can usually prevent this if, during the process of test making, they keep in mind which topics were given major emphasis in teaching and which topics were merely passed over. Some teachers systematize this phase of test making by drawing up a rough outline of the time distribution of instruction, then using this as a general guide for test emphasis. Such an outline is often called a table of specifications. The construction and use of a table of specifications is covered in Chapter 6.

Test construction should be started early.   It is doubtful whether good tests ever result when the teacher is trying to beat a deadline. Ideally, a test, after it has been completed, should be reread and criticized later. Frequently, poorly worded questions can be restructured as a result of such an examination. Some teachers ask a colleague to evaluate tests in order to improve the wording, especially in test directions. The only way a teacher can have confidence in the merit of a test is for him to have it ready early enough to give it a thorough and critical appraisal before it is administered.

Mechanics should be kept as simple as possible.   The construction of specific types of test items will be discussed later. It is a general principle, however, that simplicity in structure is highly desirable. For example, the directions should be clear, direct, and complete. Some students demonstrate an amazing degree of ingenuity in misunderstanding directions.

Another application of this principle is in the wording of test items, which should be straightforward, without verbiage. For example, a teacher who uses double negatives in true-false questions is probably testing the ability of students to cope with double negatives—and little else. A student faced with a long, complicated item was heard to remark that he didn't know the answer, because he couldn't figure out what was being asked. The teacher who wrote this item, regardless of his intent, was actually testing the student's proficiency in certain verbal skills.

Did you ever take a test in which multiple-choice, true-false, and completion items were mixed together? Happily, this is seldom done. There is no purpose—other than that of confusion—to be served by such a procedure. In order to keep the efforts of the student centered on the content rather than on the incidental procedure, it is highly desirable to have all items of a particular type grouped together in a test.

One other way in which attention to mechanics can improve the usability of a test is in the method the student uses to record his answers. Answers written in a column are far easier to check than answers randomly scattered over a page. If the students are mature enough to use a separate answer sheet designed to fit the test, the teacher can check responses without having to turn pages.

ADMINISTER THE TEST

Of course, the key operation in the measurement of achievement with the teacher-made test is the actual use of the instrument by students. Regardless of the quality of the test, poor planning of the administrative process can lead to spurious results. A few features worthy of special attention are discussed here.

Time of testing. One beginning teacher explained his method of scheduling tests by saying that he gave them when he had to. Although this procedure may have served to keep the teacher from violating certain administrative requirements, it fell far short in the effective use of testing. Ideally, when should a test be given? A common-sense answer is that a test should be given when it can make a unique contribution to the teaching-learning process. In most situations, the judgment of the teacher is the best indicator of this time. The practice, fairly common in some schools, of "giving a test every Friday" or of "giving a test the last

Thursday of the month" is somewhat hard to defend. Suppose the date, automatically fixed by such a formula, finds the class in the middle of a major unit of work. Certainly it would be psychologically sound to defer the test until the unit had been completed. If a teacher has no choice but to conform to some preset pattern of testing, probably the best procedure is to limit the material covered to major units that have already been completed. This reduces the chance of having the "monthly test" cover parts of units, some of which may have been fragmentized the previous month. In essence, it is good practice to test after predetermined units of material have been covered rather than after a predetermined period of time.

Another problem in the timing of major tests has to do with the scheduling of other events within the school. How effective would you expect a test to be if it is administered late Friday afternoon, just before the football team is to meet its traditional rival? Some students have enough self-discipline to handle such a situation, but many do not. Generally, it is considered to be good testing procedure to avoid major tests just before or just after major distractions.

Should students participate in setting the date of the test? There is nothing wrong with such a procedure, in case it can be kept under proper control. But the authors recall the case of a teacher who permitted students to waste literally hours of class time during a school year in endless—and pointless—debate on when they would take a test. If you find that, on your preferred date, many members of your class will be away on a field trip that is part of another course, it is only a matter of common sense to find a more appropriate date for your test. Frequently, it will be adequate in such a situation to give the class a choice between two dates, with attention to the fact that some students would love to debate the matter at length. What happens if some or all of your students have several other tests scheduled for your preferred date before your announcement? There is little to be gained by stacking another one on top of an already heavy load. Are you giving your test to measure student achievement, or to demonstrate your inflexibility to faculty colleagues?

Place of testing.   The usual place for test-taking is the regular classroom. Indeed, in many respects, this is the best place, since it provides an environment with which the student is familiar. It is not unusual, however, for several class-size groups to be combined for certain tests. These groups would usually exceed the capacity of an ordinary classroom. Whatever the location of the room, it should be comfortable as to light and temperature. It should be large enough so that students can be well spaced; this frequently forestalls any efforts to cheat during the test. It occasionally happens that a lunchroom or gymnasium will be used as a site for testing. Frequently, these places are noisy, which can be a definite distraction to students. Further, the surroundings are associated in the minds of the students with physical activity or with food, so that the "academic atmosphere" would probably be lacking. If large groups are to be tested, an oversized classroom makes a better place than a lunchroom or gymnasium.

Another requirement of a good location for test-giving is a minimum of distractions outside the room. If the windows overlook a construction project, a busy playground, or even a major traffic artery, some students will find the view more interesting than the test, with a resulting reduction in measured achievement. Every effort should be made to reduce the effect of this type of distraction.

Conditions of testing.   The student has a right to be tested under conditions that allow his work to be a true indicator of his achievement. Frequently, this is not the case, and sometimes the teacher unwittingly contributes to the confusion.

At the risk of seeming a bit negative, let us consider some of the practices of certain teachers that have led to reduced achievement on tests. One is the endless talker. He passes out the tests, points out corrections that should be made, warns students about cheating, tips them off about certain trick questions, tells them where they should be by midperiod, and finally, lets them start. Yet, at regular intervals, he breaks in to tell the time or to warn students that there are only 20 minutes left and generally disturbs the operation. With the fond hope of being helpful, this teacher is producing the opposite effect. Another problem along this line is the pacer. In view of the fact that, at the moment, he is not actively teaching, this teacher works off his nervous energy by walking or jingling keys and coins. If things get too dull for him, he cracks his knuckles or hums a tune. The captive audience, already laboring under an unusual strain, will, no doubt, be even more nervous as a result of such test administration.

Let us now consider the role of the teacher in setting up good testing conditions. Students should be seated rapidly and quietly as they arrive. If reseating is necessary, this, too, should proceed quietly. After everything is in readiness—all students properly seated, with pencils sharpened and desks cleared of books and papers—the tests are distributed. If corrections are to be made, this should be done as soon as students receive their tests. Then the role of the teacher becomes one of silent vigilance. He should take a position permitting him to view the entire group and then, as far as possible, stay there. If questions arise, the student should raise his hand, and the teacher should, as silently as possible, move to the student, answer the question in a soft voice, then return to his position. Incidentally, the presence of a vigilant teacher will usually forestall any attempts at cheating.

Students also frequently contribute to poor testing conditions. A few cases that need to be guarded against are (1) the student who wants to tramp noisily to the pencil sharpener during the test; (2) the student who blurts out a question from his seat, thereby disturbing the entire class; and (3) the student who wants to "negotiate" with the teacher during the test. This last case is typified by the student who calls the teacher over to ask, "Is this right?" after every answer. One special problem in this regard is the early finisher. Because of the wide variation in speed of test-taking, a test designed so that all students can finish in the designated time will be completed by some students by midperiod. The elementary teacher can usually divert the early finisher to another task, but junior and senior high teachers are usually "stuck" with him. He is a potential source of disturbance, simply because he has time on his hands. One useful device is to have ready a supply of reading matter (even "funny books" have been used), so that when the student turns in a test paper, he is given another task to keep him occupied until the testing period is over.

In general, then, good testing conditions prevail when the room is quiet and as free of distractions as possible, with the teacher available, alert, and inconspicuous. Only under such conditions are we reliably testing achievement. Otherwise, we are testing primarily the student's ability to perform under adverse conditions.

INTERPRET THE TEST DATA

The results obtained from administering teacher-made achievement tests can be interpreted in a wide variety of ways. Interpretations can vary from a highly statistical approach, described elsewhere in this book, to a simple entry of a score or letter by each student's name. The proper approach in interpreting test data is determined largely by the teacher's purpose or purposes in giving the test. The primary purpose for which most teacher-made tests are given is the assignment of grades. Many teachers properly prefer to attempt no interpretation on the basis of one test. They prefer to maintain a record of raw scores until the end of a grading period, then transfer the composite score into a predetermined system of interpretation.

A well-constructed teacher-made test can also serve, to a degree, as a diagnostic test. If the teacher looks for patterns of errors, then he is interpreting the test results diagnostically. For example, an arithmetic test involving work in addition, subtraction, multiplication, and division could serve not only as an overall measure of achievement but could also yield valuable information as to which of the fundamental operations were giving trouble.

Some teachers are inclined to overinterpret test scores. Several decades ago, the giving of number grades was more common than it is now. One teacher gave a first grader 93.5 on a report card. Obviously, he had a great deal more faith in the exactness of his tests than was justified. Under the very best of circumstances, achievement testing is relative. For example, what teacher can say, "This is *exactly* what my class should have achieved during this testing period"? Since tests are almost always based upon a sampling, can we be sure that a sample other than the one actually used would have yielded the same result? While many other such questions could be asked, they would add up to this very simple principle: We should not put more faith in the accuracy of a test than is actually justified.

EVALUATE THE TEST

Some teachers begin every test from a new beginning. Others find it feasible, by using proper security measures, to reuse certain portions of tests. Unfortunately, there are a few teachers who use the same instrument, year after year, without the slightest change.

Many teachers insist that "a good test is hard to come by." They frequently use a revised version of an earlier test or selected questions from such a test. Note that the test in question undergoes constant revision. Reuse of the same test for a prolonged period, even if adequate security measures are taken, would tend to freeze the teaching into a fixed pattern. In other words, the test would dominate the teaching, since the teacher would always try to cover those points that are on the test.

In evaluating a test, a few key questions need to be asked. One is simply, "How well did it measure?" If the scores were extremely high, the test was too easy for the class. If the scores were very low, the test was probably too difficult. If the scores of individual students differed markedly from their normal pattern of achievement, the test may have contained trick questions, subject to varying interpretations. Many other such points involved in evaluating a test are discussed in Chapter 12.

Another point that must be given attention is the practicality of a test. Some relevant questions are the following: Was the test too long? too short? Was the print clear and readable? Were the directions clear on such matters as placement of answers? Did the administration of the test require frequent interruptions of the students? *How would you handle the student who doesn't finish a test in the allotted time?*

As a result of such an examination of a test, the teacher should arrive at certain specific points that need improvement. These should be noted on a file copy of the test, so that the information will be available when needed.

It should be emphasized again that, in evaluating and improving a testing instrument, the teacher is *not* indicating his intention of using the same test throughout his career. But as long as he can, by continuous revision, keep improving it as an instrument, it would be good testing procedure to use this approach. Of course, if the time comes that "the copyright is violated" and students obtain copies, there is no alternative but to start over with a new test.

QUESTIONS AND ACTIVITIES

1. On the basis of your experience as a student, compile a list of instances in which teachers have practiced poor test administration.

2. How would you, in your own classroom, deal with these problems: (a) the early finisher; (b) the student who does not finish a test; (c) the student who writes, as an answer to a particular question, "Never heard of it"; and (d) the student who says the test was unfair?

3. On the day that a major test is scheduled, a student brings a note from his mother asking that he be excused from taking the test, because his activities as a member of the basketball team have not left him time to prepare for the test. What would you do?

4. If you need to give a make-up test to some absentees, should you use the same test that was given the class? Explain.

SUGGESTED READINGS

Bloom, Benjamin S., et al., *Formative and Summative Evaluation of Student Learning,* McGraw-Hill, 1971.

This text covers measurement and evaluation procedures in twelve elementary and high school subject areas. The treatment is excellent and in depth.

Chase, Clinton I., and H. Glenn Ludlow, *Readings in Educational and Psychological Measurement,* Houghton Mifflin, 1966.
"Unit Seven: Test-Taking Behavior" contains articles that treat topics such as the effect of disturbances during testing and the effect of changing one's initial answers on a test. These should be of interest to many teachers and students.

Dobbin, John E., and Antonia Crater, *The Improvement and Uses of Tests by Classroom Teachers: Implications for Teacher Education,* Report of Special Group C, the DeKalb Conference, Northern Illinois State College, June 29-July 2, 1955; National Commission on Teacher Education and Professional Standards, National Education Association, 1955.
This is a very succinct discussion of the most crucial aspects of constructing teacher-made tests and interpreting standardized tests. Excellent illustrations of specific, behaviorally stated objectives are to be found here.

Ebel, Robert L., *Measuring Educational Achievement,* Prentice-Hall, 1965.
This well-written text covers all the major topics and procedures in achievement testing. Each topic is pursued in considerable depth, but the interested teacher with limited background will find it easy to follow.

Green, John A., *Teacher-Made Tests,* Harper & Row, 1963.
A general discussion of test planning may be found in chapters 1 and 2. This entire little book was written specifically for teachers in terminology that they can understand.

Hornacks, John E. and Thelma Schoonover, *Measurement for Teachers,* Merrill, 1968.
Chapters 5 through 12 present an excellent discussion and description of procedures in achievement testing in various areas. Topics such as estimating readiness, and testing for skills in reading, mathematics, and the language arts are treated.

Lien, Arnold J., *Measurement and Evaluation of Learning,* Brown, 1967.

Chapter 2 presents an overview of the steps in planning effective measurement procedures.

Lindquist, E. F., "Preliminary Considerations in Objective Test Construction," in E. F. Lindquist (ed.), *Educational Measurement,* American Council on Education, 1951.

Basic principles and issues involved in achievement testing are discussed in chapter 5.

Swain, Enoch L., *Evaluation and the Work of the Teacher,* Wadsworth, 1970.

The evaluation of objectives is stressed in this text, but attention is also given to assessment of the unplanned effects of teaching.

FORMULATING OBJECTIVES FOR
THE CONSTRUCTION OF
TEACHER-MADE TESTS

Perhaps the most important aspect of planning for teaching or testing is the determination of the general and specific objectives of the course. Teaching or testing in the absence of objectives is analogous to beginning a trip before deciding where you want to go—you may expend considerable effort and accomplish very little. Proper planning is important to the success of any major endeavor. It is necessary, then, for us to consider the formulation of objectives before proceeding to the techniques of item writing.

GENERAL AND SPECIFIC OBJECTIVES

Educational objectives may be placed on a continuum from the most general to the most specific. When objectives are properly used, the specific ones are classified under the more general ones which they promote. Objectives are quite interrelated. One specific objective may promote several different general objectives. The teacher, however, should have a clear idea of the particular objectives he is trying to further. He should know what school-wide objectives his course is designed to promote, what course objectives various units of the course are designed to promote, and what unit objectives are being advanced by daily activities.

General objectives

The most general objectives are the aims of the total educational effort. These are the purposes for which society establishes and maintains schools. In a totalitarian society, schools are instruments of the state and are used primarily to promote the ends of the state. In the United States, this has not generally been the case, and the aims of education reflect the needs of the individual as well as the needs of society.

At various times in United States history, educational leaders and others have met to formulate statements of general educational aims for the whole society. Two of the most significant of these statements are the Seven Cardinal Principles of Secondary Education and The Purposes of Education in American Democracy.

Most students of American education are familiar with the Seven Cardinal Principles: (1) health, (2) command of the fundamental processes, (3) worthy home membership, (4) vocational efficiency, (5) good citizenship, (6) worthy use of leisure time, and (7) ethical character. This statement of the aims of education in America, which was issued by the Commission on the Reorganization of Secondary Education in 1918, has probably exerted more influence on the schools of the United States than has any other statement. You will notice that the aims describe what might be considered characteristics of the ideal citizen of a democracy.

The Educational Policies Commission, which was formed for the purpose of considering national educational direction and policy, issued its first statement in 1938. This publication, entitled "The Purposes of Education in American Democracy," listed four aims of education: (1) self-realization, (2) human relationships, (3) economic efficiency, and (4) civic responsibility. This classification is quite similar to the Seven Cardinal Principles. Both are stated in terms of characteristics of the ideal citizen, and both reflect the same general characteristics. The 1938 statement does have the advantage of listing specific objectives under each category. By studying this classification, the teacher can gain insight into the kinds of student behavior associated with each general aim.

The past two decades have witnessed a great deal of controversy over the goals of American education. In the 1950s much was written about the failure of education to sufficiently emphasize the "basics." In 1957 when it was feared that the United States was considerably behind the Russians in space technology, the schools were blamed for the lag. It was charged that schools had overemphasized "life adjustment" and neglected hard-core subjects such as mathematics, the sciences and languages. During the 1960s the issues revolved around curricular meaningfulness, relevancy, and the disadvantaged child. Nearly every subject has been analyzed by some national committee and then reorganized to make it "more meaningful." Students as well as their parents want courses that are relevant, that is, courses that offer solutions to current problems. It has become apparent that many children, because of their meager cultural environment, are ill equipped to learn in school. A great many programs were devised during the 1960s in an attempt to help these children.

One of the most significant trends of the current period is an increased emphasis on the quality of life. Modern schools are expected to do more than just impart knowledge. "The fullest development of the unique potentialities of each individual" is probably the most generally stated goal of education in America and requires a great deal more of a student than the acquisition of superficial and meaningless facts.

The general objectives of education reflect the values of the society that supports the educational system. As social unrest increases, the basic goals of the society and its schools should be seriously considered and clearly articulated. After such statements have been made, it then becomes the job of professionals to determine the types of curricula and learning experiences that promote these desired aims. What are the *specific* knowledges, skills, and attitudes that promote good citizenship, ethical character, or whatever the general objective might be?

Specific objectives

Specific objectives are different from general objectives in that they usually contain only one kind of knowledge, one skill or one attitude, whereas general objectives may involve several. Good citizenship, for example, involves knowledge of numerous facts about the structure and functions of government, attitudes toward institutions of government and toward other people, ability to read and understand current periodicals, and numerous other types of knowledge, attitudes, and abilities. Whole books could be written describing the qualities of a good citizen. It should be obvious that this objective is too broad to accomplish in one day's lesson, in any one unit of instruction, or perhaps in any one course. It is also too broad to use in test construction, at least until its specific components are enumerated.

In order to build a test that accurately measures achievement of what you want students to learn, your objectives must be stated in terms of specific student behavior that you can observe. It is the student who achieves, and it is the student who will exhibit his achievement by taking a test. Objectives you will use to build your test must, therefore, be stated in terms of a particular kind of behavior that you will ask the student to exhibit in a testing situation. By revealing explicitly the kinds of behaviors the student is supposed to be able to demonstrate at the end of a learning experience, the problem of test design can be greatly simplified.

Remember the discussion in Chapter 2 concerning the role of measurement in promoting learning? Tests affect the student's mode of study. If you write vague, nonbehavioral objectives, then you will not know exactly what kind of behavior the student is supposed to demonstrate at the end of a learning unit. The chances are rather high in this situation that the only behavior you will require on your tests will be recall of facts. This is acceptable if your sole objective was to have the student memorize and recall. If you wanted him to develop some mental skill, however (and you probably will in today's schools), you have failed. If teachers are going to teach in accordance with the new emphases in every subject today, they must go beyond memorization of content to the higher levels of mental functioning. And in order to accomplish these higher aims, teachers must be able to state explicitly the mental skills they wish their students to develop.

This is why the task of writing objectives is vital for today's teacher. The student will learn primarily that which is required of him on a test. If the teacher writes vague objectives and tests which require the memorization of trivia, then the student will learn very little that is important or lasting. The rest of this chapter concerns specific objectives which determine the type of testing exercise that will be used. In Chapters 7 and 8, procedures for measuring the possession of knowledge and mental skills are discussed.

WRITING SPECIFIC BEHAVIORAL OBJECTIVES

Before a teacher begins to consider the technical problems of writing behavioral objectives, he must first determine just what kinds of behavior he wants his students to develop in the course of their learning. This is basically a curricular decision. Curriculum designers should give at least as much consideration to specific behaviors to be developed as they give to general objectives and content to be covered. Unfortunately this is not always the case;

however, there are two published statements of specific objectives which teachers may find helpful.

The elementary teacher will find much help in formulating specific objectives from the report of the Mid-Century Committee on Outcomes in Elementary Education. This report, entitled *Elementary School Objectives,* was compiled and published in 1953 for the purpose of aiding the process of educational measurement and evaluation in the elementary school. The objectives are usually stated in terms of specific student behavior or observable conditions and are considered attainable by average children during the first 15 or 16 years of life. The interested elementary teacher should find the study of this volume useful in designing teaching units as well as measurement procedures.

A similar volume for secondary education was published in 1957. The report, entitled *Behavioral Goals of General Education in High School,* classifies specific objectives under three major headings, called maturity goals, and four areas of behavioral competence. Although the report deals with objectives only in general education, reference is made to specific areas of the school program. Each objective is illustrated with specific behaviors. This should be very useful for the teacher attempting to design teaching units and tests.

Professional associations of educators have become concerned with the problem of specific objectives. The literature of these associations contains excellent articles on the topic. Teachers seriously interested in improving their competence are referred to this literature, some of which is listed at the end of this chapter.

Common mistakes in writing specific objectives

After several years of teaching courses in educational measurement, the authors have noted certain mistakes that are commonly made when people first attempt to formulate specific objectives for use in test construction. Perhaps a knowledge of these will help you avoid some of them.

1. *The objective is not stated in terms of student behavior.* Consider this objective written by a third-grade teacher: "To teach

the importance of daily health habits." This may be a desirable thing to do, but teaching is a function of the teacher. What are the *students* supposed to accomplish? What will they be asked to do on a test—recall ten rules of daily health? Would such test performance demonstrate the real aim the teacher has in mind?

2. *The objective is not clearly and specifically stated.* The following objective for an English class may illustrate this point: "Increased word power." What specifically does the teacher have in mind? Does he wish his students to be able to recall the definitions and correct spelling of ten new words each week? Does he want the students to determine the meaning of new words from the context in which they are used? What will he ask his students to do in a testing situation to demonstrate achievement toward this objective? The answer to this last question will indicate the actual objective.

Another illustration of this error is the following statement written for the first grade: "To learn the importance of arithmetic in our daily lives." There are several points of confusion here. In the first place, the objective is too broad for a unit test or probably for the entire first year. A complete comprehension of the full impact of mathematics on modern society would be a task worthy of the whole 12 years of elementary and secondary school. Further, to learn the importance of something implies a belief in its value. Does the teacher want the children only to know something they did not know before, or does he also want them to possess an attitude they did not previously possess? The objective does not state clearly and specifically what the students are supposed to accomplish, nor does it imply what behavior they may be asked to exhibit in order to demonstrate achievement toward it.

Perhaps the mostly widely misused expression in connection with the writing of objectives involves the term *understanding.* Many teachers frequently write something similar to this: "The student should understand the causes of World War II." As a specific objective, this is poor practice because "understanding" is not a behavioral term. On the day that the teacher is ready for the students to demonstrate their learning, he can hardly say,

"Children, understand the causes of World War II." What *will* he ask the students to do? If he is a typical teacher, he will probably ask them to *list* the causes of World War II. And all he will know is that his students have *memorized* something. If the teacher really wants his students to go beyond memorization in their learning, he *must* state his objective in terms of the behavioral manifestation of the skill to be learned.

3. *A list of objectives often contains only subject matter to be memorized and includes nothing about mental skills to be developed.* Much stress is being placed today on intellectual skills, such as comprehension, application, and synthesis. Schools are often criticized because they do not teach students to "think." The "new" mathematics, physics, and social studies programs all stress mental skills to be developed in the *use* of subject matter as well as its acquisition or memorization.

A list of specific objectives should be more than a detailed content outline of the course. It should also include the mental skills, attitudes, and physical skills, if any, that are to be developed in conjunction with learning the content.

Techniques of writing specific behavioral objectives

For teachers who have for years thought only in terms of learning *content,* the task of stating objectives in terms of *behavior* may be difficult. One technique which may be helpful is for the teacher to ask himself, "Exactly what do I want the student to be able *to do* at the end of this learning experience?" In this context, the content becomes more than something to be "covered" or just memorized. It becomes a body of material to be *used* to promote certain desirable skills and attitudes in the life of the student. This does not mean, however, that students no longer need to know anything. Content must be "known" or memorized to some degree before it can be used. We are not saying that knowing something is unimportant, but that it is *insufficient* as an objective of education today.

Techniques of writing specific objectives would also include avoiding the common mistake discussed above. This involves three positive actions: (1) The teacher should make sure that his objectives include skills and attitudes to be developed rather than just content to be covered. (2) He should concentrate on the activity that the student is supposed to be able to perform at the end of the learning experience. (3) He should use concise, explicit phrases and "action" verbs. Words such as "know," "understand," and "realize" are not behavioral verbs. They are accepted in statements of general objectives. They are inadequate for specific objectives. Specific objectives should provide the behavioral definitions of the more general objectives which they promote. Terms such as "list," "explain," "write," and "define" are better for specific objectives because they are more direct indicators of action or behaviors.

A common practice in writing objectives is to state a general objective, then describe or define it in behavioral terms through the use of specific objectives. An illustration of this practice is:

(General)   The student knows specific historical facts.

(Behavioral)   1. He lists events in chronological order.
                   2. He relates events to their probable causes.

Note that in the general statement, we used a nonbehavioral verb ("knows"), while "lists" and "relates," used in the statements of supporting specific objectives, describe behaviors.

An illustration of this same principle might be taken from the area of elementary school mathematics.

The student extends his knowledge of measurement.
1. He measures length to the inch and half-inch.
2. He reads temperature on a thermometer.

Again, a nonbehavioral statement has been brought into focus by supporting it with behavioral statements.

Let us consider one more illustration, this time from the area of reading.

The student comprehends stories.
1. He recalls specific information from stories.
2. He predicts outcomes of stories.

When a person is writing course and unit objectives he should remember this important point: *General objectives define the universe of content and behaviors to be promoted; specific objectives define the particular behaviors from the universe which the teacher will use to design his tests and other measurement procedures.* Specifics have been emphasized here because these relate directly to measurement procedures and because teachers generally find the task of stating specific objectives more difficult than stating general objectives. However, the teacher should not become so involved in specifics that he loses the more general perspective. Unrelated specific activities may well be as bad as vague generalizations. The teacher should be able to relate every specific objective to the more general student characteristic which it promotes. One excellent means for doing this is through the framework provided by the *Taxonomy of Educational Objectives* which is discussed later in the chapter.

Aids for writing objectives

Fortunately, books and other aids are being developed to assist teachers with the problem of stating behavioral objectives. One such book, *Preparing Instructional Objectives* by Robert Mager, uses a programed learning format which the teacher may find helpful. Mager states that a well-written instructional objective should have three characteristics:

1. It should describe the terminal behavior of the student.
2. It should indicate the conditions under which the behavior is to be exhibited.
3. It should indicate the quality of performance that is to be expected.

Another book which should be helpful is *Stating Behavioral Objectives for Classroom Instruction* by Norman Gronlund. This book emphasizes the use of specific objectives to define the behavioral manifestations of general objectives. Gronlund takes several statements, such as "understand basic principles," and shows how they may be broken down into behavioral components. The appendix of that book contains a list of action verbs.

A service of great potential benefit to teachers is being developed at the Center for the Study of Evaluation of the University of California at Los Angeles. This service, called the Instructional Objectives Exchange, collects behaviorally written instructional objectives in all subjects and levels. Sets of objectives with test experiences designed to measure each may be purchased from the Exchange for a nominal fee. The Exchange is not attempting to say what objectives *should* be promoted in a given subject. The sets are intended to furnish the teacher with well-written objectives from which he may draw his own, or which may suggest others to be written.

THE TAXONOMY OF EDUCATIONAL OBJECTIVES

Perhaps the most intensive study of educational objectives yet made is that undertaken by a committee of college and university personnel working in the field of educational measurement. *Taxonomy of Educational Objectives,* two sections of which have been published, was developed to provide a common framework to facilitate communications among teachers and others working with educational measurement. (See Appendixes A and B.) It is highly recommended as an aid to the teacher in determining the type of student behavior his objectives imply. Further, it should help the teacher direct his students beyond mere acquisition of facts to the development of desirable skills, abilities, and attitudes.

At the beginning of this study in 1948, some educators doubted whether a taxonomy or classification on the order of those used in the biological sciences could be compiled in an area as varied as education. This problem was largely overcome, however, by stating the categories strictly in terms of student behavioral outcomes. Stating the categories in this manner enabled the group to encompass practically all subject fields and educational levels.

The Taxonomy group first classified behavior into three major domains: cognitive, affective, and psychomotor. The cognitive domain, covered in *Handbook I,* includes all those activities generally thought of as *mental functions,* such as knowing, understanding, and analyzing. The affective domain includes the *emotional* or *feeling* aspects of an individual—such things as attitudes and beliefs. The classification of affective objectives is covered in *Handbook II.* The psychomotor domain includes, generally, *physical activities.* Objectives in the psychomotor domain would be expected not only in physical education courses but also in such courses as writing in the primary grades and typing in high school. Objectives in the psychomotor domain will, no doubt, be classified in *Handbook III* when it is developed.

Handbook I: The Cognitive Domain was published in 1956. It is divided into two main parts. Part I presents a general introduction and orientation to the work, and Part II presents the actual classification of cognitive objectives. The teacher will find Part II particularly helpful in formulating objectives and designing tests. Each category is well illustrated with sample objectives and sample test items which measure achievement toward objectives in that category.

The cognitive domain is divided into six major levels, from the simplest behavior to the most complex. A brief explanation of each level follows. You will notice that these are not mutually exclusive. In many cases the more complex behaviors are dependent on prior attainment of the simpler ones. For instance, if a student is to evaluate a poem he must have *knowledge* of criteria for evaluating, he must *comprehend* the knowledge, he must be able to *apply* what he understands, and he must be able to *analyze* the poem.

Knowledge. The behavior involved here is primarily that of remembering and being able to recall information. No understanding or comprehension of the information is implied at this level. Objectives classified in this category would include the following examples:

When called upon, the student can list the five major causes of death in the United States.

When presented with any of the 100 addition facts, the student should be able to write the answer immediately.

When presented with a list of authors and novels, the student should be able to indicate which author wrote each novel.

When presented with a list of terms the student should be able to write the textbook definition of each.

Comprehension.   This is usually what teachers call understanding. It basically involves getting the meaning of something. Generally speaking, isolated facts are not comprehended—only memorized. Relations among facts, implications of factual information, generalizations, procedures, concepts, and ideas are the kinds of things that are comprehended. A student may demonstrate comprehension in three primary ways. If he comprehends something he can *interpret* it, for example, explain it or summarize it. He can *translate* it, that is, put it into a form different from that in which he received it. Or he can *extrapolate* or predict on the basis of the information. Among sample objectives in this category are the following:

Presented with information written in French, the student can translate it into English.

The student can explain a scientific principle learned at the college level to a high school freshman.

The student can use information presented in tabular form to determine the truth or falsity of statements made about the information.

Given certain information about the weather, the student can predict the probability of rain.

The student can write a summary of a short story read in class.

Application.   The behavior implied here is the student's ability to use in a concrete situation the information, procedures, and ideas which he has acquired and comprehended. Objectives stressing application include:

Presented with a list of sentences and a choice of verbs in each, the student can select the correct verb according to the rules of English grammar.

When confronted with a simple problem in plane geometry and the necessary information for its solution, the student can solve the problem.

Analysis.   This involves an investigation and determination of the *structure* of something—the *method* or *procedure* of a communication rather than the message communicated. We may analyze something by determining its structural components, by noting their interrelationships, and/or by determining its type. Objectives which involve the behavior of analysis are found in all subjects and at all levels of education. Some examples are:

When presented with a list of sentences, the student can classify each as interrogative, exclamatory, imperative or declarative.

Given a news report of legislative action, the student can classify it as written from an unbiased, a liberal, or a conservative viewpoint. The student can then select the words and phrases that demonstrate its biased or unbiased nature.

After having read a novel, the student can give its setting, its plot, and its climax.

Given a complex problem in physics or algebra, the student can list the knowns and the unknowns.

Synthesis.   This is what some call invention or creative thinking. Synthesis is the creation of something new; new, at least, for the person creating it. It might involve writing a story, discovering a procedure, formulating a new hypothesis, or drawing a generalization. Objectives illustrating synthesis are:

When called upon, the student can write a short story.

Given the dimensions, shape and function of a room, the student can select and arrange furnishings for it.

Given the strengths and weaknesses of an opposing football team and one's own team, the student can devise a game plan to defeat the opposing team.

The student should be able to design a table of specifications for a teaching-learning unit.

Evaluation.   Once something has been created, it may be evaluated. Evaluation is considered to be the most complex behavior in the cognitive domain. It involves most if not all of the other cognitive behaviors. For example, before something can be evaluated, one must have sufficient *knowledge* of it, must *comprehend* what he knows about it, and must be able to *apply* the procedures of *analysis* and *evaluation.* Things are evaluated in terms of criteria established for their evaluation. These criteria may involve the *internal consistency* of the thing, which is the way we evaluate a theory or argument in a debate. Or the criteria may be established externally to the thing evaluated, being derived from one's taste, values or some logical process. Examples of objectives involving evaluation are:

Given a proposed legislative act, the student can determine its desirability in terms of the safeguards to liberty found in the first ten amendments of the Constitution of the United States.

When presented with an achievement test and a table of specifications for the test, the student can determine the validity of the test in terms of the table.

When presented with a short story, the student can determine the plausability of the action in terms of the setting.

MAKING A TABLE OF SPECIFICATIONS

It will, of course, aid test construction very little for the teacher to formulate clear, specific objectives and then not use them. One of the most efficient ways to utilize well-written objectives in test construction is by means of a table of specifications. A table of specifications is essentially a two-way grid, with the content outlined along the vertical axis and the behaviors the student is supposed to accomplish along the horizontal axis.

Tables 8, 9, and 10 are examples of tables of specifications in three different subjects. Table 8 was designed for an elementary social studies unit, Table 9 was designed for a typing unit, and Table 10 covers a secondary biology unit. The percentages along the top and the left-hand margin of each table indicate the relative amounts of emphasis to be placed on each behavior and each area of content. The x's indicate cells in which an area of content and an objective are meaningfully related.

If you examine the tables, you will note that they differ in the amount of emphasis placed on each domain and each cognitive area. One or more areas may even be omitted in each table. Table 9 has no objectives in the psychomotor domain, while Table 8 has a large number of objectives in this domain. It should be obvious that different objectives are usually taught with different units. No unit *must* include objectives from all domains or all areas of the cognitive domain. Each table should have only those objectives that the teacher proposes to teach in that unit. Minor differences in style of wording objectives are found among the different tables. The particular style of wording an objective is not crucial, as long as the objective contains only one student behavior, explicitly stated.

A table of specifications is simply a convenient way of placing the content outline of a unit in relation to the behaviors to be promoted with that content. Since it contains the unit outline and objectives, it should be constructed at the very beginning of the unit plan.

The teacher uses the table of specifications to guide his teaching and measurement procedures. This is one way to insure that his testing parallels his teaching. Each item on each test given in connection with the unit may be related according to the content area and behavioral objective which the item measures. The table may be used to plot one large unit test or several

Table 8

Table of specifications for a sixth-grade unit on the Soviet Union

Content (Percentage)	Knowledge 15% — Ability to recognize and recall names of people, places, and events of the unit	Knowledge — Ability to recall facts about ways of making a living in country studied	Knowledge — Ability to recall characteristic features of the natural regions	Comprehension 25% — Ability to translate information on maps from graphic to verbal form	Comprehension — Ability to locate physical and political regions on a map	Comprehension — Ability to summarize the main ideas of a given reading selection	Analysis 20% — Given a novel political situation, the student can identify the form of government illustrated	Analysis — Given a novel description of a person's daily activities, the student can identify the most likely region in which the person lives	Analysis — Ability to differentiate between statements of fact and opinion in a given reading selection	Synthesis 5% — The ability to illustrate a social problem by creating a cartoon or anecdote	Evaluation 20% — Given a novel description of different governmental procedures, the student can judge which ones show more respect for the rights of individuals	Evaluation — Ability to compare major generalizations about a country with facts about life in the country	Affective Domain 15% — The student will have enough self-confidence to express himself during class discussion	Affective — The student will show interest in the topic studied by voluntarily contributing related information about the topic from newspapers, radio, TV	Affective — The student will demonstrate that he values the democratic process by practicing it during class discussion
I. Physical Features (25%)															
A. Size	X														
B. Location				X	X										
C. Natural regions			X												
II. History (20%)															
A. Early	X														
B. Russian Revolution										X					
C. Recent											X				
III. People (15%)															
A. Nationalities	X														
B. Occupations		X						X							
C. Customs															
IV. Cities (15%)	X					X									
V. Government (25%)															
A. Characteristics of Communism						X	X								
B. Comparison with other forms of government									X	X	X	X			

Table 9

Table of specifications for a unit in basic typing

Content (Percentage)	Knowledge 5%: Ability to recall or recognize facts and procedures taught in the unit	Application 3%: Ability to use the 5 checkpoints when getting ready to type	Ability to use the 5 checkpoints when leaving the desk	Ability to figure horizontal spaces across varying sizes of paper	Ability to figure lines (vertically) on varying sizes of paper	Evaluation 1%: Ability to correct his own typed material	Ability to state his strengths and weaknesses in using conditioners to typing	Ability to state his strengths and weaknesses in using techniques to typing	Psychomotor Ability 90%: Ability to demonstrate correct use of the 3 techniques to typing	Ability to demonstrate correct use of the 5 conditioners to typing	Ability to demonstrate correct use of the 7 operative parts of the typewriter	Ability to demonstrate typing direct dictation according to the correct procedures	Ability to demonstrate typing on the exploration level to increase speed	Ability to demonstrate typing on the control level to increase accuracy	Ability to space correctly before and after punctuation marks when typing	Ability to demonstrate the typing of an alphabetic sentence using the correct finger for each key	Affective Domain 1%: Sufficient self confidence to participate in class discussion	Enough interest in his education to be present regularly and bring the materials needed	Sufficient self-direction so that he is increasingly able to work independently	Sufficient self-control so that he is increasingly able to use behavior which makes him an acceptable member of his school community
I. Organization of Work (1%)	X	X	X															X	X	
II. Typewriter Parts and functions (2%)	X	X	X	X	X						X					X				
III. The Keyboard (80%)	X					X						X	X	X	X	X				
IV. Techniques and Conditioners (10%)	X						X	X	X	X		X	X	X						
V. Typing Levels (4%)	X											X	X	X	X	X				
VI. Spacing (1%)	X			X	X	X											X			
VII. Vocabulary (1%)	X						X	X									X	X	X	
VIII. Attitude Toward Self and World (1%)	X																X	X	X	X

Table 10

Table of specifications for a unit in biology

Behavioral Area / Percentage of Emphasis — Content	Recognition of names and works of important men in bacteriology	Recognition of the general characteristics of bacteria	Recall of the general structure of a bacterial cell	Recognition of some facts about the general nature of rickettsiae	Recognition of some facts about the general nature of spirochetes	Recall of the three types of defenses a human body has against disease	Recall of the kinds of immunity from disease	Recognition of the two ways in which artificial immunity can be produced	Recognition of the names of some chemicals used in the treatment of disease	Recall of the role of the electron microscope in studying bacteria
I. Nature of Bacteria and Related Organisms										
A. History	X									X
B. Pasteur's work	X									
C. General characteristics		X								
D. Bacterial classification system		X								
E. General structure		X	X							
II. Generalized Functions in Bacteria										
A. Locomotion		X								
B. Nutritional processes		X								
C. Conditions for growth		X								
D. Bacterial respiration		X								
E. Reproduction in bacteria		X								
1. Asexual		X								
2. Sexual		X								
3. Conditions affecting reproduction		X								
F. Comparison of bacteria, spirochetes, and rickettsiae				X	X					
III. Infectious Diseases Caused by Microorganisms										
A. Pasteur's germ theory of disease	X									
B. Koch's work	X									
C. Koch's postulates	X									
D. Methods of spread (infectious organisms)										
E. Body defenses against disease						X				
F. Immunity from disease										
1. Jenner, Pasteur, Von Behring	X									
2. Kinds of immunity							X	X		
G. Chemotherapy and infectious diseases									X	
H. Antibiotics and infectious diseases										

Comprehension 34%				Application 3%	Analysis 6%					Synthesis 10%			Evaluation 3%		Affective Domain —				
Ability to restate Pasteur's germ theory of disease in words other than those of the text	Ability to recognize definitions of important terms when they are stated in words other than those of the text	Ability to predict the effects of variations in environmental conditions on bacterial growth	Ability to predict the effect of environmental conditions on reproduction in bacteria	Ability to predict the amount of bacterial contamination caused by different methods of spreading infection	Ability to predict the results of antigen–antibody reactions in hypothetical situations	Ability to classify bacterial colonies according to shape, size, and texture	Ability to distinguish between bacterial and viral infections upon visual inspection of a contaminated agar plate	Ability to analyze a situation to determine which method of spreading infection has been used	Ability to analyze a situation to determine which, if any, of the body's defenses could effectively be used to fight a certain type of infection	Ability to formulate a hypothesis	Ability to devise an experiment to determine if immunity has been produced	Ability to formulate an experiment designed to test the effectiveness of some antibiotics and chemicals on certain bacteria	Ability to evaluate a laboratory experiment to determine if a hypothesis has been substantiated or disproven	Ability to evaluate a hypothetical situation in terms of Koch's postulates in order to determine whether a certain organism is causing a specific disease	Appreciation of the importance of scientific equipment to research	Appreciation of the importance of the scientific method	Desire for personal hygiene	Desire for better personal protection against harmful bacteria (better methods of control)	Appreciation of the influence microorganisms have over human welfare (beneficial vs. harmful)
	X				X	X													
	X																		
	X																		
	X																		
	X																		
	X	X																	
	X																		
	X		X																
	X																		
	X																		
	X																		
	X																		
X																			
	X												X	X					
	X			X				X											
	X							X											
	X						X												
										X	X								
	X																		
	X									X		X							
	X									X		X							

Source: Data prepared by Janet Becnel, science teacher, Lafourche Parish, Louisiana.

subunit tests. Several advantages may result from the proper use of a table of specifications, the more important of which are discussed next.

Advantages of a table of specifications

If a test is to be valid, it should measure what the teacher attempts to teach. The major advantage of a table of specifications is that it enables the teacher to build content validity into his tests. The table of specifications defines the universe of content and behaviors from which test exercises may be drawn. If test exercises are classified in a table of specifications as they are written, then the teacher can easily see if he is drawing from the universe which has been defined. He can also see if he is neglecting a significant objective or overemphasizing a minor one.

Another advantage of a table of specifications is that it enables the teacher to have a clear perspective of a unit of work and the specific behavioral changes he hopes to bring about through it. This more precise picture enables him to do a more efficient job of both teaching and testing.

A third advantage of a table of specifications is its diagnostic value for both teacher and student. One of the most valuable functions of tests is the opportunity for discussion of incorrect answers when the teacher returns corrected papers to his students. If the test items have been classified in a table of specifications, the student can determine the particular content areas and behaviors in which he is having difficulty. In the same way, the teacher can check on his own effectiveness by noting areas and objectives in which substantial numbers of the class are having difficulty.

Finally, as we have implied previously, tables of specifications should not be major, time-consuming undertakings just before a large end-of-unit examination. They should be constructed during the planning stage of the unit; then the teacher can classify and make validity checks on the questions he asks on small daily and weekly tests as the class progresses through the unit.

QUESTIONS AND ACTIVITIES

1. Write several specific objectives of your academic field and have other class members criticize them.

2. Develop a list of well-written specific objectives and classify them according to the three domains of behavior. Classify those in the cognitive domain according to its categories.

3. Develop a complete table of specifications for a unit in your teaching field.

4. Using one of the Seven Cardinal Principles, write several intermediate and specific objectives that will contribute to this end. Can you *prove* that accomplishment of the specific and intermediate objectives will contribute to growth toward the general objective? How? Try to find several research studies on the relationship between specific and general objectives.

SUGGESTED READINGS

Bloom, Benjamin S., et al., (eds.), *Taxonomy of Educational Objectives, Handbook I: Cognitive Domain,* McKay, 1956.
Part I discusses the development of the Taxonomy and the nature of the cognitive domain. Part II presents the Taxonomy in the cognitive domain and excellent illustrations of items designed to measure achievement in the various categories.

Dressell, Paul L., and Lewis B. Mayhew, *General Education: Explorations in Education,* American Council on Education, 1954.
Chapters 3-8 present a comprehensive discussion of desirable objectives in the major areas of general education and of their use in educational measurement.

French, Will, *Behavioral Goals of General Education in High School,* Russell Sage Foundation, 1957.
In this text, the secondary school teacher can find helpful suggestions for objectives he may wish to incorporate into his course.

Gronlund, Norman E., *Stating Behavioral Objectives for Classroom Instruction,* Macmillan, 1970.
A useful little book that explains behavioral components.

Kearney, Nolan C., *Elementary School Objectives,* Russell Sage Foundation, 1953.
The elementary school teacher will find this book helpful in formulating specific objectives.

Koran, John J., Jr., et al., *How to Use Behavioral Objectives in Science Instruction,* National Science Teachers Association, 1969.
This is a practical, concrete discussion from which all elementary teachers can benefit.

Mager, Robert F., *Preparing Instructional Objectives,* Fearon, 1962.

Noll, Victor H., *Introduction to Educational Measurement* (2nd ed.), Houghton Mifflin, 1965.
The teacher can get a good introduction to the importance and functions of objectives in educational measurement from chapter 5.

Remmers, H. H., N. L. Gage, and Francis Rummel, *A Practical Introduction to Measurement and Evaluation* (2nd ed.), Harper & Row, 1965.
An excellent discussion of the formulation of general and specific objectives is to be found in chapter 7.

7

CONSTRUCTING TESTS TO MEASURE KNOWLEDGE

The measurement of knowledge is a major part of general educational measurement. While sheer memorization is featured less than was the case 50 or 100 years ago, the acquisition of knowledge is still a major goal in the education process. And, as has been mentioned earlier, if this is a goal in teaching, it is also a goal in testing.

In recent years, there has been a marked increase in the use of standardized tests of various types; however, the "backbone of the testing program" in most classrooms is the tests made by the teacher. Many of these tests are designed to measure knowledge.

125

SELECTING THE TYPES OF ITEMS TO USE

Colleges and early public schools in America made extensive use of the oral examination, but the inefficiency of this process doomed it to failure, because the procedure usually meant that a committee of teachers could examine only one student at a time. The oral examination was replaced by the familiar essay test. (One student described an essay test as being of the "short-question, long-answer type.") During the first several decades of this century, various studies pointed out certain weaknesses of the essay test as a measuring instrument. Concurrently, certain authorities were discussing the merits of the short-answer types of test items. The result is that both types of tests—essay and short-answer—are widely used in today's schools.

Advantage of short-answer items

One area in which the short-answer item is superior to the essay item is in the matter of *sampling*. It is difficult to imagine a situation in which, for a particular unit of work, a student is tested on every item of information he may have gained. Dependence upon a sample drawn from the larger body of material is almost inevitable. It is important that the test be adequate in scope and based upon a valid sample. Because of the amount of time and effort required to take an essay test, students frequently complete such tests with a feeling of frustration in that they have had little opportunity to demonstrate the extent of their knowledge. But the short-answer item requires far less student time in the process of simply recording answers. Hence, it is possible to achieve a more extensive sampling in the short-answer test than in the essay test.

Another advantage of the short-answer test is in *reliability of scoring*. Studies repeatedly demonstrate that teachers do not agree with each other in scoring essay tests and frequently disagree with themselves when later rescoring tests. With short-answer items, on the other hand, there is little likelihood that such variations would occur, since scoring is essentially a matter of applying a previously prepared key to a student's answer sheet.

Related to this advantage is the fact that short-answer tests give little opportunity for *bluffing*. All of us have had contact with individuals, who, whether speaking or writing, can inundate us with a flood of impressive verbiage. This can be a problem in scoring essay tests, as the scorer can become so taken up with the skill of the writing that he fails to observe the deficiencies in content. It is said of a former business leader in America that, as a lad, he had to take an examination in a subject about which he knew nothing; however, the essay test gave him ample opportunity to "spread his wings" in high-sounding prose. He later admitted that he was passed on the examination because he said "I don't know" in an impressive manner. Certainly, there is little opportunity for this problem to arise in the short-answer test.

Another strength of the short-answer test is its special usefulness in *diagnosis*. In part, this follows from the factor of extensive sampling. Certainly, if we are trying to search out weaknesses in achievement, it is necessary that we test on all major aspects of the material being taught. The gaps in sampling that are inherent in the essay test establish definite limitations on the diagnostic value of such tests.

One other point of view regarding the short-answer test has to do with the teacher rather than the student. When a teacher is faced with the task of preparing to give a short-answer test, there is *little likelihood of his being overly casual about it*. Selecting topics worthy of inclusion, wording of items so they can be interpreted in one and only one way, typing, duplicating, and assembling the test—all make up a task of sufficient magnitude to challenge the teacher. On the other hand, there is always the tendency to procrastinate when faced with the task of preparing an essay test. One teacher used to send a student to the board; then he flipped through the book and dictated his essay questions at random for the student to write. Sometimes this farcical procedure was still going on at midperiod. While this was an extreme case, it does illustrate the danger of slothfulness on the part of the teacher where an essay test is forthcoming.

Advantage of essay items

One of the advantages of the essay test has been touched upon somewhat sketchily in an earlier section. This is the *apparent ease of construction* of this type of test. This can be deceptive, since it does take considerable time to develop a good essay test; however, it certainly would be less demanding on teacher time and effort to prepare a few essay questions than to prepare several pages of short-answer items.

Another advantage is that the essay item is more effective than the short-answer items in testing *achievement on certain types of skills.* Included in such a list of skills is ability to organize and relate information, ability to select information that is pertinent to a particular topic, and ability to make applications. It should be pointed out, however, that these merits do not apply automatically to any essay test item. These advantages are realized only when the item is skillfully constructed, with particular attention to testing on the higher levels of achievement.

It has been emphasized earlier that teaching objectives and testing objectives should be closely related. It would follow that the use of essay tests as measures of achievement in the foregoing skills is justified only if growth in such skills is an objective in the teaching that has preceded the test.

Another advantage of the essay test is that the use of such tests *may motivate the student to emphasize larger units of subject matter.* When a student is preparing for a short-answer test, he is inclined to learn isolated facts, since these are easier to test with the short-answer item. When preparing for an essay test, on the other hand, he would probably be more concerned with trends, relationships, and generalizations. Indeed, such concern could be of benefit to both pupil and teacher. *(Do you think students should be told what type of test they are to take?)* A more detailed discussion of the characteristics of the essay item is given in Chapter 9.

Since this chapter is concerned with tests to measure knowledge, and since the short-answer test is generally considered to be a more efficient device for measuring knowledge, the emphasis here will be on that type of test.

Types of tests affected by level of learning

It has been mentioned that learning can occur at a variety of levels, ranging from the bare ability to recognize a seen answer to such higher levels as application or appreciation. While there is no set formula as to which type of test functions best for each level, it is obvious that certain types of items function better at some levels than at others. For example, have you ever taken a test in which you wrote, essay style, a series of definitions of terms? This procedure does not make use of the unique qualities of essay tests. Probably a simple-recall type of test would have been adequate. Four levels of learning and their relation to item types are mentioned below.

Recognition.   Knowledge that has been mastered only to the degree that you can recognize a correct answer when you see it has been learned only at a rudimentary level. In realistic terms, teachers frequently need to test at this level, however. Under such circumstances, the true-false or matching item is probably satisfactory. While the matching item can be made to function at a higher level, it is frequently used for measurement at the recognition level.

Recall.   Material that you are able to remember without clues has been learned at the recall level. A case in point might be the student in elementary school who is trying to achieve mastery of the facts of addition in arithmetic. This requires that the facts be so well learned that they can be produced by the student when he needs them. Frequently useful at this level is the family of items of the simple-recall type—completion, label, list, arrange, and others. In the final analysis, calling upon a student to complete a multiplication or addition table is essentially a completion type of testing.

Comprehension.   This learning is at a considerably higher level than the other two types. With a true-false test, could you tell whether or not a student actually understood the operation of an electric motor? Among the short-answer types of items, probably a skillfully constructed multiple-choice question has most to offer in this kind of situation. Also, The constant-alternative type (essentially a multiple-choice item with the same set of alternatives applied to a series of questions) is sometimes used. The essay item clearly has a role in testing at this high level, too.

Application.   A student must have achieved a very high level of learning when he can take a set of learned principles and actually use them. You have probably noted that, as we have proceeded up the learning scale, the value of certain types of items, notably true-false, has steadily diminished. Others, however, have gained in utility. At this level, the constant-alternative and multiple-choice types are still useful. The essay item is extremely valuable here. Also, a problem-solving test would be most useful. This might be a verbal problem in algebra, a laboratory problem in physics, or a design problem in a shop course. All of these illustrate the point that, if we want to test a student at the application level, we must confront him with a situation in which he is called upon to "apply."

GENERAL PRINCIPLES FOR CONSTRUCTING SHORT-ANSWER ITEMS

Later in this chapter, attention will be given to the construction of each of the common types of short-answer tests; however, certain rules are generally applicable to all these types. In order to minimize repetition, these rules will be discussed separately. It should be kept in mind that they apply to all types of short-answer items.

As you read this and the other sections dealing with rules and procedures, you should realize that lists of rules are to a large extent arbitrary. They do not describe the "recipe" for good tests. Rules are meaningful to one only when he understands the basic principles underlying them.

One of the basic principles underlying test construction is this: A test is essentially a communicating device. You, the teacher, must communicate to the student exactly what knowledge or skill you want him to demonstrate. You may have formed the impression that the basis of educational measurement is mathematics; it is not. The basis of good measurement in education is the creative use of language. No amount of statistical manipulation will in itself make a good test out of a collection of poorly written items. An essential component of good test construction is the ability to write well.

Another principle of test construction is elimination of the *test-taking* factor. It is recognized by nearly everyone that some students achieve well on tests not because they know any more than others, but because they are better test takers. This is particularly true when tests happen to reflect idiosyncracies in the personality and style of the teacher. The teacher should strive to make the test-taking procedure as smooth, simple and direct as possible. In as far as possible a student's test score should reflect his achievement toward the objectives of the unit only, and not his test-taking skill.

Use simple wording

It is well for a teacher to keep in mind just what it is that each item purports to test. Then, having established this, he should structure the item simply and directly.

If a short-answer item is to function effectively, it should test on one and only one bit of information. Consider, for example, this true-false question: "Measuring academic achievement, generally considered to be a vital phase of instruction, is a difficult operation." Suppose a student agrees that such measurement is a difficult operation but does not agree that it is a vital phase of instruction. How could he answer such an item? Further, the student might wonder, " 'generally considered' by whom?" If the teacher wished to get a student's response to the statement that measuring academic achievement is a difficult operation, his test item should include that and nothing more. Incidentally, statements with qualifying phrases frequently give trouble to abler students, in that they are inclined to be somewhat suspicious of the verbiage.

Further, it is important that the statement be constructed so as to get immediately to the point. This is different from the preceding example, which dealt with a statement involving two related but separate ideas. Consider this true-false question: "Because of their unique form of construction and the simplicity of the answering process, true-false tests may encourage guessing." Essentially, aren't we simply asking a student to react to the idea that true-false questions encourage guessing? Wouldn't it be a better test item if we held the words to a minimum?

Another problem in wording is to observe the essential limitations on vocabulary. Few things are more embarrassing to a teacher than to incorporate in a test terms that are unfamiliar to the students. This usually means that he must interrupt the testing to do some teaching about word meaning. If the teacher intends to test for mastery of certain vocabulary items, he can best do it by a group of questions specifically designed for this purpose. It is very important that the teacher, in test construction, keep in mind the level of achievement of the student being tested, and never replace an appropriate two-syllable word with a five-syllable word, unless testing for the meaning of the latter is a goal within itself.

Avoid tricks

There is always a temptation to work in an occasional trick question in making up tests. This practice is usually hard to justify, especially to the student. A classic illustration is the true-false question: "Edgar Allen Poe was the author of *The Fall of the House of Usher.*" This is false only because Poe's middle name was Allan, not Allen.

Another procedure that should be avoided is the use of double or triple negatives. Some teachers seem to like this type of question, and there are situations in which this device might actually serve to simplify a statement. Yet deliberately including double or triple negatives as a means of complicating the wording is very difficult to justify, unless the motive of the teacher is to test the students on their ability to interpret confused and confusing statements.

One occasionally encounters a test filled with questions based on material that is trivial or totally irrelevant. Have you ever taken a test based on footnotes? Or one in which many questions test on points that were barely mentioned in class discussion? Or one in which the teacher reused last year's test and failed to bring it up to date, so that you were asked questions on totally unfamiliar material? A basic point to keep in mind is that our testing emphases should closely parallel our teaching emphases. If teachers honestly apply this principle, there will be no tendency to test on trivia—unless, perchance, that is what they teach.

Avoid qualitative terms

In order to make effective use of short-answer tests, the statements comprising the test must be as clear as it is possible to make them. To achieve this, minimize the use of terms that can have a variety of meanings. Some terms of this sort are *seldom, most, far, near, many, much, often,* and *few.*

To illustrate the problems that might arise, consider the true-false item, "One seldom has occasion to administer artificial respiration." Suppose the class includes a student who works as a lifeguard and has used this technique several times—or suppose there is a student in the class whose life has been saved by artificial respiration. Furthermore, who is "one"? Obviously, the term *seldom* creates problems in such a question.

Consider the statement, "There were many causes for World War II." How many causes must there be in order to make this a true statement? Possibly there were one major cause and several subsidiary ones. Does this make the statement true? Or false? Many students can display an amazing degree of ingenuity in negotiating for points when tests including such statements are returned to a class. The teacher is actually inviting such problems to arise when he uses qualitative statements in a test.

Avoid absolute terms

While the use of the ambiguous terms described earlier may serve as a source of problems on a test, the same could be said of such words as *always, never, all,* and *none.* There are few statements that are *always* true—conversely, there are few that are *never* true. Such terms can be used effectively,—but they must be used consistently in the same sense. For example, in the statement, "All measurements are estimates," the term *all* is used in a true statement.

It would serve no purpose completely to exclude absolute terms from tests. But unless special care is exercised, use of these terms follows a pattern that would serve as a clue to the more observant students.

Use correct grammar

Anything that a teacher writes is subjected to careful scrutiny by an extremely critical audience, namely students. Hence, in test writing, it is important that the teacher use grammatically correct statements. Further, there are occasions when incorrect structure can provide a clue to the answer. Consider the multiple-choice question, "Eve handed Adam an (a) apple? (b) pear? (c) peach? (d) plum?" Assuming the teacher is using correct English, only one answer makes for grammatical consistency. Consequently, a student with a knowledge of English, but with no knowledge of Adam and Eve, would be able to provide the correct answer.

Keep each item independent and unified

A prime necessity in making good short-answer items is that each statement be clear and simple in construction, embracing one and only one thought. In keeping with this principle, it is important that we avoid "cross-referenced" statements. There should be no reference to "the battle mentioned in question 6" or "the author referred to in the above section." This is especially relevant to cases where an incorrect answer to a question would automatically give rise to an incorrect answer elsewhere. This has the effect of putting the student in "double jeopardy."

It should be emphasized that each statement must be unified; that is, it must deal with a single item of information. The temptation to throw in conditioning phrases or clauses has already been mentioned. These merely serve to clutter up a statement, in many cases actually obscuring the central thought. And what is the student to do when he encounters a true-false question that is both true and false? Unless a major goal of instruction is to teach the student how to deal with confused statements, such items should not be used.

Give same test, or comparable test, to all students

Insofar as it is feasible to do so, the teacher should arrange for all students in a course to take the same test. This principle is based upon the premise that, during the period preceding the test, the students have been working toward the same goals, applied to a common body of subject matter. Consequently, one would assume that the same test items would be applicable to all the students.

There are circumstances, however, under which the teacher feels that it is not advisable to give the same test to all students. For example, if a class is so large as to make monitoring the test a major problem, many teachers prefer to use alternate forms of a test, so that no student takes the same test as his neighbors. If this procedure is used, it is important that the two tests be comparable. The best way for the teacher to handle this is to make both forms of the test at the same time. This will normally serve to keep the two tests very similar in content, with the teacher making a conscious effort to vary the structure.

A similar type of logic could be applied in the case where a teacher has two sections of a course. If identical tests are used, the second section will likely profit by security leaks from the first section. However, if two forms, as described above, are used, the second section will profit little from the experience of the first. Obviously, if for any purpose the teacher plans to compare the test results from the two sections, or if he plans to merge them for purposes of "curve grading," comparable tests must be used. Merging results from two sections, one of which took a short-answer test, while the other took an essay test, would be of doubtful value.

Give careful attention to length of test

One of the most difficult tasks confronting the teacher as he prepares a test is to determine the appropriate length. Several factors enter such a determination.

One factor is the amount of material, as well as the importance of the material being covered. Obviously, a considerably longer test is necessary to adequately sample a major unit of work than is the case for a quiz about the previous day's work. Further, if the test covers material that was merely surveyed, a shorter test could be used than if the material had been given intensive treatment.

A second factor in determining test length is maturity of the class. Students at the advanced high school levels should have the reading skills as well as the test-taking experience that would enable them to move rapidly on a test. Younger students might well panic when confronted with a test which, to older students, would not seem unduly long.

A third factor, very difficult to cope with, is that of time. It is hard to judge the rate of progress of a class on a test; however, it gives rise to all sorts of difficulties if your class does not finish a test ("May I continue into the next period?"). Even teachers with years of experience occasionally completely misjudge the amount of time students will need to complete a test.

A recommended criterion is to try to set the test so that *practically* everyone will finish. Many classes include one or two students who traditionally fail to finish. Some even take pride in this. It is certainly desirable, in any case, to hold the number of unfinished tests to a minimal level. Some students will finish well before the end of the period and will have to stay in the room until the period ends. Some sort of assignment should be given to the early finishers to avoid disciplinary problems.

Give clear, specific, and complete directions

It is not unusual for a test that includes good items to prove to be of doubtful value because of inadequate directions. In test making, a teacher should use as much time as is necessary to be sure the directions say what they should say. Frequently, the help of a colleague can be enlisted for this purpose. It is safe to assume that if test directions can be misinterpreted, they will be.

The maturity of the students is, of course, a factor in deciding what type of instructions are needed. For elementary and junior high classes, instructions should be quite detailed, yet simply worded—an illustration or two might be necessary. For older students who have had extensive experience with short-answer tests, a very simple statement suffices. The key point is that every student should know precisely what he is expected to do on the test.

A beginning teacher in a senior class assumed that her students were mature enough to render instructions unnecessary. So she gave a test in which simple headings such as "completion" or "matching" were used without instructions. Most of the students responded as she had hoped they would. Some of the more technically minded, however, showered her with questions during the test, such as "Do any of the multiple-choice questions have more than one correct answer?" and "Do the matching questions come out even?" A few students saw a golden opportunity for negotiations and deliberately went off on a tangent. When the papers were returned, these students greeted the teacher with helpless looks and the question, "How was I to know?" The point of this true story is that, in working out the directions, a teacher not only is clarifying the procedure for the students, but is protecting himself in case of challenges.

A good set of test directions should meet several criteria. It should make unmistakably clear how a section of the test is to be taken, where the answers are to be recorded, and how they are to be recorded (True, False, T, F, +, 0). It should point out any potential points of confusion. If more than one answer can be correct in multiple-choice questions, this should be mentioned. If some terms in a matching test can be used more than once, this should be mentioned. Further, if the teacher is including any type of test with which the students are not familiar, he should make an extra effort to point out the unique features of this test.

Few things are more frustrating to a teacher than to check test papers in which the students have exercised an unusual degree of ingenuity in devising their own methods for recording answers. Such ingenuity normally comes into play only when the test instructions are such as to invite new patterns; that is, when the directions are not clear. The time spent by the teacher in preparing test directions is time well spent.

Group the items according to type

This point is so obvious as to require little elaboration. Did you ever take a test in which various types of test items were intermingled? This practice makes for a very confused situation and is in violation of the basic principles of test making. All items of like structure should be grouped together, with an appropriate heading and set of directions. Incidentally, can you imagine making a clear statement of directions for a section of a test in which true-false, completion, and multiple-choice questions are mixed?

Keep the system of responses as simple as possible

In designing a test, some attention should be given to the system of responses. In general, it is well to keep responses to a symbol, word, or, at most, a short phrase. If this cannot be done, it probably means that the material is better suited to some variation of the essay test.

If symbols are used, they should be selected so that there is little or no room for debate. Some students, for example, can write T's and F's so that each symbol is a compromise between the two. After a few such experiences, a teacher should change to a different set of symbols.

Many teachers like to have students use a separate answer sheet in taking short-answer tests. If the students are of such maturity that answers can be recorded on a separate sheet rather than on the test itself, there is no reason why the separate sheet should not be used. The task of checking tests is greatly simplified if the teacher can have all of the answers recorded on an answer sheet. It should be kept in mind, however, that the use of this device benefits only the teacher. The use cannot be justified if, in any way, it works a hardship on the students.

These principles are important in constructing all types of short-answer tests. Each type of short-answer item has its own peculiar characteristics, limitations, and advantages, however. The important points to be considered in connection with each type of item will now be discussed.

MULTIPLE-CHOICE ITEMS

Many experts in the field of testing consider the multiple-choice item to be the most effective type in testing a broad variety of outcomes. In structure, this type of item consists of an incomplete statement, or stem, associated with a variety of options. Normally, the latter consist of a correct answer and several "distracters."

It is hard to find many types of material to which a teacher, through the exercise of ingenuity, cannot apply a multiple-choice format. Some of the test situations to which this type of item is especially adapted are definitions, cause and effect, recognition, evaluation, differences and similarities, generalizations and discrimination.

The usual type of multiple-choice item has only one correct answer. One variation might be to have all options correct, with the student directed to indicate the one that is best. Another variation assigns to the student the task of finding the only incorrect answer. Both types are fairly difficult to construct. Generally, the teacher will produce a better test if he sticks reasonably close to the conventional pattern for multiple-choice items.

Advantages

The fact that multiple-choice items are more widely used than any other type in the newer standardized tests indicates the high regard test makers have for the multiple-choice format. There are several definite strengths that account for this popularity.

Probably the most important single advantage of the multiple-choice item is its adaptability. Practically any type of subject matter can be tested in this way. Further, by careful construction of items, almost all levels of learning from recognition to application can be tested with multiple-choice items. Another desirable characteristic of these items is that they provide an easy system of scoring. Since the student normally indicates his choice of answers by writing a simple symbol (letter or number), the scoring process takes a minimum of time and effort. This feature also makes it easy to use separate answer sheets, or, if the volume of tests is sufficient, to use machine scoring.

Further, the structure of the multiple-choice item emphasizes the value of good work habits for the student. The essay test, as sometimes used, invites verbosity. The true-false test offers such good odds that the student is tempted to guess when he does not know an answer. Neither of these procedures is, however, likely to be used in multiple-choice tests: There is a minimum of writing; moreover, when the chances of a correct guess are reduced to one in four or five, there is less encouragement to guess.

While it has become common to use the multiple-choice item in the upper grades, there is more and more use of it even at the primary level. By the use of oral directions, ample illustrations, and a simple answering system (such as encircling the correct picture), it is possible to adapt the multiple-choice item for use by the lower grades.

Disadvantages

Though it is generally considered to be the most useful of all the common forms of short-answer items, the multiple-choice test has certain weaknesses. Probably the most pronounced weakness is that good multiple-choice items are quite difficult to prepare—far more so than would be apparent to a casual observer. The major problem is to find an adequate number of good distracters. Usually, the first few options are fairly easy, but the last one or two are difficult; to provide each stem with an adequate number of functioning distracters can, therefore, be a tedious, time-consuming task.

Another problem inherent in this type of item is that it is difficult to judge the amount of time that will be required by the students. Answering a good multiple-choice item requires careful study, followed by the exercise of judgment. Frequently, the more serious students will take what appears to be an excessive amount of time in this process. While it is not a characteristic of the test as such, many multiple-choice tests are constructed so as to place undue emphasis on isolated bits of information. This, in turn, can give an undue advantage to the student who is an adept memorizer. Also, the multiple-choice items prepared by many teachers measure only at the lower (recognition) level of learning.

Principles of construction

A multiple-choice item consists of a stem and several options or alternatives. As commonly used, one of the options is a correct answer, while the others serve as distracters. In this discussion, we will deal first with the entire item (item and options) and then give special attention to the options.

The item as a whole.   In taking a multiple-choice test, the student is aware only of the total item. Preparing such a test is a complex operation involving the application of certain basic principles. Some of these, as applied to the item as a whole, are examined in the following paragraphs.

Each item should deal with one and only one central idea or theme. If there are two ideas worthy of inclusion, then each should be incorporated into a separate question. An item in which reference is made to "measurement and evaluation" might well be confusing to a student who is well informed on the differences between these terms but might be easy for a student who is less perceptive about these differences. If the item is to test a concept regarding *measurement,* then only this term should be used. Further, if the item is to serve with maximum effectiveness, all verbiage should be eliminated. The tendency to incorporate conditioning clauses or phrases (unless they serve a definite purpose) should be carefully avoided.

Direct questions frequently work better than incomplete statements. For example, the stem "A distinguishing feature of multiple-choice tests is____" might well be replaced with "Which of the following is a distinguishing feature of multiple-choice tests?" The sole purpose is to confront the student with a problem situation. Whichever structure that will make the problem stand out more clearly should be used. Many teachers of intermediate and upper elementary grades consistently use the question instead of the incomplete statement.

Each item should have one and only one correct answer. As is true of most principles of test construction, there may be situations in which an exception is justified. If there is consistency with the policy of testing on a single concept with each question, there will seldom be occasion to use an item with more than one correct response. In those isolated cases where a teacher feels justified in using more than one correct answer, he should be very careful to point out in the directions that this can occur. Otherwise, because of their limited experience with this type of item, some students would find one correct answer, then pass on to the next question.

Items should be written in clear, direct style. The story is told of a witness in a court trial who was asked a long and involved question. At the end of the question he was asked, "Do you or do you not?" His logical response was, "Do I or do I not what?" Probably all of us, at one time or another, have been confronted with test questions that were so long and confusing that it was quite difficult to figure out what was being asked. Every effort should be made to keep the items clear and concise. When this is done, the student can concentrate on the answer—not the question.

Correct grammatical construction should be used. Even students who are poor in grammar are amazingly adept in locating grammatical errors when they are made by the teacher. There are two common types of problems in this phase of test construction. If, in the stem, we make use of *a* or *an,* this could serve as an indicator. It is unlikely that the teacher would use an article that is inconsistent with the correct answer. Hence, use of the article *a* would likely eliminate the options starting with vowels. Also, if the stem makes use of a plural verb, the student could likely eliminate those options that are singular. Both of these situations can be avoided quite simply if we use the direct question rather than the incomplete statement.

Avoid clues that reveal the correct answer. If a multiple-choice test is made too hastily, some questions may well incorporate clues that give an advantage to the more observant students. For example, if Henry Clay were listed as an option on a question about compromises, or Pythagoras on a question about triangles, some students would probably associate them on the basis of general knowledge. Occasionally, *specific determiners* may appear in a multiple-choice question. This occurs when extremely broad terms (*always, entirely*) or extremely limited terms (*never, none*) serve to reduce the effectiveness of certain of the distracters.

Make each item independent. Insofar as it is feasible, each multiple-choice question should be self-contained. Again, exceptions are occasionally justifiable. For example, a map, chart, or table might serve as a point of departure for a family of questions, each of which is based upon the same material. But it is generally considered undesirable to use such terms as "Under the conditions described in question 15," since this has the effect of producing a dependent item. One can readily envision several types of difficulties this practice would present to the student. Suppose that, under the stress of test taking, he looks at question 14? or 16? Further, this type of structure might confront the student with a "double jeopardy" situation, in which a lack of information regarding question 15 might cause him to give an incorrect answer to the question referring to it.

Avoid copied statements. There is a temptation, particularly on the part of inexperienced teachers, to relate their teaching—and testing—very closely to text material. While this might serve as a kind of moral support ("I know the book is correct"), it can make for poor testing. If an item is to measure at the level of understanding rather than at the level of recognition, it must be so constructed so as to de-emphasize textbook statements.

Have you ever known a good memorizer? Many students depend upon this facility to see them through on tests. Although there is nothing basically wrong about memorizing if one wants to do it, it would be highly undesirable for a test to measure only at this level—and test items that are based upon statements "lifted" from the text do essentially this.

The entire item should make sense. While it has been emphasized that verbiage should be avoided and qualifying phrases held to a minimum, overzealous application of this principle may lead to the omission of words or phrases that are actually needed. The statement, of course, should be as long as necessary in order to present the problem. If the teacher is to meet this qualification with his test, he must keep in mind that the statement must not only make sense to him; it must also make sense to students who are working under a considerable amount of pressure and emotional stress.

The options.   Probably the most difficult part of making multiple-choice items is to provide each with an adequate number of valid options. Usually, the correct response and at least one other will be relatively easy to supply. But with the addition of each option, the task becomes more difficult. Some suggestions that apply specifically to the options are discussed next.

Each option should be plausible. Since *good* distracters are hard to come by, some teachers fall into some such pattern as: a correct option, an incorrect one, and two or more that can only be described as ridiculous. Even the weaker student can eliminate these irrelevant distracters at a glance, thereby reducing the question to an alternate response, or essentially a true-false type of item. If the multiple-choice item is to be used to its maximum potential, it is absolutely necessary that each option appear as a reasonable answer to the uninformed. The level of difficulty of a multiple-choice item is determined largely by the homogeneity of the options. The more homogeneous the options, the more difficult the item as a whole will be. Thus, the teacher can, to a large degree, control the difficulty of items through this device.

Provide several options. It was pointed out in an earlier discussion that each type of material to be covered on a test will likely adapt itself to one form of item better than to others. Hence, a key decision—one which, if made wisely, can save the teacher a great deal of time—is "Which type of structure best fits this situation?" If an item is of the "either-or" type, it would probably lend itself best to a true-false structure. If, however, there are several possible options, it could fit into a multiple-choice structure. There is no set number of options in a multiple-choice item. Many teachers will not use fewer than five; others will use three. Generally, four options is considered an acceptable pattern. It is worthy of emphasis, however, that the number of options is less important than their quality. If, for example, an item adapts naturally to three options, a better question can be produced by using only three than if a fourth option were provided that served only to increase the number. Some teachers incorporate three-option, four-option, and five-option questions into the same test. In such cases, it is probably advisable to group these items according to the number of options.

Make it clear how and where answers are to be recorded. When directions do not make clear where answers are to be listed, students either waste time by asking, or else they use their own judgment in the matter. The latter alternative can result in an amazing diversity of practices, costing the teacher a considerable amount of wasted time and effort. If answers are to be recorded on a test sheet, a set of parentheses in the left-hand margin, next to the question number, is usually supplied. The symbols used in designating the individual options should be clear and distinct. The numerals 1, 2, 3, 4, and 5 are frequently used. However, some students are quite ingenious at making 2's look like 3's, or 3's look like 5's, especially if there is hope of some bargaining when the tests are returned. Many teachers find it best to designate the options with capital letters—A, B, C, D, and E. Whatever system the teacher may decide to use, it is very important that the students be informed about it.

Avoid patterns of correct responses. The easiest option to write is the correct answer. Hence, there is a tendency to place this option early in the question. A special effort should be made to distribute the correct response randomly among the options. Some teachers set up recurring patterns of correct responses so as to facilitate scoring (1, 2, 2, 4, 1, 2, 2, 4, etc.). Certain students demonstrate amazing insight in figuring out such patterns. After a test is prepared, the teacher should examine his scoring key immediately. Any tendency to follow a pattern can be corrected simply by shifting the position of certain options before the test is duplicated.

Examine carefully any usage of *all of the above* and *none of the above*. While it is not particularly unusual to find these terms used as options in multiple-choice questions, it raises certain problems. For example, suppose that "all of the above" is used as the last option on a question. The student can dismiss this as an answer if only one of the other options is incorrect. The same system of logic could apply to "none of the above." Frequently, use of "all of the above" or "none of the above" merely means that the teacher ran out of options before he ran out of space. Under these circumstances, the "all" or "none" option is very likely to be nonfunctional. If the teacher plans to use these phrases as options, it is important that occasionally they be the correct answer—in short, if these phrases are to be used, they should actually function.

Avoid overlapping options. When writing items dealing with classification systems or numbers, caution should be used to avoid overlapping options. Consider the following example:

A butterfly may be classified as:

    A. a vertebrate
    B. an invertebrate
    C. an insect
    D. a lepidoptera

Options B, C, and D are all correct. This problem is easily overcome by eliminating all but one correct option or by rewriting the stem. In the latter case, the options could all be proper classifications of the butterfly, and the stem would direct the student to select the most general or specific category.

TRUE-FALSE ITEMS

The true-false type of test is representative of a somewhat larger group called alternate-response items. This group consists of any question in which the student is confronted with two possible answers. For example, a two-option multiple-choice item would fall into this category. But, since most of the points discussed here are equally applicable to all alternate-response items, and since students are familiar with the true-false nomenclature, this discussion will concentrate on true-false items.

Advantages

Although the true-false test is one of the oldest of the short-answer types in terms of usage, a list of its strengths would be relatively short. Perhaps this accounts for the fact that true-false tests are not used as extensively as they once were. They do have a place in a testing program, however, since certain types of subject matter are more readily adaptable to this format than to any other.

The most important single advantage of the true-false test is that it permits *extensive sampling*. All ordinary tests are necessarily based upon a sample of content rather than upon total content; however, the more extensive the sampling of a test (assuming it is a fair sample), the more likely it is to be valid. Since a student could respond to 100 true-false items in the time required to answer a single essay item, it is possible to cover a much wider range of topics with the former type than with the latter.

Another advantage of this type of test is that it can be scored with a high degree of objectivity. Since the student responds to each item with a single symbol, there is little room for subjectivity in the scoring process.

Over the years, some effort has been made to use the true-false test as a diagnostic instrument. While in theory the extensive sampling permitted by this test would serve as a diagnostic feature, the structure of the items is such as to place definite limits on the types of learning that this item can measure.

Disadvantages

Sometimes the apparent ease of construction is listed as a strength of true-false questions; however, it is probably more realistic to list difficulty of construction as a weakness. How, for example, can one be sure that the statement *is* true (or false) when read by different people with different backgrounds? In order to be doubly sure, one is inclined to add qualifying phrases as insurance. Frequently, this has the effect of making the statement obvious. Along with this, some statements can be changed from true to false just by reading them differently.

Reference has been made earlier to the fact that short-answer tests tend to measure knowledge on isolated trivial facts. This is especially the case with true-false tests. This feature would probably not be objectionable if the goals of teaching were merely the mastery of facts. Few teachers are satisfied to teach at this level only. In other words, it is quite difficult to test learning at its higher levels with true-false tests.

Another rather odd feature of the true-false test is that sometimes the weaker students do as well as, or even better than, the strong students. Apparently the poorer student finds a straightforward statement, accepts it at face value, and marks a correct answer. Meanwhile, the better student reads the same statement, becomes suspicious, reads things into it that were never intended, and marks an incorrect answer. There is definitely a tendency for the true-false item to arouse suspicion on the part of the better students.

Another weakness of true-false tests is ease of guessing. Since there are only two possible outcomes, the pupil has fairly substantial odds tempting him to guess. Hence, a question in the teacher's mind might well be, "How successful was he in his guessing?" Some teachers use a correction-for-guessing formula, and others place special penalties on wrong answers. When a student has a 50-50 chance of having a correct answer without even reading the question, the temptation to guess is hard to resist.

It is generally recommended, however, that teachers *not* attempt to use correction-for-guessing formulas with their own tests for several reasons. In the first place, the use of correction-for-guessing formulas is predicated on the assumption that students should respond only to those items of which they are absolutely sure of the correct response, and that guesses are based on an absolute lack of knowledge. From your own test-taking experience, you know that such extremes of knowing are rarely encountered in ordinary testing. On most items, the student is *reasonably* sure of the correct response but not *absolutely* sure, and his guesses are usually based on partial information rather than no information at all. In the second place, directions not to guess often introduce a personality factor into the measurement of achievement, which lowers the validity and reliability of the test. Third, when every student answers every item, correction-for-guessing formulas are not needed because there is a perfect correlation between corrected scores and raw scores.

Suggestions for construction

Despite the obvious limitations of true-false tests, they are still widely used. Indeed, well-constructed true-false items have a place in a well-rounded testing program, because they are of unique usefulness in particular types of test situations. In order to have these items function well, certain principles should be observed in their construction.

If true-false items are used, there should be a fairly large number of them. One of the chief merits of this type of test is that it permits extensive sampling. Hence, if 10 or 15 such items are used in a test, we are accepting the weaknesses but are not taking advantage of the extensive sampling feature. Some textbooks list a specific minimal figure of 50, 75, 100, or some other number. Though these figures are somewhat arbitrary, if the maximum value is to be gotten from true-false items, they should be used in considerable quantity.

Each item should contain only one idea. Everyone is familiar with this type: "Columbus, who discovered America in 1492, was seeking a shorter route to the Orient." If time *and* motive are of interest, they should be tested separately. The structure of the true-false item is such as to limit its usage in testing to one-idea statements.

Statements should not be copied directly from the text. Also, it does not improve the situation very much to use a statement from the text and insert "not" in order to change the answer. Regardless of the aims to which the teacher subscribes, use of this type of item will serve to reward memorization. Hence, this will automatically become the dominant aim of the class.

Specific determiners should be avoided. True-false items are especially vulnerable in this respect. For example, terms like *never, none, all,* and *always* are far more commonly associated with false statements than with true statements. On the other hand, such terms as *generally, as a rule, may* and *often* are frequently used in true statements, simply because the teacher uses them as a device to make sure they are true. Consequently, such terms should be used with caution. It should be pointed out, however, that the word *never,* for example, is not a specific determiner. Rather, it is the consistent usage of the word in false statements that serves as a clue. If *never* or any other such term is used in true statements as well as in false ones, then it is not serving as a specific determiner.

Statements should be clear and direct. Verbiage, double negatives, and qualifying phrases or clauses should be carefully avoided. Nothing is more frustrating to an already anxious student than vague, confusing statements.

Do not emphasize the trivial. A teacher should remind himself on occasion that testing is part of teaching. Yet it is not unusual to find in true-false tests items that are so trivial that they were ignored completely in the teaching that preceded the test.

Establish the standard or basis for judging truth or falsity of a statement. For example, a statement like "The chief issue in the Civil War was the elimination of slavery" would likely be challenged, because ample support could be found for other "chief issues." If a specific historian were cited, the statement could be defended, however.

Make the number of true statements and the number of false statements approximately equal. Many teachers prepare items without regard to number. Then they prepare a scoring key, compare the number of statements of each type, and make the necessary changes in order to achieve some degree of balance. There should be no pattern of responses. Patterns very seldom occur accidentally; however, the scoring key should be examined to make sure that they have not occurred.

True-false variants

Several variations of the true-false type of item have been developed to overcome some of the weaknesses in the original true-false format. Some of the more popular true-false variants are discussed next.

Three-response items.   In this type, a student might classify each statement true, false, or no evidence; true, false, or can't tell; or some other such pattern.

Five-response items.   Here a student classifies each item true, probably true, no evidence, probably false, and false. Different terms can be used, depending upon the nature of the material. It should be noted that, although this type of item still can be thought of as true-false, it is far removed from an alternate-response type and can measure a higher level of learning than just recognition and recall.

Cluster items.   In this type, a simple stem is set up, with a variety of statements clustered around it. Each such statement is classified as being true or false.

Correction items.   In this type of item, the student classifies each statement true or false. Then for each statement he believes to be false, he makes whatever corrections are necessary in order to make the statement true. This type of item can also test at a level considerably above that of recognition and recall; however, the scoring process can be time consuming, since the correction part is a departure from true objectivity.

SIMPLE-RECALL ITEMS

The simple-recall family of test items is fairly popular in teacher-made tests. Little use is made of such items in standardized tests, possibly because of a certain degree of subjectivity in scoring. As the name implies, these items require the student to supply an answer—one which is not before him in a list of choices. Hence, since the task of the student is to recall rather than recognize the correct answer, this type of test measures at a somewhat higher level than do some of the other short-answer types.

Simple-recall items can take a variety of forms. Probably the most common is the *completion type.* Some students refer to this as the "fill-in-the-blank" type. Another is the list or list-in-order type. This would be convenient to use in testing for chronological sequences and related materials.

Analogy types, in which part of an analogy is omitted, and simple computations (with the "answers" to be supplied) are considered to be recall items. Another type is that in which a chart, map, or diagram is supplied, with the student labeling the component parts as directed. Variations of all these types can be adapted to a wide variety of subjects.

Advantages and weaknesses

One of the chief strengths of the simple-recall item is that it reduces the problem of guessing. When the student is confronted with the task of supplying an answer on his own, there is very little likelihood of a correct guess. Another strength is that it encourages more intensive study than do recognition items, because the student must know the material well enough to supply, rather than simply recognize, the answer. Also, this type of item is versatile. Many types of subject material are well suited for some form of simple-recall testing.

There are two major weaknesses of simple-recall items. One is that, along with other short-answer types, there is a tendency for testing emphasis to be on isolated facts. The other, which can create major problems, is that scoring is relatively laborious and frequently somewhat subjective. Both of these weaknesses can be held to a minimum, if the test is made carefully and with attention to detail.

Suggestions for construction

Despite the merits of simple-recall items, they are as hard to prepare as other types of items. Here are a few suggestions that might assist in their preparation.

Omit only key words or phrases. The omission of trivial or incidental parts works an undue hardship on students and serves little purpose in instruction. Along with this, it is important that the teacher avoid mutilation. Have you ever been faced with such impossible questions as "The____ and the____ constitute the____"? One student said of a completion test that there were just enough words to hold the blanks together.

The question should be so constructed as to require a minimum of writing on the part of the student. If the item requires a student to write long statements, you probably should use a different type of test.

Have answers recorded in a column. At best, scoring completion items requires considerably more time and effort than scoring other types. But if a teacher has students write answers into blanks as they occur in the body of the test, he will need a lot of time to pick out and check responses. It is much more logical to number the blanks, then have corresponding blanks in the left-hand margin of the test sheet for the recording of answers.

Design the question so that there is only one correct response. This is by all odds the most difficult part of preparing completion items. The amount of creativity exhibited by students when taking this type of test is positively amazing. On the other hand, through poor design, some teachers actually invite a diversity of answers. Consider, for example, the endless possibilities in "George Washington was _____" or, somewhat more specifically, "George Washington was born in _____." This could be answered with "America," or "Virginia," or "1732," or in various other ways. Unless a teacher is prepared to accept a wide diversity of answers, he should be very careful to construct questions that are quite specific. Even with the most thorough preparation, he will occasionally find it necessary to depart from a prepared scoring key in checking completion items.

MATCHING ITEMS

As usually constructed, a matching item consists of two columns or listings, often called cues and responses. The task of the student is to associate each cue in Column A with an appropriate response in Column B. Hence, this could be thought of as a test of association. Some common usages of this test are relating men with events, relating dates with events, relating laws with illustrative phenomena, and relating tools with jobs.

Strengths and weaknesses

The chief strength of the matching item is that, for material which is well suited to it, this test provides maximum coverage with a minimum of space and preparatory time. Also, with sufficient effort in preparation, the matching test can be adapted to a fairly extensive range of situations.

The principal weakness of the matching item is that it is quite time-consuming for the student. It is as though he were taking a multiple-choice test with 10, 12, or more options for each stem. Particularly on the earlier matching cues, the student moves very slowly. Another basic weakness is that the matching item usually measures only recognition.

Suggestions for construction

Because of its unique features, there are definite limitations on the type of material that is suitable for testing with the matching items system. Within these limitations and with proper care in construction, however, matching items can make a valuable contribution to testing. Some suggestions follow.

Entries should be homogeneous. If a history teacher wants to test on treaties, laws, and court decisions, he should use three separate groups of matching columns—one on treaties, one on laws, and one on court decisions. Any attempt to merge them into a single group would probably be unsuccessful, because specific determiners would be abundant. For the same reason, it is also advisable to have two or three more responses than cues.

Do not make the matching part of the test too long. It is important that the entries be held to a reasonable number. As a ground rule, an average of 10 is sometimes recommended, with a maximum of 15 and a minimum of 5 as corollary recommendations.

Since the student must make continuous use of all items in each column, it is recommended that the entire matching part of the test be on a single page.

Make it clear what is to be matched against what, and where the answers are to be recorded. If entries from Column A are matched against entries from Column B, the scoring key will be quite different from one used if the matching were reversed. Incidentally, if it is made clear in the instructions, there is no reason why the same entry in Column B should not be matched with more than one entry in Column A.

Some teachers occasionally make use of a three-column matching item. For example, an English teacher might want to test on the student's ability to associate authors and principal characters with titles of various novels. In such cases, extra care should be taken to ensure that the directions are clear, since this type of item can be quite confusing.

ARRANGEMENT ITEMS AND OTHERS

The arrangement type of item is well described by its title. Frequently, several statements are presented, with the student being expected to arrange them in some prescribed sequence. For example, a list of former Presidents of the United States might be presented, with directions that they be arranged in some order. This type of test can be effective in such material as placing events in chronological order, putting steps of an operation in logical sequence, or describing the order of operations in the solution of a problem or experiment. This type of item is of primary value in those situations where sequence is of major importance.

One difficulty with the arrangement item has been to avoid double jeopardy on the part of the student. For example, if he is asked to assign a chronological sequence to a group of Presidents (Polk, Lincoln, Cleveland, Garfield, Taft), it is impossible for him to make a single error. If one name is erroneously placed, at least one other would also be misplaced. Further, if the student should list Taft first, then all the others would be incorrectly placed, even though they were in proper sequence. In order to cope with this problem, it is usually suggested that arrangement items be in clusters, each containing a maximum of three names, steps, or events. The cluster, not the separate entries within the cluster, could carry a point of credit. This would reduce the double-jeopardy feature.

One other type of short-answer item that is gaining wider usage is the interpretation type. Frequently, this type of test is based upon a chart, map, or diagram, accompanied by statements for student evaluation. These statements do go considerably beyond the extracting of information, since the emphasis is on the interpretation of information. For example, the school marks of three students, by subject areas, are shown as a group. A sequence of statements about the achievement of these students accompanies the group. Each statement might be classified as "true," "probably true," "can't tell," "probably not true," or "not true." Instead of pictorial material, the teacher might use a statement of a principle, a description of a phenomenon, or some other such background statement. Because it is particularly useful in measuring intellectual skills, the interpretation item is more fully discussed in Chapter 8.

This chapter has been devoted largely to a description of the more commonly used types of short-answer tests; however, there is no way to tell how many other types may be in use. A teacher should strive to adapt his tests to his own situation. If this means that he needs to devise an entirely new type of test, he is encouraged to do so, as long as the basic principles of item writing are followed. Always remember that the *test-taking* factor should be reduced as much as possible, so that the student's score will be a valid indication of his achievement toward course objectives and not his ability to respond to poorly written items.

QUESTIONS AND ACTIVITIES

1. Write several items of the different types discussed in this chapter and have your colleagues criticize them.

2. Develop a list of items in your teaching field and classify them according to the level of learning measured. Reclassify them according to the categories of the Taxonomy in the Cognitive Domain.

3. On the basis of your own test-taking experience, compile a list of errors in test making you have encountered. Do you find any one type of item occurring more frequently than others on your list? Explain.

4. Write a set of test directions for a multiple-choice test which would be appropriate for students at the (a) fourth-grade level, (b) junior high level, (c) senior high level. Have these criticized by a colleague.

SUGGESTED READINGS

Ahmann, J. Stanley, and Marvin D. Glock, *Evaluating Pupil Growth* (3rd ed.), Allyn and Bacon, 1967.
> Chapter 3 has excellent illustrations of "poor" and "improved" short-answer items.

Ahmann, J. Stanley, Marvin D. Glock, and Helen L. Wardenberg, *Evaluating Elementary School Pupils,* Allyn and Bacon, 1960.
> Chapters 11, 12, and 13 present excellent illustrations and measurement procedures in language, arts, mathematics, and other content areas at the elementary school level.

Gerberich, J. Raymond, *Specimen Objective Test Items,* Longmans, Green, 1956.
> This text is an excellent source of short-answer items. It presents illustrations of items, classified according to level, academic field, and type of achievement.

Gronlund, Norman E., *Measurement and Evaluation in Teaching,* Macmillan, 1965.
> The student wishing to read more about test construction and item writing will find a thorough and comprehensive treatment in part II of that text.

Payne, David A. and Robert F. McMorris (eds.), *Educational and Psychological Measurement,* Blaisdell, 1967.
> Unit six of this book of readings presents four excellent articles on different aspects of item writing and test improvement.

Stadola, Quentin, *Making the Classroom Test,* Evaluation and Advisory Service, Series No. 4, Educational Testing Service, 1961. This little pamphlet contains one of the best treatments of the subject to be found. Excellent illustrations are presented, along with discussions of what content and type of reasoning the items measure. The pamphlet may be obtained free from Evaluation and Advisory Service, E.T.S., Princeton, New Jersey.

8

CONSTRUCTING TESTS TO
MEASURE ACHIEVEMENT
OF INTELLECTUAL SKILLS

Chapter 7 covered techniques involved in writing the most commonly used short-answer test items. An attempt was also made to indicate the kinds of achievement each type of item can be used to measure most effectively. For example, matching items are effectively used to measure recognition; simple-recall items are most effectively used to measure recall information; and essay, multiple-choice, and problem-type items are most effectively used to measure achievement in such areas as comprehension and application. Most of the items discussed in Chapter 7, however, are used primarily in determining various types and amounts of *knowledge* possessed by a student. This chapter will deal specifically with the construction of tests to measure achievement of *intellectual skills*.

NATURE OF INTELLECTUAL SKILLS

In the past, intellectual skills have been referred to in many ways. Some writers have described them as the "higher mental processes." In the *Forty-Fifth Yearbook of the National Society for the Study of Education,* they were referred to by the very general term "understandings." John Dewey used the term "reflective thinking." With the hope of promoting some degree of order and consistency, we have chosen to use the terminology and the structure found in the *Taxonomy of Educational Objectives: Cognitive Domain.* We have done this, first, because we feel that order and consistency (one of the original purposes of the Taxonomy group) are desirable ends to be promoted. Second, we feel that the Taxonomy satisfactorily meets the criterion of completeness. Practically all intellectual skills that teachers want their students to acquire can be classified here. Third, we feel that the Taxonomy provides a framework of student behavior that the classroom teacher can use, without too much difficulty, to clarify and systematize his teaching and testing procedures.

Intellectual abilities and skills are included in categories 2-6 in *Handbook I* of the Taxonomy. These are comprehension, application, analysis, synthesis, and evaluation. To review the meaning of these terms, see Chapter 6 of this book, where each is explained and illustrated, or Appendix A, where a complete outline of the cognitive domain is given.

Regardless of the terms used for them, intellectual skills and abilities may be generally described as those behaviors involving problem solving. The individual who has developed intellectual abilities and skills can, when confronted with a problem, determine its nature and bring up from his past experience information and techniques for solving it. This may, in some cases, involve all the behaviors outlined in the Taxonomy. In others, it may involve only one or two of them.

IMPORTANCE OF MEASURING INTELLECTUAL SKILLS

Recent trends in education make it essential for a work on educational measurement to include a discussion of testing procedures designed to measure the achievement of intellectual skills. These trends, which have occurred in all academic fields and at all educational levels, emphasize the direct and purposeful teaching of intellectual skills.

The procedures and objectives—in mathematics developed by the School Mathematics Study Group; in physics developed by the Physical Science Study Committee; and in biology, English, and foreign languages—all have as their essential purpose the teaching of intellectual skills.

The recent emphasis on teaching for intellectual skills has been the result of one of the most serious and persistent criticisms of education. Throughout most of American history, schools have been criticized for not teaching students to "think." Schools, it is said, stress only the more superficial learning outcomes. They teach students only to memorize great quantities of unrelated, unmeaningful, and often trivial facts. There is too little stress, the critics say, on teaching for understanding and application. This criticism has been made by people both within and without the field of education. In the 1950s the academicians were making the charge, but John Dewey was saying the same thing in the early part of the twentieth century.

There is evidence to indicate that the charge has been largely justified. For example, you undoubtedly have heard of "boners" made by schoolchildren in which words are used in situations completely unrelated to their meanings. Two examples of such "sayings" quoted in the *Forty-Fifth Yearbook of the National Society for the Study of Education* are: "Socrates died from an overdose of *wedlock*" and "Pompeii was destroyed by an eruption of *saliva* from *the Vatican.*"[1] What do these "sayings" imply? They imply precisely that they are mere verbalizations, indicating little or no real understanding on the part of the child who says them.

Another source of the emphasis on teaching intellectual skills is the growing body of research evidence that knowledge alone is an insufficient goal of education. Available evidence on the subject indicates that the mere possession of knowledge (that is, the ability to recognize or recall) does not assure understanding. Neither does possession of knowledge assure the ability to apply it. Understanding and application may accompany the possession of knowledge in some students, but the relationship is too imperfect to be relied on when understanding and application are not purposefully taught.

Another indication of the insufficiency of knowledge as an educational goal is the retention factor. Studies comparing the relative retention of gains in knowledge and gains in intellectual skills have demonstrated fairly consistently that gains as measured solely by a test of knowledge tended to shrink drastically as months went by after the period of instruction. Gains in intellectual skills generally did not tend to be lost and, in some cases, actually increased. Knowledge alone, as most of us know from our own experience, tends to be forgotten if it is not continually used. Intellectual skills are much less apt to be forgotten.

It can also be reasoned that the transfer potential of intellectual skills is much greater than that of knowledge alone. Intellectual skills are applicable to all content areas, while knowledge of a particular piece of information has much more limited applicability.

The nature of contemporary United States society justifies the emphasis on intellectual skills. In the second half of the twentieth century, we find ourselves in a rapidly changing and unpredictable

---

[1]Nelson B. Henry, "The Measurement of Understanding," *Forty-Fifth Yearbook of the National Society for the Study of Education,* Part I, University of Chicago, Press, 1946.

culture. Who can foresee today the kinds of problems that individuals will face 10 or 20 years from now? Unable to make confident predictions about the future, we must equip children of today with the most generalized learning possible. Students must develop skills and acquire knowledge that will be useful in the widest number of possible situations.

In a democratic society, we also value individual initiative and independence. If a person is to operate as a democratic citizen by evaluating the events of the day, drawing his own conclusions, and acting on the basis of them, he must have developed the intellectual skills necessary for the task.

Once again, let us forestall any assumption that an emphasis on intellectual skills implies that knowledge is unimportant. It implies not that students should learn less but that they should learn more. You will remember that although knowledge comprises only one-sixth of the *Taxonomy of Educational Objectives: Cognitive Domain,* it is placed *first.* The logic of this arrangement is obvious: One cannot comprehend nor apply what he does not know. Neither can one analyze, or evaluate in the absence of knowledge. An emphasis on intellectual skills implies that students *should* have knowledge but that they not stop with mere knowing. They should go beyond knowing to understanding and application—the development of intellectual skills in the use of the knowledge they are taught now and in the acquisition and use of new knowledge needed to solve unforeseen problems of the future.

CONSTRUCTING ITEMS TO MEASURE INTELLECTUAL SKILLS

No doubt the reason many teachers test only for recognition and recall is that constructing tests to measure intellectual abilities and skills is a time-consuming and difficult task. The task is well worth the effort involved, however, in the teacher's sense of professional pride and satisfaction that follow the realization that he has been instrumental in promoting a significant aspect of a student's development.

Items designed to measure intellectual abilities and skills may be classified generally as the problem type. In this type of item, the student is presented with a problem he must solve. In order to solve the problem, he must utilize the skill or ability he has been expected to achieve. *Problem* is used here in a very broad sense, meaning any situation in which a student must perform with intellectual skills beyond just recognition and recall. It may involve data to be interpreted, principles to be used, conclusions to be drawn, concepts to be explained, or other intellectual processes. Generally, it should involve the utilization of knowledge or skills which the student has been previously taught; but *the problem itself must be novel to the student.* Novelty is the distinguishing feature of this type of item. If the problem is one the student has previously worked through, or one that was worked in class, then the exercise becomes only one of remembering.

All the suggestions pertaining to clear and concise item writing presented in Chapter 7 should be utilized in writing problem-type items. Beyond these general rules, each type of problematic situation that the teacher contrives may require special consideration. Examples of items pertaining to various levels and fields are presented subsequently, with appropriate comments. The reader who wishes more information concerning the measurement of a particular intellectual skill is urged to consult *Handbook I* of the *Taxonomy of Educational Objectives.* For information on items peculiar to an academic field, consult the *Forty-Fifth Yearbook of the National Society for the Study of Education.*

Illustrative items for measuring intellectual abilities and skills

The following items were selected because they appeared to be representative of intellectual abilities and skills that are taught most widely at the various educational levels and academic fields. No attempt has been made to present an exhaustive list. It is hoped that the teacher will obtain ideas from these illustrations he can use to design his own tests to measure those particular skills he is helping students develop.

In writing items to measure mental skills, one should not overlook the common types already described. The matching item may be used to measure a type of comprehension, if one column of the things to be matched is novel to the student. If terms are presented in one column and *novel* definitions are presented in the other, the student must have comprehended the meaning of the terms to do the matching.

The multiple-choice item readily lends itself to the measurement of intellectual skills and abilities. This type of item, however, does not automatically measure intellectual skills and abilities.

Consider the following example:

The President of the United States during World War I was:
A. Franklin Roosevelt
B. Woodrow Wilson
C. William H. Taft
D. Theodore Roosevelt

An item such as this does not require any mental activity beyond recognizing the correct name.

The following item requires the student to interpret the meaning of certain historical events and draw valid conclusions from them.

Considering the fact that the United States did not enter World War I until approximately three years after it began and considering the strenuous efforts of President Wilson in behalf of the League of Nations, which of the following most probably would describe Wilson's attitude toward war?

A. War is desirable because it provides the greatest opportunities for demonstrating the true qualities of manhood.
B. War, although undesirable, is an economic necessity.
C. War, although undesirable, is inevitable.
D. War is terrible, and man's greatest talents and efforts must be used to prevent future wars.

Excellent illustrations of multiple-choice items used to measure intellectual skills and abilities have been presented in a pamphlet published by the Educational Testing Service, entitled *Multiple Choice Questions: A Closer Look.* The interested teacher is referred to this pamphlet for more illustrations of multiple-choice items.

Comprehension.   You will remember from Chapter 6 that comprehension is demonstrated by the ability to translate something from one form to another, the ability to interpret or get the meaning of something, and by the ability to extrapolate or predict from given data.

The following essay item requires a student to translate from one level of abstraction to a simpler level:

In your own words, explain the meaning of test reliability to a school board member who has no background in educational measurement or statistics.

This multiple-choice item requires a student to translate from a graphic form to a numerical form:

The shaded area of the above pie is represented by which of the following fractions?

   A. 1/8
   B. 1/4
   C. 1/3
   D. 1/2

The preceding situation could also be set up as a matching item, with several pies and fractions.

The type of item commonly used to indicate a student's ability to interpret is called "the interpretation of data item." In this type of item, the student is presented with data in some form—a paragraph, a chart, a table, a line graph—and asked to judge the truth or falsity of statements based on the data. In the following item, the student is asked to interpret a chart showing average temperatures in four large cities.

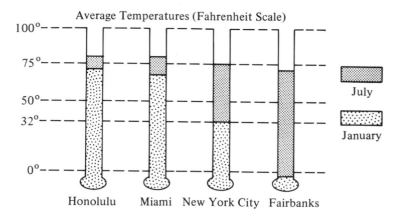

Average Temperatures (Fahrenheit Scale)

Directions: Using only the information presented in the chart, judge each statement presented below, and mark it in the following manner:

T—if the information presented in the chart is sufficient to make the statement TRUE;

CT—if, using the information presented in the chart, you CAN'T TELL whether the statement is true or false;

F—if the information presented in the chart is sufficient to make the statement FALSE.

1. The average July temperature in Miami is about 80 degrees.
2. Of the four cities shown, the greatest difference between the average July and average January temperature occurs in Fairbanks.
3. It never gets colder than 32 degrees in New York City.
4. The climate in Miami is about the same as the climate in Honolulu.
5. The average July temperature in Fairbanks is about the same as the average January temperature in Miami.
6. People in Fairbanks would dress like people in Miami when they go outside in January.

Instead of the preceding 3 categories, some teachers may wish to make the item more subtle by adding "probably true" and "probably false." But these are best used only with senior high school students, who have had experience with this type of item. Students inexperienced in using these categories are likely to use them to express doubt about their own judgment rather than to indicate limitations of the data.

Application.   Almost all teachers hope their students will be able to apply or use their knowledge and skills in a concrete situation. Items requiring students to apply what they have learned are not extremely difficult to construct and are found quite frequently in teacher-made tests. The ability to apply the rules of grammar may be tested by requiring students to supply the proper form of a noun, verb, adjective, etc., in a series of sentences. Punctuation may be tested by requiring students to supply the proper punctuation for a group of sentences or a paragraph. The ability to apply computation skills and arithmetical reasoning may be tested by well-designed problems. The following item requires the student to utilize basic arithmetical techniques and reasoning:

> Mother went to the store and bought three shirts for $10.00. The brown shirt cost $2.50, and the blue one cost half as much as the white one. How much did the blue one cost?
>
>   A. $2.50
>   B. $3.00
>   C. $3.50
>   D. $4.00
>   E. $4.50

Application of scientific principles may be tested by presenting students with a concrete situation and asking them to explain why a certain action should be taken or why a certain consequence should be expected. The following item deals with the application of principles concerning the effect of temperature on a confined body of air:

> If you were starting to cross the Mojave Desert on a hot summer day in an automobile with worn tires, what would be a wise precaution to take regarding the air pressure of the tires? What scientific principle is involved in this situation?

The following item concerns application of principles of educational measurement:

Directions: Four results are listed below. Below these are listed six practices. On your answer sheet, blacken the letter of the result which would be the most likely and specific outcome of each practice.

- A. Increased validity
- B. Increased reliability
- C. Decreased validity
- D. Decreased reliability

1. Using a table of specifications when constructing a test.
2. Giving a test in a hot, overcrowded room.
3. Using ambiguously written items.
4. Using the test of another teacher.
5. Giving a test the afternoon before the Christmas holidays.
6. Constructing a test in the absence of specific objectives.

Analysis.   A teacher might find, among the objectives he desires his students to accomplish, such behaviors as the following:

1. The ability to determine the major points in an argument.

2. The ability to distinguish between statements of opinion and statements of fact.

3. The ability to recognize the point of view of a writer.

4. The ability to recognize the form and pattern in a work of literature or art.

In such a case, he needs to design items that will indicate ability to analyze material. You will remember from Chapter 6 that analysis is divided into three types: (1) the ability to determine the major components of something, (2) the ability to determine the relationships among the components, and (3) the ability to determine the general structure or organizing principles.

Analysis is of particular importance in language, literature, and speech, wherein a student is expected not only to comprehend a story, poem, or speech, but also to determine its structure. It is true that a teacher can analyze all the beauty out of a literary piece by overstressing analysis, but it is also true that appreciation is enhanced when one can become aware of basic structure and elemental relationships. Analysis is also important in social studies classes in which students are expected to be able to distinguish between objective and biased articles and speeches. In physical science classes, analysis is important in situations where the nature of the problem has to be determined prior to proposals for its solution.

Ability to determine elements and their relationships may be indicated by presenting the student with a short composition and asking him to outline it. In speech class, a student may be asked to distinguish between major points and supporting data in an argument. Ability to determine basic structure and organizational principles may be tested by asking a student to determine the point of view of the author. In art, a student may be asked to determine the artistic style of a painting and to indicate the purpose of color, shading, and form.

This item requires the student to determine the basic literary style of a passage:

A writer of realism would most likely begin his story with which of the following?

  A. Today, I saw an old man who was begging for money. His clothes were tattered and torn; his shoes had paper-thin soles.
  B. Today, I saw an old man who was begging for money. His face revealed his innermost cruel thoughts.
  C. Today, I saw an old man who was begging for money. His clothes were old, and his face lined, but I knew that he enjoyed his simple existence, because I saw a twinkle in his eye.

The following item, adapted from *Handbook I* of the *Taxonomy of Educational Objectives,* requires the student to determine the relationship between a resolution and arguments concerning it:

Resolved: *That the voting age should be lowered from 21 to 18 years.*

Directions: Some of the statements below could be used to support the resolution, some could be used in arguing against the resolution, and some have no bearing on the issue at all. Mark each statement according to the following scale:
- A—if you feel that the statement could be used by the AF-FIRMATIVE side in a debate on the resolution;
- N—if you feel that the statement could be used by the NEGATIVE side;
- X—if you feel that the statement has no bearing on either side of the argument.

(Note: You are not asked to judge the truth or falsity of the resolution or the statement.)

1. A person who is old enough to fight and die for his country is old enough to vote in it.
2. Universal suffrage does not include the immature.
3. Successful schools require mature teachers.
4. Our advanced educational system has lowered the age at which people are able to make mature judgments.
5. The electoral college system is out of date.
6. A person still dependent on others for his livelihood is not in a position to make independent judgments.

Synthesis.   Synthesis is another intellectual skill commonly found among teachers' objectives. It is quite frequently what the behavior teachers have in mind when they refer to creativity. It involves such activities as writing a short story, composing a poem or piece of music, formulating a hypothesis or a plan for solving a problem, writing lesson plans, and designing a dress. The essential element of synthesis is the creation of something new—at least to the person who creates it. Writing a story about some experience fits here, since the story itself must be created, even though it is based on past events.

Most of the items that test objectives in this category are of the essay type. In language arts and English classes, a picture may be placed in front of the class, and the student directed to write a short story or poem about events suggested by the picture. Students may be presented with several lines of poetry and asked to finish the verse. They may be asked to relate the most important, funniest, or most delightful thing that happened to them during the past summer.

In other courses, students may be presented with a problem and asked to formulate a hypothesis and a plan for solving the problem. In bookkeeping, for example, they may be asked to design a bookkeeping system for a given size and type of business enterprise. In social studies, students may be presented with a social problem and asked to formulate proposals for social action to eliminate or reduce the problem. In industrial arts, they may be asked to design a tool with certain qualities to do a particular job. In home economics, students may be asked to decorate a room, plan a menu, or design a dress. In chemistry, they may be asked to formulate a hypothesis to explain a given reaction, and to design an experiment to test the hypothesis. The *creative teacher* will be able to design many more items to test the ability to synthesize.

Evaluation.   Although evaluating or judging is a common human activity, it is not frequently found among teachers' objectives. Teachers are, however, interested in their students' ability to distinguish between such things as "good" and "bad" behavior, literature, art, or music. You may remember from Chapter 6 that the ability to evaluate involves most of the behaviors in the Taxonomy that precede it. That is, the student must know the criteria for evaluation and something of the process of evaluating; he must be able to comprehend what he is to evaluate, as well as the process of evaluating; he must be able to apply the techniques of evaluating; and when the thing to be evaluated is of some degree of complexity, he must be able to analyze it. Furthermore, if his evaluation involves writing a critique, he must have some facility to synthesize a novel communication. You may also remember that evaluations may be made in terms of internal criteria or external criteria.

Those things most frequently judged in terms of internal criteria are literary works, such as essays and debates. One way to test for ability of students to evaluate in terms of internal consistency is to present them with the outline of an essay or debate, and ask them to determine which of the major points are logically inconsistent with the others. Another technique is to require them to evaluate the logical consistency of several conclusions which might be drawn from a problem or event in science or social studies.

Evaluation in terms of external criteria is probably more commonly taught in elementary and secondary schools than is evaluation in terms of internal consistency. The ability to use criteria in the actual evaluation of a work of art, literature, or music may be tested by presenting a model to students and asking them to write a short critique of it. They may also be asked to describe the good and bad features of a model. In social studies, students may be presented with some individual action, or a political policy, and asked to evaluate it in terms of religious or democratic principles. A student teacher may be asked to give a critique of a test, using the criteria of reliability, validity, and usability. At a more subtle level, students may be asked not only to evaluate something in terms of predetermined criteria but also to determine which criteria are appropriate to its evaluation.

It is evident from these examples that testing for intellectual skills and abilities requires a great deal of thought and effort. These kinds of items cannot be written during a short study period on the day the test is to be given. One would do well to secure the cooperation of other teachers in a continuing process of developing items to measure intellectual skills appropriate to a particular level and academic field. If the recent developments in mathematics and the new emphasis of understanding and application in the other academic fields are not accompanied by tests measuring achievement in their new areas, there will be nothing "new" about them at all. We will have only a new set of verbalizations to be superficially memorized.

QUESTIONS AND ACTIVITIES

1. Make a list of five items you have studied recently. For each, prepare a series of questions testing at several levels.

2. Have you taken any tests that you thought were unusually effective in testing at the higher levels? Describe them.

3. What is your reaction to the statement, "Extensive testing at the recognition level is an effective method of testing at higher levels"?

4. Prepare a report on recent research dealing with measuring achievement of intellectual skills.

SUGGESTED READINGS

Ahmann, J. Stanley, and Marvin D. Glock, *Evaluating Pupil Growth,* (3rd ed.), Allyn and Bacon, 1967.
> Chapter 4 reviews and illustrates some of the principal procedures used in measuring intellectual skills.

Bloom, Benjamin S., et al. (eds.), *Taxonomy of Educational Objectives, Handbook I: Cognitive Domain,* McKay, 1956.
> The illustrations in Part II should be invaluable to a teacher attempting to write items which will measure achievement of intellectual skills.

Dressell, Paul L., and Lewis P. Mayhew, *General Education: Exploration in Evaluation,* American Council on Education, 1954.
> All chapters have some discussion of measurement of intellectual skills, and chapter 7 deals specially with "Critical Thinking." Chapter 10, in attempting to indicate future trends in general education, gives critical thinking a basic role.

Dutton, Wilbur H., *Evaluating Pupils' Understanding of Arithmetic,* Prentice-Hall, 1964.
> Arithmetic teachers and others interested in measuring for understanding in the area will find this book helpful. The appendix contains some excellent illustrative items.

Henry, Nelson B., "The Measurement of Understanding," *Forty-Fifth Yearbook of the National Society for the Study of Education,* Part I, University of Chicago Press, 1946.

    In Section I, the importance of teaching for understanding, the nature of understanding, and methods of indicating understanding are discussed. In Section II, each chapter is devoted to measuring achievement of understanding in a particular subject.

Horracks, John E. and Thelma I. Schoonover, *Measurement for Teachers,* Merrill, 1968.

    Chapter 8, 9, and 10 present procedures for testing skills in reading, mathematics, and language arts which the teacher should find helpful.

Morse, Horace T. and George McCune, *Selected Items for the Testing of Study Skills and Critical Thinking,* Bulletin 15 (4th ed.), National Council for the Social Studies, 1964.

    Teachers of English and language arts, as well as social studies teachers will find the suggestions and illustrations in this bulletin of great value.

Smith, Eugene R., and Ralph W. Tyler, *Appraising and Recording Student Progress,* McGraw-Hill, 1942.

    The procedures developed during the "Eight-Year Study" to measure certain intellectual skills are described in chapter 2.

Stoker, H. W., and R. P. Kropp, "Measurement of Cognitive Processes," *Journal of Educational Measurement,* June, 1964, pp. 39-42.

    Elementary teachers and secondary English teachers may find this study interesting and valuable. It deals with the classifying of reading comprehension test items according to the major categories of the *Taxonomy of Educational Objectives: Cognitive Domain.*

9

CONSTRUCTING AND USING ESSAY TESTS

The essay test has had an unusual life history. Appearing upon the educational scene at a time when the oral test was proving too unwieldy, the essay test became extremely popular. Indeed, for the first several decades of the twentieth century, many teachers used only this type of test. Published studies indicating the unreliability of the scoring process contributed to the gradual decline in usage of the essay test; however, it has not been superseded and probably will not disappear from the scene, since this type of test has a unique contribution to make in a testing program.

STRENGTHS OF THE ESSAY TEST

The literature related to testing has for several decades placed considerable emphasis on the problems associated with using essay tests. It is important in maintaining proper perspective, however, that we take note of the fact that this type of test also has some major strengths.

Guessing creates few problems.   It would be impossible to eliminate guessing entirely from the testing process. But the essay test offers the student a minimum of temptation in this regard, since the probability of a correct guess is relatively slight.

Maximum freedom of response is allowed.   One occasionally encounters a teacher who is highly critical of his students' skills in self-expression. Yet many of the same teachers use short-answer tests exclusively—tests in which a student's opportunity to express himself is limited to writing a single letter or numeral. Several years ago, a graduate of a large high school who was taking an essay test during her freshman year in college remarked to the instructor that this was the first time she had taken this type of test. The student had been denied a type of experience that could have made a real contribution to her development in the area of communications.

Helps develop a variety of skills.   In addition to its self-expression feature, the essay test calls upon students to use several other important skills. Some of these are selecting pertinent material, organizing this material into a coherent discussion, and arriving at conclusions. All of these are important, yet are frequently overlooked in a testing program that excludes the essay test.

Encourages good study habits.   Oddly enough, one of the major strengths of the essay test has to do with the way a student prepares for the test rather than with the test itself. It has been mentioned earlier that, regardless of a teacher's stated goals, students are inclined to study for the type of test the teacher uses. If tests emphasize unrelated items of factual information, test preparation is essentially a matter of memorizing such facts. But if a student is preparing for an essay test, he is likely to stress larger units, look for relationships, and exercise judgment in deciding points of emphasis.

WEAKNESSES OF THE ESSAY TEST

If we could view tests in the abstract, the essay test would appear to be more valuable than it actually is. When we view tests as devices the teacher uses in order to measure pupil progress toward stated goals, however, the essay test begins to display certain weaknesses. In short, it is difficult to evaluate a test without simultaneously considering such items as difficulty of scoring. Many proponents of the essay test claim that the chief criticisms of this test have to do with the scoring of the test, rather than with the test itself. Such discussions probably serve little purpose, since the testing operation necessarily includes both the instrument and the processing of the results. Some of the commonly accepted weaknesses of this type of test are described next.

Sampling is limited.   The theoretical aspects of sampling as a vital part of testing have already been cited. Also, it has been pointed out that adequate sampling is essential in good testing. But time limitations make it impossible to achieve good sampling in an essay test, assuming that a substantial body of the subject matter has been covered.

Danger of bluffing.   The "gift of gab" can be encountered in written as well as in oral communication. Some students, well endowed with this attribute, can gild ignorance with such high-sounding verbiage as to sound most persuasive. Most teachers using essay tests have encountered test papers written in a convincing manner, implying (but never actually stating) a vast storehouse of knowledge. Only upon close inspection does the teacher realize that nothing is being said.

Difficult to score.   Numerous studies have demonstrated that the same paper will receive a wide range of values when scored by a group of teachers. Others have found that, if the same teacher scores the same tests twice, he will likely disagree with himself. Some other factors that are believed to affect the score on an essay test are the quality of the preceding paper, the quality of the handwriting, the position of the paper in the stack (high standards gradually erode away during a long evening of test reading), and the degree to which the views expressed agree with those of the grader. Even its most vocal proponents concede that consistency in scoring the essay test is difficult to achieve.

OBJECTIVES MEASURED MOST EFFECTIVELY

It has been mentioned previously that each type of test functions more effectively in some situations than in others. An attribute of good test construction is that each type is used for maximum effectiveness. For example, if you wanted to test a class for mastery of a group of definitions, you would probably not use an essay test, because the real strength of this test is its ability to measure at levels higher than recall. What are some of the desired outcomes of education regarding which the essay test is a useful tool of measurement?

Ability to select appropriate material.   It is the hope of the teacher that the pupil will have a considerable amount of background knowledge in the general area of the test; however, just knowing a multitude of facts is not adequate to produce a good answer. The ability to draw from background knowledge those items of information that are applicable to a particular situation is also necessary. Probably no one would question the importance of this type of skill, yet many types of test items are relatively ineffective in this area of measurement.

Ability to organize material.   Many teachers have had experience with the student who takes a quick glance at an essay test question, then wildly dives into a great floundering of words. Such a reaction seldom leads to a well-organized discussion. Many teachers advise students to take several minutes to think through the question before they start writing. Others even insist that the student write out a simple outline before he launches into the discussion. Certainly, the development of skill in organization is a highly desirable outcome of teaching. In order to test on this phase of education, the student must be given an opportunity actually to organize material. Good essay tests provide this opportunity.

Ability to present material.   A student can have a vast accumulation of facts, along with good organizational skill, and yet do poorly on an essay test. He must be able to present the material with clarity, using correct grammar and spelling. Some critics of education point out cases of students who are deficient in these skills. Doubtless, there are such cases. One of the best means of locating those students who need remedial work in these areas is the essay test.

Ability to respond with uniqueness.   It is a generally accepted principle that education is an individual process, despite the fact that, in practice, we put students in groups or classes for instruction. The uniqueness of each student comes to be recognized and, in varying degrees, appreciated by the teacher. But the short-answer types of tests give students only the barest opportunity to display their individuality. The essay test gives students a good chance to use their favorite expressions and respond each in his own way. This highly desirable outcome of education—that is, the development of uniqueness—sometimes gets lost in pressures for conformity.

SPECIFIC USES OF THE ESSAY ITEM

You may have heard of teachers who made very confusing use of essay items. There was the physics teacher whose examination consisted of the single statement, "Discuss the electron." Or, even more general, the literature teacher whose test consisted of the single word, "Poetry." Obviously, both left the student guessing as to what was expected of him.

A complete listing of situations that are well suited to essay testing would be impossible. Some types of test situations in which the essay test is widely used are illustrated here.

Compare. This might take the form of comparing two philosophies, two or more procedures, or many other things. One point worthy of special attention is that the student should be clear on the *basis* of comparison.

Contrast.

Summarize. Development of the ability to compress major units of study into fairly brief statements is a highly desirable outcome of education. Hence, it is worthy of inclusion on occasional tests.

Support a position. A popular form of question in this area is to lead off with a statement of an issue, then ask the student to agree or disagree. Finally comes the "why?" When well constructed, this is a very challenging type of question.

Use a basic principle to explain a phenomenon.

Use one or more phenomena to arrive at a basic principle.

Describe a procedure. While this type can serve a useful purpose, care should be exercised to assure that this is not used in a simple recall situation.

SUGGESTIONS FOR CONSTRUCTION

As has been pointed out earlier, no type of item is so good that it cannot be rendered ineffective. One factor that can reduce effectiveness is using a type of question in a situation or on material for which it is not suited. Another factor, frequently encountered in essay tests, is that the apparent ease of construction causes the teacher to approach his test-making task too casually. There are several basic principles that should be observed in making this type of test.

Be sure the test is neither too general nor too specific.   This, of course, should be influenced by the maturity of the group being tested. An item that is general enough for an advanced graduate student would probably mystify a junior high student. If a test item is to give a student an opportunity to select and organize, however, it must be more general than a written statement of memorized facts. Extremely specific material should probably be tested with some sort of short-answer items; extremely broad questions should be used only when they serve a definite purpose and with groups that are sufficiently mature to handle them effectively.

Define the direction and scope of the response.   Frequently, a question may look quite specific to a teacher, yet the student may not be clear as to what is expected of him. In an actual case, a college class taking an essay test submitted papers varying in length from 2 pages to 40 pages. (Incidentally, the 2-page paper received the better mark.)   While the question seemed fairly specific, there was no limitation in the scope of the discussion. The student with the short paper presented a discussion that definitely applied to the question; the other interpreted the test as an open invitation to write everything he knew. Some teachers limit the scope of a question by asking a "topic question," then adding several subsidiary questions of a more specific nature.

Consider the time factor.   The problem of judging the length of time students will need in order to complete a test is especially difficult with essay questions. Students who generally operate at about the same achievement levels frequently differ widely in their ability to write. Or, even with comparable quality of writing, they frequently differ in the speed with which they write. The safest approach, to make the test of such length that everyone *should* finish, may well require that the test be somewhat shorter than one would like it to be. Further, it is well to prepare for two special cases: those who finish early, and those who, despite all the teacher's efforts, do not finish. The earlier suggestion (that the teacher spell out in some detail the scope of the expected response) has important applications in controlling the length of time required to write the test.

Try to have all students take the same test.   Many teachers have traditionally made use of optional questions ("answer three of the following five," etc.). While this practice might serve to give students a "break," it is hard to justify, since it means that a wide variety of combinations is possible. How, for example, could one compare the achievement of Joe, who answered questions 1, 2, and 3, with that of Larry, who answered questions 3, 4, and 5? Further, if the test is to serve a diagnostic purpose, how could you discover Joe's weaknesses on questions 4 and 5, neither of which he answered?

Some teachers make use of a challenge question or problem for those students who finish early. While this practice has some commendable features, it should be made clear that the student works on this question *after* he has completed the remainder of the test. It should not be included as a possible substitute for some part of the test.

SUGGESTIONS FOR SCORING ESSAY TESTS

The scoring of short-answer items is primarily mechanical in nature, but there is nothing mechanical about scoring essay items. It is a tedious and demanding operation. And it is, in the final analysis, a subjective process. One teacher, after trying a variety of methods, finally concluded that "you can't carry out a subjective procedure objectively." In order to achieve as much consistency as possible, there are a few scoring suggestions that should be considered.

Be clear about minimum essentials of an acceptable answer.   By stretching a point, this might be considered a scoring key. Before he begins reading the papers, the teacher should make a list of all the points that, in his opinion, should be dealt with in each answer. In the absence of any such guidelines, there is danger that major omissions might go undetected. Further, if some points are more important than others, the key should indicate the relative weights assigned to each.

Preferably, keep tests anonymous.   While the accusation that teachers have "pets" is seldom valid, there is danger that a teacher might subconsciously be influenced by certain emotions. Many teachers, in scoring essay tests, have found themselves thinking such things as, "Joe has been absent a great deal," "Mary always has trouble expressing herself," and "Sally writes so slowly." While probably true, such sentiments do not make for an unbiased evaluation of a test paper. If the teacher does not know whose paper he is reading, such factors cannot affect the result.

Some teachers strive to keep tests anonymous by assigning students numbers, so that the name is not used. Others have papers folded in such a way as to hide the name. But there does not seem to be any way around the fact that, after a period of time, such factors as handwriting and word usage are likely to serve as identifiers to an alert teacher, whether or not the name of the student is visible.

Score all responses to each item before going on.   If there are several questions on a test, the scorer is far more likely to be consistent if he follows this pattern than if he reads each paper in its entirety at one time. Further, having fixed in mind the minimum essentials of an acceptable answer, the teacher will find that he can proceed through a stack of papers quite rapidly by checking a particular question on each paper. Some teachers object to this method on the grounds that it makes for a great deal of "paper shuffling." While this is true (if there are five questions, each paper must be handled five times), it is outweighed by the gain in consistency and efficiency.

Inform students about the method of scoring before giving the test. For example, if a student's mark is to be influenced by spelling, grammatical usage, and quality of handwriting, he should know this before taking the test. If such factors are considered to be of importance in the course, it is perfectly defensible to use them as marking criteria. It is never safe to assume that the students understand this, however. Not only should they be told the criteria upon which marking will be based, but they should also be told the weight assigned to each factor.

Many teachers make use of a dual marking system for this purpose. Under this system, the student is given one mark on the basis of content and another based on mechanics. Others prefer to use the single mark as an indicator of overall quality.

It is impossible to include in a discussion of this kind all the features of the essay test. When an individual teacher reviews this type of item for his own use in his own classes, he may well discover uses that are uniquely valuable in his own set of conditions. It is very important that the teacher be willing to try new approaches in all of his testing. The essay test is no exception.

QUESTIONS AND ACTIVITIES

1. Prepare a class report on some of the research studies dealing with the unreliability of scoring of essay tests.

2. Prepare a list of test situations in your own teaching field, in which you feel that essay tests could serve a valuable purpose.

3. Prepare a set of essay questions that you feel to be of good quality. Ask a friend to analyze them for weaknesses.

4. Show by illustration how, in the same measurement situation, you could make use of essay items and various types of short-

answer items. Overall, which do you think would function best? Why?

SUGGESTED READINGS

Ahmann, J. Stanley, and Marvin D. Glock, *Evaluating Pupil Growth* (3rd ed.), Allyn and Bacon, 1967.
> Chapter 5 presents a comprehensive discussion of the essay test aimed at aiding the teacher to use it more effectively and reliably.

Downie, N. M., *Fundamentals of Measurement: Techniques and Practices* (2nd ed.), Oxford University Press, 1967.
> Chapter 9 presents an excellent introduction to the strengths, limitations, and uses of essay tests.

Green, John A., *Teacher-Made Tests,* Harper & Row, 1963.
> Chapter 5 has a thorough and understandable treatment of the uses, construction, and scoring of essay tests.

Gronlund, Norman E., *Measurement and Evaluation in Teaching,* Macmillan, 1965.
> Chapter 10 presents excellent illustrations of essay items and suggestions for constructing and using them.

Karmel, Louis J., *Measurement and Evaluation in the Schools,* Macmillan, 1970.
> A general discussion of the essay exam is presented in chapter 14.

Stecklein, J. E., *Essay Tests: Why and How?, Bulletin on Classroom Testing, No. 2,* Bureau of Institutional Research, University of Minnesota, 1955.
> This publication presents rationale and techniques for constructing and using essay tests.

10

MEASURING ACHIEVEMENT BY
DIRECT OBSERVATION OF
PERFORMANCE AND APPRAISAL
OF A SAMPLE PRODUCT

The point was made in Chapter 2 that there are certain objectives in education that do not lend themselves readily to measurement by means of paper-and-pencil tests. Measurement of such objectives frequently requires the use of direct observation of performance or appraisal of a sample.

Direct observation of performance is the appropriate method in a variety of learning situations, from kindergarten through the university, where the ability to exhibit a technique under realistic conditions is the objective. Examples of such objectives in the primary grades involve simple psychomotor functions, such as forming letters and numerals, coloring and drawing; as well as more complex kinds of behavior, such as working cooperatively on a group project. Examples in upper elementary and secondary grades include skills in physical education classes and procedures in music, art, typewriting, public speaking, home economics, and industrial arts. The ability to handle certain classroom situations is an excellent example of an objective in teacher education which is best measured by direct observation of performance.

Many of these procedures lead to the completion of a product that also requires assessment and evaluation. This is particularly true in art, typing, home economics, and industrial arts classes. English, history, and civics classes may also include objectives calling for production of finished products in the form of completed essays and reports. When the objectives of a course include the ability to produce a finished product, then assessment of a sample produced by the student is a necessary part of the teacher's measurement program.

MAJOR PROBLEMS INVOLVED IN APPRAISING PROCEDURES AND PRODUCTS

Research in the measurement of procedures and products has not been carried on as extensively as that involving paper-and-pencil tests. As a result, much more information is available about the proper construction and use of paper-and-pencil tests than about the other two methods. Teachers can improve their measurement techniques in these areas, however, if they are willing to expend some effort in applying relevant principles.

The major problems involved in appraising procedures and products are similar to those of any other measuring effort in education: reliability and validity. In order to make a reliable appraisal, one must know specifically the qualities of the procedure or product that are to be appraised. Too often a teacher evaluates a report, speech, or performance according to his "general impression." This is the kind of evaluation that produces both unreliable and invalid results. The teacher's feeling about the personality of the student may influence his judgment of the student's product. If the teacher happens to be in a bad mood, the student may start off with a 10-point handicap. It is not hard to imagine the effect this has on the student and his motivation to learn. *In your own experiences as a student, were you ever confronted with such an evaluation of your efforts?*

The best way to overcome such poor evaluation practices is to have written down before the evaluation begins the specific features of the product or procedure by which it is to be judged. These features of evaluative criteria should include the significant aspects of the thing to be judged, and these should be specifically related to the objectives of the unit.

After the criteria are listed, a second vitally important step is the weighting of the criteria. Some will be more important than others; hence, more "weight" or points should be assigned to them. In a civics report, for example, content may be the most important feature, so it is given a maximum of 50 points. Organization and presentation may be worth 25 points each. Each of these three major features should be subdivided into its components, and these should be weighted in the same way. The weight assigned to each feature will depend on the values of the teacher and should reflect the stress he had placed on each during the presentation of the unit.

TECHNIQUES OF PERFORMANCE AND PRODUCT APPRAISAL

Throughout the first half of the twentieth century, there have been many attempts to develop formal, standardized procedures for assessing performances and products. Some researchers have been successful in producing scales by which the product or performance of a student may be observed and evaluated. More often than not, however, these scales have been more effective in assessing personal behaviors or attitudes which were of interest to the researchers. Consequently, such scales are of little help to the teacher interested in measuring student achievement toward specific objectives of a unit of work. The teacher should know, better than anyone else, the specific objectives he has stressed; therefore the most valid scales should be the ones constructed by the teacher. Excellent illustrations of weighted objectives and scales for specific subjects may be found in the *Forty-Fifth Yearbook of the National Society for the Study of Education*, to which reference has already been made.

There are four primary techniques that may aid in the direct observation of student performance and the evaluation of products: (1) ranking, (2) check lists, (3) rating scales, and (4) anecdotal records. The qualities and uses of each of these will be discussed.

Ranking

As a method of collecting and ordering information about a student, performance or product ranking has been one of the least reliable. The principle problem involved in ranking has been the lack of clearly defined specific qualities by which a performance or product is to be ranked. More reliable rankings of public speaking, for example, may be obtained if the teacher has defined specific criteria, such as loudness, enunciation, posture, movements, and organization, rather than broad criteria, such as delivery and content.

Ranking has an advantage in that different degrees of quality of a characteristic are recognized, rather than the mere presence or absence of the characteristic. In some cases, such as the proper form for a particular kind of typed letter, the characteristic is either present or absent. The letter has been typed in the proper form or not. In many cases, however, the characteristic is present in greater or lesser degree, such as the gracefulness of a movement in physical education.

In ranking a performance or product according to different degrees of a particular characteristic, a procedure that may improve reliability is that of noting the extremes. In ranking a set of student products (birdhouses, pictures, cakes, or reports) on a particular characteristic, it is not too difficult to select those at the extremes—the very best ones and the very worst ones. The teacher may, in this manner, classify all products into three groups, such as superior, average, and inferior. If he desires, the teacher may classify the products on all the characteristics he considers important, assigning a given number of points each time a product is classified. He may assign 15 points for each rating of superior, 10 points for average, and 5 points for inferior, or he may vary the number of points for each superior, average, and inferior ranking, depending on the importance of the character-istic. Thus he may, by totaling the points assigned to each product, determine fairly reliably an "overall" or general ranking of the product.

While we have considered performance ranking and product ranking together, the two have certain basic differences. Suppose, for example, you are a speech teacher and you want to list your 30 students in rank order as to performance on some 3-minute speeches. Technically, you could not be sure of anyone's rank until all the speeches were finished; and by then you might have forgotten the earlier ones. In ranking products, however, you have the benefit of a second look. Hence, in some ways, it is easier to rank products than it is to rank performances.

Check lists

The distinct advantage of using a check list in judging the per-formance or product of a student is that the specific features to be judged are written down. The teacher evaluates the quality of a performance or product by checking each characteristic in turn. This can ensure that the teacher does not overlook some essential characteristic. This procedure is particularly helpful when there are many diverse characteristics of a thing that must be "checked on," or when the teacher's evaluation must be completed in minimum time.

A check list for evaluating a performance usually consists of a series of actions listed in the order in which they may be expected to occur. The teacher usually checks *yes* or *no,* indicating that the action did or did not occur or that it was or was not satisfactorily performed. Another kind of check list indicates the sequence of the activities. On this check list, the teacher places a number by each activity which indicates the sequence in which it occurs. This type of check list is particularly helpful in evaluating student performances in which the sequence of activities is important, such as setting up a laboratory experiment, making a cake, or planting a tree.

The following example illustrates the use of a check list for evaluating a speech. It is to be checked by the teacher as he observes the student's delivery. It is not intended to include all the features of a speech that might be evaluated, since those would depend, to some extent, on a particular teacher's objectives. It is intended to illustrate how general features may be subdivided into more specific aspects that can be observed. You will notice that the two general features to be evaluated with this check list are delivery and content. Notice also that the subdivisions of these general features are stated in specific behavioral terms, making them more readily observable.

Check List for Evaluating an Informative Speech

Key:

      1—Speaker's exhibition of this feature was poor throughout the speech.

      2—Speaker exhibited the feature satisfactorily throughout most of the speech.

      3—Speaker exhibited this feature well and continuously throughout the speech.

A. Delivery
    1. Poise
      (a) Does speaker exhibit poise
———— approaching the stand?
———— at the stand?
———— leaving the stand?
———— (b) Does speaker maintain eye contact with listeners?

_____ (c) Does speaker control signs of nervousness in his voice?

_____ (d) Does speaker control signs of nervousness in his hands, face, and body?

   2. Gestures: How well does speaker add meaning to his speech with appropriate gestures and expressions of

_____ (a) hands?

_____ (b) face?

_____ (c) body?

   3. Voice

_____ (a) Does speaker speak loudly enough for everyone in audience to hear?

_____ (b) Does speaker enunciate clearly?

_____ (c) Does speaker have a pleasant voice?

_____ (d) Does speaker appropriately use voice fluctuation and tone to emphasize feeling and meaning?

B. Content and Construction

   1. Is speaker's coverage of the topic sufficient for his audience

_____ (a) in scope?

_____ (b) in depth?

_____ 2. Is speaker's choice of words appropriate to level of his audience?

_____ 3. Does speaker use appropriate illustrations?

_____ 4. Is the organization of the speech appropriate for its content?

_____ 5. Does speaker overemphasize minor points and neglect major ones?

You will note that this check list incorporates some of the features of a rating scale, which is discussed next.

Rating scale

Rating scales can be very useful devices for evaluating the performance or product of a student. They incorporate the advantage of ranking, in that different degrees of a feature are considered, and the advantage of a check list, in that the specific features of the thing to be evaluated are listed. The rating scale also permits a performance to be evaluated while the performance is going on.

Rating scales can be designed only by a person who is thoroughly familiar with the product or procedure to be judged. Usually two or three teachers working together can obtain better results than one teacher working alone. The first step in constructing rating scales is to list the important features of a procedure or product by which it is to be judged. Each feature is then placed on a continuum representing degrees of quality from minimum to maximum. The continuum may be divided into three parts (good, average, and poor); five parts (superior, above average, average, below average, and inferior); or as many as seven or more parts. Each category along the continuum should be defined more specifically than superior, good, average, or poor. For example, "good" posture during a speech should be defined, perhaps, as "stands up straight and faces audience." "Poor" posture may be defined as "tends to slouch and hangs head down while speaking." Each of the categories along the continuum may be identified by a number. The rater then observes the procedure or product and marks the number or description that best describes the degree of quality he observes.

When using a rating scale, one should guard against two problems often associated with them: (1) the halo effect and (2) the tendency to avoid the extremes of the scale and rate all performance in the middle ranges. The halo effect is a tendency to generalize from one or two attributes of a person to everything else about him. For example, teachers tend to give higher achievement ratings to pupils who are nice, neat, clean, and honest, and to give lower ratings to those who are the opposite. This does not mean simply that nice, neat, honest pupils are necessarily lower achievers than others. Indeed these qualities may well reflect their general excellence. However this is not *necessarily* the case. The point is this: When one rates a pupil's performance, he should rate it objectively. Rate the performance, not the pupil. The second problem, the tendency to lump all ratings in the middle range, may result from a reluctance to be either harsh or generous. If one can realize that rating is simply recording information, not evaluating, he may be able to be more realistic. A fair evaluation can be made only after a series of ratings are available, and the evaluation is more reliable if two or more persons have contributed.

The rating scale shown below illustrates some of the qualities mentioned above. This example was adapted from a much longer one in use at Louisiana State University. Notice that each feature to be rated is placed on a continuum (very poor to excellent). The quality of the scale is improved by descriptions of the areas along each continuum.

A RATING SCALE FOR YOUR INSTRUCTOR

This is a rating scale for your instructor to be used by him for the purpose of improving his teaching techniques. If you make the ratings conscientiously, individually and honestly, it will be of great value to you and the many students who will take this course after you.

It is necessary in each case merely to place a check mark at the point of the line which seems most accurate.

DO NOT SIGN YOUR NAME OR MAKE ANY OTHER MARK WHICH MIGHT SERVE TO IDENTIFY YOU.

1. Does the instructor indicate careful preparation for the class meetings?

No preparation	Little preparation	Preparation often inadequate	Usually well prepared	Meetings very carefully planned

2. Does the instructor show an interest in his subject?

Subject irksome to him	Very seldom shows enthusiasm	Only mildly interested	Frequently shows enthusiasm	Very enthusiastic and interested

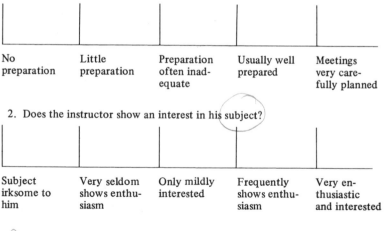

Profession
"   al attitude

3. How are plans and assignments determined?

Very in-definite and usually hurriedly given	Rather in-definite and autocratically given	Definite: often hurriedly given by instructor	Carefully given but indefinite, though co-operation of students is sought	Clear and definite; students and instructor plan together in light of students' needs

4. Does the instructor arouse the interest of the students?

Majority inattentive most of period	Students seldom in-terested	Students occasionally show interest	Students frequently show interest	Interest usually runs high

5. How is the time in the class meeting apportioned?

Often neg-lects subject for other irrelevant topics	Spends more time on details than on important topics	Stresses important topics and details equally	Spends most of time on important topics, stresses few details	Stresses fundamental or important topics, dis-regards trivial details

6. Is the instructor's speech clear and distinct?

Words very indistinct, often im-possible to hear	Words some-times indis-tinct and not easy to hear	Loud enough but not distinct	Distinct but not loud enough at times	Speaks very clearly and distinctly

7. Is the instructor self-confident?

Timid	Often confused by trainees	Fairly self-confident, occasionally disconcerted	Seldom, if ever, disconcerted	Sure of himself; meets difficulties with poise

8. How well does the instructor express his thoughts?

Meaning almost never clear	Much hesitation for words; meaning often not clear	Some hesitation; meaning at times not clear	Some hesitation; meaning always clear	Words come easily; meaning always clear

9. Does the instructor stimulate the students to do original thinking and to express their own opinion?

Easily aroused to temper by opposition	Sometimes impatient when views are opposed	Shows no personal response to opposition	Welcomes differences of opinion	Invites differences of opinion

10. How would you describe his personal appearance?

Usually slovenly— clothes and person	Often quite untidy and careless in appearance	Sometimes careless in appearance	Usually tidy and careful in appearance	Well groomed; clothes neat, clean, in good taste

Is instructor available to student outside of lecture?

What is relationship of instructor to student

attitude

11. How would you rate your instructor on his general overall performance?

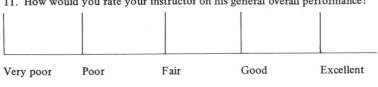

Very poor   Poor   Fair   Good   Excellent

Add here any additional or explanatory comments.

_____

_____

_____

Anecdotal records

Of the four techniques discussed in this section, the anecdotal record is the least systematic. It has one distinct advantage, however, over the other three. It presents the teacher with a method of recording his observations of spontaneous behaviors that may be significant in evaluating achievement. Check lists and rating scales usually require some preplanned structure regarding the time and place where they are to be used. However, the teacher may observe significant evidence of achievement toward certain objectives at unusual times and places during the course of the school day. Anecdotal records provide a convenient method of collecting and recording this kind of evidence. They also may be used to collect evidence of performance that occurs during a long period of time, such as a semester or school term. The assessment of student teachers and the assessment of pupil conduct may be improved by the use of anecdotal records. An evaluation can be made much more fairly at the end of a grading period if the supervisor or teacher has collected evidence of performance instead of having to rely solely on his memory. However, anecdotal records, like any other assessment technique, should not be used without purpose. The procedure of having each teacher turn in three or four anecdotal records on each pupil taught during the year just to fill a student folder is a rather poor practice.

Anecdotal records should be written, when at all possible, at the time the teacher observes signíficant behaviors. That is, the teacher should record the behavior when he sees it, rather than waiting until the event has been partially forgotten. The main thing to keep in mind when writing anecdotal records is that there is a tendency for a person to confuse a report by writing his opinion or judgment of an event, rather than objectively recording the event as it occurred. The useful anecdotal record is the one that gives an objective report of an event, rather than one which tells only how the *teacher felt* about it. (Sometimes anecdotal records reveal more about the people who write them than they do about the subjects of the report.) Mimeographed forms on which anecdotes are to be recorded help to improve their objectivity and insure that important information is not omitted. A sample anecdotal record form is presented below:

```
+---------------------------------------------------------------+
|                     ANECDOTAL RECORD                          |
| _____ Name    Date _____         |
| _____ Place   Time _____         |
| Incident   _____    |
|                                                               |
| Comments _____    |
|                                                               |
| Signature  _____    |
+---------------------------------------------------------------+
```

It should be evident that assessment of procedures and products is an important part of the measurement program of many teachers. It is, however, often the most difficult part. The techniques involved are much less objective and refined than paper-and-pencil tests. Their reliability is much more dependent on the ability of the teacher to use them than is the case with paper-and-pencil tests. Actually, they are only aids that help the teacher make more systematic and objective observations. As with other measurement procedures, several samples of a student's performance or product should be noted before a final evaluation of his achievement toward a given objective is rendered.

QUESTIONS AND ACTIVITIES

1. In your own educational experience, describe situations in which your efforts were evaluated by check lists or rating scales. Do you feel that the end result was fair to you? Explain.

2. Describe a situation in your teaching area in which effective use could be made of a rating scale. Then design such a scale for presentation to a class.

3. The story is told of a young girl attending a finishing school who was graded "B" in horseback riding. What information, if any, does this convey? Would a rating scale have worked better? Why?

4. Suppose you were asked to help judge a science fair at either the elementary or secondary level. What are some features that you would look for in rating the projects?

SUGGESTED READINGS

Ahmann, J. Stanley, and Marvin D. Glock, *Evaluating Pupil Growth* (3rd ed.), Allyn and Bacon, 1967.
> Principles and techniques of evaluating procedures and products are discussed in chapter 7. Several standard illustrations are presented.

Green, John A., *Teacher-Made Tests,* Harper & Row, 1963.
> Chapter 4 presents an informative introduction to the techniques of systematic observation of performance, along with some excellent illustrations.

Horrocks, John E. and Thelma Schoonover, *Measurement for Teachers,* Merrill, 1968.
An excellent discussion of testing procedures in subjects stressing the psychomotor domain is presented in chapter 12.

Remmers, H. H., and N. L. Gage, *Educational Measurement and Evaluation* (rev. ed.), Harper & Row, 1955.
Chapter 6 presents a discussion of the assessment of products and procedures, plus several illustrations that should prove helpful.

Ryans, David C., and Norman Frederiksen, "Performance Tests of Educational Achievement," in E. F. Lindquist (ed.), *Educational Measurement,* American Council on Education, 1951.
Chapter 12 is an advanced and very thorough discussion of the construction and use of performance tests. Several illustrations are presented, along with six logical steps for developing a performance test.

Tyler, Ralph W., "A Skill Test in Using a Microscope," *Educational Research Bulletin,* November 19, 1930.
A rather old, but still excellent, illustration and discussion of a technique of assessing performance in the science laboratory.

11

APPRAISING ACHIEVEMENT
IN THE AFFECTIVE DOMAIN

You will remember that human behavior is divided into three major classifications or domains: the cognitive, the psychomotor, and the affective. Measuring achievement in the cognitive domain, which includes intellectual behavior, was discussed in Chapters 7-9. Chapter 10 discussed measuring achievement in certain aspects of the psychomotor domain. In this chapter, some of the problems and procedures of measuring achievement in the affective domain will be discussed.

NATURE OF THE AFFECTIVE DOMAIN

Those behaviors commonly thought of as emotions are classified in the affective domain. Terms often used in education to describe behavior in this domain are *feelings, attitudes, interest, appreciations, beliefs,* and *values.* Objectives involving these types of behavior probably will be found most frequently, though not exclusively, in courses of literature, art, and the social studies. In all courses, the teacher hopes that her students will develop positive attitudes about the value of the subject. In physical science courses, we strive to develop positive attitudes concerning the use of the scientific method. Throughout elementary school, objectives involving the affective domain are found.

Relationship between cognitive and affective achievement

Discussions of the relationship between cognitive and affective achievement have sometimes sounded like the chicken-or-the-egg argument. Some people maintain that positive attitudes toward a subject automatically follow knowledge of the subject; that is, the more one knows about a subject, the more he appreciates it. Others maintain that motivation is the key. If a person is convinced of the importance of a subject, he will automatically learn more about it. There is, of course, an element of truth in each position. Your own past experience as a student, however, has probably indicated that neither result is automatic in all learning situations. It is quite possible to enjoy a course while learning very little about the subject matter; or, conversely, one might learn a great deal about a subject and develop a considerable distaste for it at the same time.

Whether or not a student develops interest in and liking for a subject depends not only on his cognitive behavior concerned with the subject but on many other things as well. Perhaps more important than knowledge of the subject are such factors as the attitudes of other persons who are important to the student, the satisfaction the student gains from working with the subject, and the manner in which the subject is taught.

Examples of affective objectives

The following list of objectives should help to clarify further the type of behaviors usually classed as affective. The objectives are drawn from representative academic fields and various grade levels and are stated in terms of student behavior to be achieved.

Literature
> The student has a desire to read good literature.
> The student reads literature to discover variations in literary style.

Music
> The student enjoys vocal harmonizing with a group.
> The student endeavors to create variations on a musical theme.

Social Studies
> The student develops an awareness of possible effects his actions may have on others.
> The student develops a sense of responsibility for participation in local, state, and national political affairs.
> The student is willing to perform for the benefit of the group rather than solely for himself.

Grammar
> The student prefers to use correct grammar when speaking or writing.

History
> The student has pride in the cultural contributions of his forebears.
> The student believes that a knowledge of history is necessary if a society is to avoid repeating its past mistakes.

General Science
> The student has a scientific curiosity — he wants to know the how and why of phenomena.
> The student has an attitude of suspended judgment—he does not jump to conclusions before the facts have been collected.

The kind of objective involving the affective domain deserves special mention because of the frequency with which it is erroneously classified. This objective usually begins, "The student develops an understanding of the importance of ___," and ends with whatever concept or subject the teacher is teaching. Teachers often teach and test for achievement toward this objective as if it were a cognitive behavior. Students are made to memorize the "reasons" for the thing's importance and to repeat these reasons on a test. Because of this misclassification, the essential element in the objective is achieved by the student incidentally, if at all. What the teacher really desires the student to achieve is a realization, an attitude, a belief that the thing is important; therefore the essential element in the objective involves affective rather than cognitive behavior. A teacher's efforts are much more likely to be effective if he clearly understands the results he is trying to help his students achieve. Ambiguity of terminology used to describe behavior in the affective domain is one of the chief problems in its measurement.

THE TAXONOMY OF EDUCATIONAL OBJECTIVES: AFFECTIVE DOMAIN

Primarily to overcome the problem of ambiguity of terminology and to stimulate research, *Handbook II* of the *Taxonomy of Educational Objectives* was published in 1964. (See Appendix B.) *Handbook II* does for the affective domain what *Handbook I* did for the cognitive. That is, it sets up a hierarchical classification system of specific objectives stated in terms of student behavior.

The organizing principle used in the affective domain is *internalization*. This term refers to the process of "incorporating something within the mind or body, adopting as one's own the ideas, practices, standards, or values of another person or of society."[1] Used as the continuum in the affective Taxonomy, internalization

[1]David R. Krathwohl, Benjamin S. Bloom, and Bertram B. Masia, *Taxonomy of Educational Objectives, Handbook II: Affective Domain,* McKay, 1964, p. 29.

appears to be broader than the definition given above. In the affective Taxonomy, it refers to behaviors ranging from mere *awareness* of something, through *responding* to something with *positive feeling* and *increasing commitment* to it, until it is *organized* with increasing complexity into one's philosophy of life. Of course, every idea of which a person becomes aware will not be responded to with positive feeling nor be incorporated ultimately into his philosophy. The affective Taxonomy merely describes possible behavior along a continuum of increasing internalization.

The five categories of the affective Taxonomy, with their subdivisions, follow:

1.0 Receiving
   1.1 Awareness
   1.2 Willingness to receive
   1.3 Controlled or selected attention

2.0 Responding
   2.1 Acquiescence in responding
   2.2 Willingness to respond
   2.3 Satisfaction in response

3.0 Valuing
   3.1 Acceptance of a value
   3.2 Preference of a value
   3.3 Commitment

4.0 Organization
   4.1 Conceptualization of a value
   4.2 Organization of a value system

5.0 Characterization by a value or value complex
   5.1 Generalized set
   5.2 Characterization

The lowest level in Taxonomy is 1.0, receiving. The student is at this level of internalization when he first encounters an idea or phenomenon. As long as the student remains at this level, he makes no emotional response to the idea, although he may move quickly to the higher levels where emotional response is classified. (Of course, he may continue to be disinterested also.) At the second level, 2.0, responding, the student begins to behave in terms of the idea—he responds to it. For example, in category 1.0, a student would become *aware* of certain rules of safe driving; at category 2.0, he would drive in accordance with those rules. As the process of internalization continues, he reaches the 3.0 level, valuing. When the student has internalized the rules to this degree, he is often described as attaching *worth* to them, believing in them, or having faith in them. Feelings of patriotism and loyalty would be classified in this category. At the 4.0 level, organization, the student begins to organize various values he has assimilated into a *system* of values. The highest stage on the internalization continuum is 5.0, characterization by a value or value complex. When a person reaches this stage, he has begun to behave in a consistent manner, and he may be said to have developed a consistent philosophy of life. He may also be described as having achieved full maturity.

Objectives in categories 4.0 and 5.0 are not often found among an individual teacher's list of objectives. These objectives are not usually attainable as the result of one course but are more appropriate as goals for the total educational process as carried out by schools and all the other agencies of social development. Perhaps most of the affective objectives an individual teacher would hope to promote would be found at levels 1.0, 2.0, and 3.0. Even at these levels, however, it probably takes more than the efforts of any one teacher to effect any lasting change.

PROBLEMS INVOLVED IN MEASURING ACHIEVEMENT
IN THE AFFECTIVE DOMAIN

There is extensive discussion of measuring achievement in the cognitive domain presented in Chapters 7, 8, and 9, while the affective domain is given limited treatment in this chapter. This contrast indicates that a great deal more is known about cognitive achievement. Our relatively meager knowledge about the affective domain complicates the currently recognized problems of obtaining evidence of achievement toward affective goals. As has been stated, perhaps the most serious problem encountered in attempts to measure affective achievement is the vagueness of the terminology used to describe behavior in the affective domain. Terms like *interest* and *appreciation* are difficult to translate into specific, observable behavior. It is to be hoped that *Handbook II* is a beginning in the reduction of this problem.

Another problem encountered in measuring achievement toward affective goals is the lack of complete consistency between affective qualities and their behavioral manifestations. We are not always sure that a given behavior is the result of a given affective quality. The same attitude or feelings may produce different behaviors in different persons; and, conversely, the same overt behavior may be caused by different feelings and attitudes in different persons.

Certain philosophical issues also contribute to the difficulties of measurement and evaluation in the affective domain. One is the issue of education versus indoctrination. In a democracy, especially a heterogeneous one such as ours, education is supposed to serve the ends of free choice and independent decision making. Indoctrination implies a limiting of free choice, an attempt to persuade or coerce the individual to accept one particular belief or set of values over others. Indoctrination dealing with the promotion of particular attitudes and beliefs is quite intimately associated with the affective domain. Because of American society's negative view of indoctrination, teachers are understandably hesitant about teaching and testing in the affective domain. In many cases, also, a person's beliefs are considered to be his private concern. The privacy of one's beliefs is of particular significance when political or religious issues are involved.

Finally, measurement is difficult in the affective domain, because here we are concerned that a student *will do* a task or *does hold* an attitude. In the cognitive domain, we are interested only in determining if a student *can perform* a task, *can state* a belief for himself. In the cognitive domain, a teacher can present him with a task and determine whether or not he can perform it. In the affective domain, however, the matter is much more complicated. How can we determine whether or not a student holds a given attitude? We can ask him a series of questions designed to reveal his attitude, and this is the method often used. It is quite easy, however, for the student to answer the questions to indicate the attitude desired by the teacher while he believes just the opposite. A more valid technique to determine a student's feelings or attitude toward something would be to make systematic observations of his behavior in relation to that thing. The difficulty with this technique is the time involved in the systematic observation of each student and the fact that many feelings the teacher would like to determine involve behaviors that cannot always be observed during school hours.

The necessary use of questionnaires to determine affective achievement brings us face to face with the problem of honesty, that is, "Are the student's responses accurate reflections of the way he actually feels and behaves or is he only giving answers he thinks the teacher wants him to give?" This problem can be diminished in two ways. In some cases, the questions can be written so subtly that the student has difficulty determining the desired response and must, therefore, give an honest one. In all cases, however, it can be made clear to the students that their responses will be used in no way in determining their course grade. Not using responses concerning student's values in determining grades may also be philosophically desirable in many situations.

OBTAINING EVIDENCE OF ACHIEVEMENT
TOWARD AFFECTIVE GOALS

For the teacher who is interested in assessing achievement toward affective goals, two major activities are necessary. First, he must define precisely the affective objectives. This definition must be in terms of specific student behaviors that can be observed directly or inferred from other behaviors. Second, he must create situations in which the behavior can be directly observed, or he must ask the student questions about behavior that cannot be observed directly.

Since many affective objectives imply covert rather than overt changes and involve behavior outside the school, written questions will probably be the chief technique, especially in junior and senior high school.

To illustrate the process, a simple but commonly found objective in elementary school can be used: "The pupil realizes the importance of regular dental care." The first thing to be determined is the behavioral manifestation of this objective. What can be expected of a child who realizes that regular dental care is important? He might be expected to possess a toothbrush, to brush his teeth properly after every meal, and to visit his dentist twice a year. (The cooperation of parents is assumed in this case, though not always be forthcoming.) Second, the methods by which evidence of these behaviors can be collected must be determined, such as by observation or direct question.

More abstract kinds of objectives, such as appreciation, may be handled in the same manner. This has been done in two major studies, the Eight-Year Study of the Progressive Education Association (1933-1941) and the Cooperative Study in General Education of the American Council on Education (1939-1944).

Those who are interested in pursuing the assessment of achievement in the affective domain beyond the scope of this text are referred to the reports of these studies listed in the bibliography at the end of this chapter and to *Handbook II* of the *Taxonomy of Educational Objectives.* One example from each of the studies is presented here.

Appreciation of literature

During the course of the Eight-Year Study, it was found that many of the educational objectives the committees wanted to assess were not usually tested in schools. It was necessary, therefore, to define these objectives in terms of student behavior and to develop instruments for their assessment. Such was the case in attempting to assess appreciation of literature. In this endeavor, the Committee on the Evaluation of Reading selected seven reactions to reading which they considered to be important manifestations of appreciation of literature. These reactions are presented here, with certain overt acts demonstrating each.[2]

1. Satisfaction in the thing appreciated
   1.1 He reads aloud to others, or simply to himself, passages which he finds unusually interesting.
   1.2 He reads straight through without stopping or with a minimum of interruption.
   1.3 He reads for considerable periods of time.

2. Desire for more of the thing appreciated
   2.1 He asks other people to recommend reading which is more or less similar to the thing appreciated.
   2.2 He commences this reading of similar things as soon after reading the first as possible.
   2.3 He reads subsequently several books, plays, or poems by the same author.

3. Desire to know more about the thing appreciated
   3.1 He asks other people for information or sources of information about what he has read.
   3.2 He reads supplementary materials, such as biography, history, criticism, etc.
   3.3 He attends literary meetings devoted to reviews, criticisms, discussions, etc.

4. Desire to express oneself creatively
   4.1 He produces, or at least undertakes to produce, a creative product more or less after the manner of the thing appreciated.
   4.2 He writes critical evaluations.
   4.3 He illustrates what he has read in some graphic, spatial, musical, or dramatic arts.

5. Identification of oneself with the thing appreciated
   5.1 He accepts, at least while he is reading, the persons, places, situations, events, etc., as real.
   5.2 He dramatizes, formally or informally, various passages.

[2]Reproduced by permission from Eugene R. Smith and Ralph W. Tyler, *Appraising and Recording Student Progress,* copyright © 1942 by McGraw-Hill Book Company, pp. 254-255.

5.3 He imitates, consciously and unconsciously, the speech and actions of various characters in the story.

6. Desire to clarify one's own thinking about the life problems raised by the thing appreciated
   6.1 He attempts to state, either orally, or in writing, his own ideas, feelings, or information concerning the life problems with which his reading deals.
   6.2 He examines other sources for more information about these problems.
   6.3 He reads other works dealing with similar problems.

7. Desire to evaluate the thing appreciated
   7.1 He points out, both orally and in writing, the elements which in his opinion make it good literature.
   7.2 He explains how certain unacceptable elements (if any) could be improved.
   7.3 He consults published criticisms.

In assessing these behaviors, the students were presented with questionnaires about their reading. A portion of the "Questionnaire on Voluntary Reading" is presented here. The original questionnaire consisted of 100 ungrouped items. In this illustration, the items are grouped under the seven types of behavior presented in the preceding example. The seven types of behavior were worded in the questionnaire to place emphasis on what students actually do, rather than what they desire to do.[3]

Questionnaire on Voluntary Reading

Directions: The purpose of this questionnaire is to discover what you really think about the reading you do in your leisure time. Altogether, there are 100 questions. Consider each question carefully and answer it as honestly and frankly as you possibly can. *There are no "right" answers as such.* It is not expected that your own thoughts or feelings or activities relating to books should be like those of anyone else.

The numbers on your Answer Sheet correspond to the numbers of the questions on the questionnaire. There are three ways to mark the Answer Sheet:

[3] Ibid., pp. 251-252.

A—means that your answer to the question is Yes.
B—means that your answer to the question is Uncertain.
C—means that your answer to the question is No.

If it is at all possible, answer the questions by Yes or No. You should mark a question Uncertain only if you are unable to answer either Yes or No.

Please answer *every* question

"Derives satisfaction from reading"
1. Is it unusual for you, of your own accord, to spend a whole afternoon or evening reading a book?
2. Do you ever read plays, apart from school requirements?

"Wants to read more"
1. Do you have in mind one or two books you would like to read soon?
2. Do you wish you had more time to devote to reading?

"Identifies himself with his reading"
1. Have you ever tried to become in some respects like a character whom you have read about and admired?
2. Is it very unusual for you to become sad or depressed over the fate of a character?

"Becomes curious about his reading"
1. Do you read the book review sections of magazines or newspapers fairly regularly?
2. Do you ever read, apart from school requirements, books or articles about English or American literature?

"Expresses himself creatively"
1. Have you ever wanted to act out a scene from a book which you have read?
2. Has your reading of books ever stimulated you to attempt any original writing of your own?

"Evaluates his reading"
1. Do you ordinarily read a book without giving much thought to the quality of its style?
2. Do you ever consult published criticisms of any of the books which you read?

"Relates his reading to life"
1. Has your attitude toward war or patriotism been changed by books which you have read?
2. Is it very unusual for you to gain from your reading of books a better understanding of some of the problems which people face in their everyday living?

In order to assess student honesty in answering a questionnaire such as the one on voluntary reading, the committee developed another questionnaire on which students were asked to respond to questions about their reading behavior and then write an illustration or example of each behavior. It was assumed that the nature of the illustration would indicate whether or not the student had actually engaged in the behavior. The following example illustrates the format and first few items of such a questionnaire.[4]

Directions: This is not a "test" but an attempt to discover more about your reading interests. Obviously, no two persons have exactly the same reading interests; consequently *there are no "right" or "wrong" answers, as such, to these questions.*

Please answer each question as carefully and as honestly as you can. Mark your answer to each question by checking the space under Yes, No, or Uncertain at the right of the sheet. If your answer to a question is Yes, please give the additional information asked for in the question. If your answer is No or Uncertain, go on to the next question.

	Yes	No	Uncertain
1. Do you have in mind one or two books you would like to read?	_____	_____	_____
If you do, please give the author and title of one:		_____	
2. Do you ever read adventure novels in your spare time?	_____	_____	_____

[4]Ibid., pp. 271-272.

If you do, please give
the author and title of
one you have read: _____

3. Do you ever read essays,
apart from regular school
requirements?
    If you do, please give   _____   _____   _____
the author and title of
one you have read: _____

4. Is there any author whom
you like so well that you
would like to read any
new book he might
write?
    If there is, please give   _____   _____   _____
his name and the title of
one of his books you
have read: _____

5. Do you ever of your own
accord read humorous
stories or books of satire?   _____   _____   _____
    If you do, plaese give
the author and title of one
you have read: _____

Assessment of art appreciation was also attempted in the Eight-Year Study. This was done by asking students to pair 40 colored pictures and noting the kinds of similarities to which the students were sensitive. This technique was based on the primary assumption that "it is possible to understand the nature of and degree to which the art experience of an individual is developed by ascertaining the degree to which he is able to see and appreciate significant similarities and differences in art objects."[5] The students were also asked questions about their preferences among the pictures, and their reasons for these preferences. The total

[5]Ibid., p. 283.

process of selecting the pictures, administering the test, and interpreting the results was quite involved, and beyond the scope of this text to describe, but the teacher interested in assessment of art appreciation will find pages 276-312 in Smith and Tyler both interesting and helpful.

Health attitudes

The group of college representatives participating in one phase of the Cooperative Study in General Education in 1939-1941 was attempting to determine the content most appropriate for science courses taken by nonscience majors. During the course of this study, it was decided to ascertain the knowledge, interests, and attitudes toward personal health possessed by certain groups of college students. Six inventories were developed during the course of the study, according to the same general procedure used in the Eight-Year Study and that which is recommended in most texts on educational measurement. First, the specific objectives to be assessed were listed, and their behavioral manifestations were determined. Then items were written that required the demonstration of the behavior or that yielded information from which the behavior could be inferred. It should be noted that such a procedure is not easy, especially in a relatively uncharted area, such as the affective domain, and is best done by the combined efforts of several teachers working as a team.

The example presented here is adapted from "Inventory 1.3," which was designed to obtain information about students' interest in, and willingness to consider, certain types of health problems.[6]

Inventory 1.3

Health Interests

Directions: Your school wants to determine the kinds of health problems that are of greatest interest to you. Your

[6]Cooperative Study in General Education: American Council on Education, *Determining Personal Health Needs and Developing Means of Meeting Such Needs in College Programs,* University of Chicago, 1941 (mimeographed). Reprinted by permission of American Council on Education.

reaction to the questions below will aid us in defining such interests. Imagine that you were to seek the answer to each question. If the question interests you and you believe it should be dealt with in school, blacken the space under "A" on the answer sheet corresponding to the number of the question; if the question interests you but you think it should not be dealt with in school, blacken the space under "U"; if the question holds little or no interest for you or if you are indifferent to the question, blacken the space under "D."

A—the question is *interesting* and *should* be dealt with in school.

U—the question is *interesting* but *should not* be dealt with in school.

D—the question is *not interesting.*

1. Do certain diseases of the skin result from beauty parlor or barber shop treatments?
2. Are pimples caused by poor digestion?
12. What is the best way to remove superfluous hair?
22. Does the use of deodorants cause skin irritation?
36. Do certain foods cause cancer?
57. Is it harmful to be a blood donor?
75. Will drinking coffee before bedtime keep a person awake?
102. Is a coat of tan healthy?
123. When should children be told about reproduction?
125. Can well educated persons have feeble-minded children?

There were 129 items in the complete inventory.

Both the Questionnaire on Voluntary Reading and the Health Interests Inventory are, of course, fairly elaborate instruments. Such instruments probably would not be used by an individual teacher in his routine testing program, but rather as a part of the annual measurement program of several teachers working together in the same academic field or level of school.

Music appreciation

So that you will not form the conclusion that all assessment in the affective domain is beyond the scope of the teacher's routine measurement activities, a less elaborate illustration is presented next.

In a music appreciation class at Louisiana State University, it is desired that students become aware of the use of different styles of music to communicate various moods and ideas. This objective is assessed by "listening" items, such as the following:

> *Directions:* Three passages will be played on the phonograph. Listen to each one carefully, and classify it according to the most appropriate category listed.
> A—a fairy dance
> B—impending doom
> C—an approaching army
> D—a love theme
> E—a victory celebration

Similar items may be designed to assess awareness of the uses and values of almost any subject. It should be remembered, however, that in the assessment of awareness, as in the assessment of intellectual skills, the situation in which the student is required to respond must possess some degree of novelty for him. Requiring students merely to list *x* number of contributions of the Greeks or to outline a sequence of steps on material which has been memorized from the text or lecture is not an assessment of awareness but only of recall. Positive feeling toward something is best indicated by the student's own discovery of its uses and values.

QUESTIONS AND ACTIVITIES

1. What kinds of behavior would you expect a student who appreciates music to exhibit? Perhaps the list of activities for appreciation of literature will provide suggestions.

2. Assume that, in a teaching position, you are expected to give a letter grade in art appreciation. How would you arrive at such a grade?

3. Which of the categories in the *Taxonomy of Educational Objectives: Affective Domain* are pertinent to your teaching field?

4. An English class studied *A Tale of Two Cities* at length, using a paperback edition as a text. After the unit was finished, the students lit a bonfire and burned their copies of the book. If you had been their teacher, how would you have reacted?

7

SUGGESTED READINGS

Dunkel, Harold B., *General Education in the Humanities,* American Council on Education, 1947.
> This is the report of the humanities phase of the Cooperative Study in General Education. Of particular interest for educational measurement is the report of the development of inventories to assess general life goals, religious concepts, beliefs about fiction, and beliefs about art. The educational implications of the findings presented here should be of value to teachers of the humanities. Each inventory is illustrated in the appendix.

Gerberich, J. Raymond, Harry Greene, and Albert Jergensen, *Measurement and Evaluation in the Modern School,* McKay, 1962.
> Most of the chapters dealing with measurement in specific subjects have some discussion of assessing affective outcomes. Chapter 21 discusses assessment of outcome in music, art, and literature.

Krathwohl, David R., Benjamin S. Bloom, and Bertram B. Masia, *Taxonomy of Educational Objectives, Handbook II: Affective Domain,* McKay, 1964.
> Part I discusses the development of the Taxonomy and the nature of the affective domain. Part II presents the Taxonomy in the affective domain along with illustrative test items for each category.

Smith, Eugene R., and Ralph W. Tyler, *Appraising and Recording Student Progress,* McGraw-Hill, 1942.
> The procedures used in the Eight-Year Study to assess social sensitivity, appreciation, interests, and personal-social adjustment are described in chapters 3, 4, 5, and 6, respectively.

12

EVALUATING THE TEST

Among the most serious errors made by teachers in their efforts to measure achievement is their failure to "test their tests." Few teachers analyze the results of a test to discover whether or not it has been effective. Teachers often cite the lack of available time and the complicated statistics involved as reasons for this failure. It is true that a teacher's time is limited. It is also true that a teacher could not undertake the elaborate procedures used by test publishers in the statistical refinement of standardized tests. But the teacher can and should find time to utilize a few simple techniques to indicate whether a test has really done the job it was supposed to do.

You will remember the three criteria for evaluating a test: reliability, validity, and usability. The last of these, usability, can be determined as the test is being administered and scored by answering the questions pertaining to this quality. Were most students able to finish the test without being rushed? Were the directions easily interpreted? Was the manner of indicating answers easily understood? Was the test easy to score objectively and accurately? The determination of the other two, validity and reliability, requires an analysis of the test scores and the individual items of the test.

RELIABILITY

Are the test scores accurate indications of the students' actual achievement? This is the question of reliability. How can the teacher determine whether or not the scores are reliable? It is usually not feasible for him to use the procedures of test publishers, but there are less complicated methods that he can use. These methods should be sufficient for classroom use.

If the teacher is inclined, he can use a formula developed by Kuder and Richardson.[1] To use this formula, one needs first to compute the mean and standard deviation of the test. These computations are described in Chapter 3. The formula for estimating reliability follows:

$$r_{tt} = \frac{n \, \sigma_t^2 - M \, (n - M)}{\sigma_t^2 \, (n - 1)}$$

r_{tt} = reliability of the test
n = the number of items on the test
M = the mean of the test scores
σ_t = the standard deviation of the test

[1] G. Frederic Kuder and M. W. Richardson, "The Theory of the Estimation of Test Reliability," *Psychometrika*, September, 1937, pp. 151-160.

This formula may appear to be more complicated than it actually is. To illustrate, let us suppose that we had a test of 60 items, with a mean of 40 and a standard deviation of 8. Substituting these values, we have $n = 60, M = 40$, and $\sigma = 8$.

$$r_{tt} = \frac{[60 \times (8)^2] - [40(60 - 40)]}{(8)^2(60 - 1)}$$

$$= \frac{[60 \times 64] - [40 \times 20]}{64 \times 59}$$

$$= \frac{3840 - 800}{3776}$$

$$= \frac{3040}{3776}$$

$$= .81$$

The coefficient of .81 would not be considered very high for a standardized test. It is probably about as high as would be expected on most teacher-made tests, however. Furthermore, this formula nearly always underestimates reliability, so the teacher may assume that this test, along with others of equal quality, will give a fair indication of the actual achievement of his students.

A more direct, though more superficial, method of estimating the reliability of a test is to rank the students on the test and compare their rankings on similar tests. This method was illustrated fully in Chapter 4 and will be briefly reviewed here. Let us assume that an American history teacher gives four tests during a study of the colonial period, all designed to measure similar objectives. He can logically expect the better students to make the higher scores and the poorer students to make the lower scores on all four tests. If the rankings on one of the tests are quite different from the rankings on the others, then the reliability of those test scores would certainly be in doubt. Minor variations in rank are to be expected, and on any one test a top student may drop to the bottom because of illness or perhaps failure to study. But generally, we can expect top students to remain near the top, average students to be around the middle, and poor students to remain near the bottom. Of course, this assumption can be made only in cases where the different tests measure achievement of similar objectives on similar material.

If preliminary investigations cause the teacher to doubt the reliability of a test, he should make further investigations to discover the cause of the low reliability. Perhaps the test is too short, maybe the directions are not clear, or perhaps many of the items are ambiguous, causing the students to guess. If it is an essay test, it may not have been scored properly.

One of the best procedures for discovering poorly written items on a test is reviewing the test in class, generally an excellent way to help students become aware of their strengths and weaknesses. If there are items that are poorly written, the students will probably make them known to the teacher. Reviewing a test in class is also a convenient way of checking the validity of items. If an item deals with material that has not been previously covered, the teacher may be fairly certain that the students will call his attention to this fact.

VALIDITY

Did the test measure what it was intended to measure? This is the question of validity. You may remember from the discussion of validity in Chapter 4 that the most important type of validity to be considered in an achievement test is content validity. An achievement test should measure all major objectives in an instructional unit in terms of emphases. If the test exactly reflects the unit as it was taught, then the test has content validity. At the time a test is given, its content validity should not be in doubt. Content validity can be *insured* if the teacher has well-written, behavioral objectives and uses a table of specifications when constructing the test. Some teachers may wish to check the validity of their tests by additional methods. Test scores may be correlated with other measures of achievement on the same subject matter. Such measures as standardized tests that the class has taken, as well as grades and tests given by former teachers of the class, may be used. The logic behind this procedure is that, if two different tests are valid measures of the same thing, a group of students should make similar scores on both tests. This same reasoning is used when the discrimination power of individual test items is studied.

ITEM ANALYSIS

A test is no better than the items that compose it. A test that is generally reliable and valid may be improved by discovering individual items that do not function properly. Two qualities by which individual items are judged are *discrimination power* and *difficulty level.*

Discrimination power

Determining the discrimination power of an item is a technique for indicating its validity. If the teacher is reasonably sure that the test has content validity, then he may logically assume that the scores on a particular item should, in general, agree with scores on the total test. If the test is valid, then an item that agrees with the test is also valid. If an item "agrees" with the test, then a larger proportion of high scorers than low scorers will have marked it correctly.

For illustration, let us suppose that we have given a test, scored it, and arranged the papers in order from the highest to the lowest score. We may consider the top quarter the high group, and the bottom quarter the low group. In a class of 32 students, we would take the top 8 papers and the bottom 8 papers. We would then check to see how many persons in each group marked the item correctly. Let us now suppose we find that item 3 was answered correctly by six of the top group and only three of the bottom group. We may then conclude that the item discriminates positively—that it "agrees" with the test. For item 9, let us suppose we find the opposite results. There were only two correct answers in the high group and five correct answers in the low group. This item discriminates negatively—it does not agree with the test. Something is wrong with such an item. If an item is sufficiently difficult to be missed by a majority of the top group, it certainly should be missed by at least a majority of the low group.

The usual cause of negative discrimination is ambiguity. There is something about the item which causes the better student to see implications that were not intended. He is actually being penalized for thinking too well. The less able student considers the item more superficially, does not concern himself with extended implications, and marks it correctly.

Knowledge of the discrimination power can be very helpful when a student challenges the validity of an item. While you are reviewing a test with your class, some student may say, "Question number _____ is bad. You should give us credit for it, because it can't be understood." This type of comment is not unusual, especially when an item is difficult. A check on the item's discrimination can indicate quickly whether or not the charge is true. Let us suppose you found that in your class of 32 students, only one in the low group, but three in the high group, marked it correctly. You may conclude, then, that the item is not "bad"; it is just difficult. A check would probably reveal that only about 20 percent of the entire class marked it correctly.

The teacher may find that the task of determining the discrimination of every item on every test is too time consuming. If he reviews his tests in class, however, and checks the discrimination of each item that is challenged, he will find that the quality of his tests is greatly improved.

Difficulty Level.   *Difficulty* refers to the number of persons who missed the item. Ideally, an item should have a difficulty level of about 50 percent, since maximum discrimination power is possible only at this level. Items marked correctly by all students or missed by all students are generally considered to be poor items. A test composed of such items would have everyone making the same score, perfect or zero, and would, therefore, tell you nothing about the differences in achievement existing among the students. A test on which every class member makes a perfect score is obviously too easy for the class. The students have not been allowed to demonstrate the full extent of their achievement. A test on which every class member makes zero is too difficult. It is beyond the capacity of the students.

In actual practice, a teacher-made test will not be composed entirely of items with a difficulty level of 50 percent. In some instances, it may not even be desirable. A teacher may include in a test some very easy items to give his weak students some experience of success, and he may include some very difficult items to provide challenge for his strong students. Where there are extreme differences among class members, the teacher may divide his class into groups and teach and test each group separately.

The difficulty level of every important test should be checked. This may be done by studying the distribution of the test scores. Perhaps the most convenient way of doing this is to list the scores from highest to lowest, locate the median (midpoint), and visually examine the spread of the scores. If the median is somewhere near the middle of the possible test range and there are not a large number of zero or perfect scores, the teacher may feel fairly sure that the test is suitable for the group. The point also should be made that there are some teaching situations in which it is hoped that all of the scores will be perfect. This is the case when the teacher establishes some minimum goal or standard to be attained by all students. Examples of this would be: (1) the ability to recall the 100 addition facts or (2) the ability to type 30 words per minute with no more than four errors. In these situations the teacher hopes that every student will accomplish the objective perfectly. Even in these situations, however, the teacher should provide for those students who will be able to perform better than the standard. Those wishing to pursue this topic further are referred to the section on criterion referenced measurement in Chapter 2 and to the article by Popham and Husek listed in the Suggested Readings.

The following example illustrates a convenient way of scoring and running an item analysis on a test. Figure 3 is a reproduction of one-half of a test answer key used by one of the authors. Students are required to mark their test responses by blackening the appropriate letter on sheets similar to this one. (The actual answer sheet has two columns allowing space for 50 items.) Holes are punched in the key corresponding to the positions of the correct answers. Each answer sheet is scored by placing the key over it. If a correct response has been made, the blackened area appears beneath the hole in the key. If the space beneath the key is blank, a red mark is placed on the student's answer sheet indicating both an incorrect answer and the position of the correct answer. By letting the red pencil slide off the edge of the key, the incorrect response is also recorded. Using this method, a person can score answer sheets and obtain the difficulty level of each test item very quickly. After the papers are scored, they are ranked, and the discrimination power of each item is determined. This information is recorded in the margin of the answer key, as illustrated.

The 25 items shown do not represent an actual test, but do represent the pattern of difficulty an actual test might take. If you will examine the figure closely, you will notice that items numbered 1 through 5 are too easy to discriminate. Those missed by only one or two students were not checked for discrimination. This set of easy true-false items was placed at the beginning of the test to encourage poorer students. The latter items are much more difficult. Some of these were missed by nearly everyone in the class. This, too, was planned. All of the items of sufficient difficulty discriminate positively except numbers 6, 17, and 23. Item 6, missed by only 3 of the 32 persons in this class, is probably too easy for proper discrimination. Item 23, marked correctly by only three persons is probably too difficult. A check with the class would probably reveal that item 17 was worded so poorly that different interpretations of meaning were made. Such items must be eliminated or reworded the next time this test is given. Any item that discriminates negatively or does not discriminate at all

Name _____ Course _____ Date _____ Score _____

Read instructions carefully.

						Number Missing in Each Item	
						High Group	Low Group
1.	(a)	(b)	(c)	(d)	(e)	1	1
2.	(a)	(b)	(c)	(d)	(e)	1	3
3.	(a)	(b)	(c)	(d)	(e)	0	3
4.	(a)	(b)	(c)	(d)	(e)	1	3
5.	(a)	(b)	(c)	(d)	(e)	3	6
6.	(a)	(b)	(c)	(d)	(e)	2	5
7.	(a)	(b)	(c)	(d)	(e)	2	4
8.	(a)	(b)	(c)	(d)	(e)	3	7
9.	(a)	(b)	(c)	(d)	(e)	4	7
10.	(a)	(b)	(c)	(d)	(e)	5	8
11.	(a)	(b)	(c)	(d)	(e)	4	6
12.	(a)	(b)	(c)	(d)	(e)	5	4
13.	(a)	(b)	(c)	(d)	(e)	3	7
14.	(a)	(b)	(c)	(d)	(e)	3	6
15.	(a)	(b)	(c)	(d)	(e)	2	4
16.	(a)	(b)	(c)	(d)	(e)	6	8
17.	(a)	(b)	(c)	(d)	(e)	0	7
18.	(a)	(b)	(c)	(d)	(e)	7	6
19.	(a)	(b)	(c)	(d)	(e)	5	8
20.	(a)	(b)	(c)	(d)	(e)	6	8
21.	(a)	(b)	(c)	(d)	(e)		
22.	(a)	(b)	(c)	(d)	(e)		
23.	(a)	(b)	(c)	(d)	(e)		
24.	(a)	(b)	(c)	(d)	(e)		
25.	(a)	(b)	(c)	(d)	(e)		

Figure 3
Test answer sheet.

reduces the general quality of the test and the usefulness of the test results.

KEEPING A FILE OF TEST ITEMS

Test construction may be made easier and test quality improved by building a file of good test items. Each item may be written on a 3 X 5 card and filed by subject matter or objective. On the back of each card, data concerning the item's difficulty level and discrimination may be recorded each time the item is used. After a few years, the teacher will have collected a set of items of known reliability, validity, and difficulty. Each time the teacher begins to construct a new test, then, he may use appropriate items in the file as a nucleus around which the test can be built. Of course, for each test new items should be written to take care of changes in emphasis, technique, and subject matter. The best of the new items may be added to the file and some of the older items deleted in order to keep the file current and valid.

QUESTIONS AND ACTIVITIES

1. In your experience as a student, can you recall any instances in which a teacher exhibited evidence of having evaluated his test? If you can, what procedures were used?

2. Can you recall any times when you wished the teacher had evaluated his own test? In what ways could the test have been improved?

3. In a certain university, a professor is said to have used the same final test for 20 years. What does this tell you about the teacher, the teaching, and the examination?

4. Do you see any danger in a teacher's keeping a file of test items?

SUGGESTED READINGS

Ahmann, J. Stanley, and Marvin D. Glock, *Evaluating Pupil Growth* (3rd ed.), Allyn and Bacon, 1967.
   Chapter 6 presents the basic procedures for analyzing individual items and using the results to improve one's tests.

Diederich, Paul B., *Short-Cut Statistics for Teacher-Made Tests,* Evaluation and Advisory Service, Series No. 5, Educational Testing Service, 1960.
   The first part of this pamphlet describes a method of item analysis the teacher can easily use without spending excessive amounts of time and effort.

Ebel, Robert L., *Measuring Educational Achievement,* Prentice-Hall, 1965.
   Chapter 11 of this text presents a thorough discussion of the principles and techniques of item analyses.

Katz, Martin, "Improving Tests by Means of Item Analysis," *The Clearing House,* January, 1961.
   This article presents a detailed description of a method by which the classroom teacher can make an item analysis of his tests.

Mehrens, William A. and Robert Ebel, *Principles of Educational and Psychological Measurement,* Rand McNally, 1967.
   Unit Five presents 7 articles on item analysis and selection procedures which would be of value for the person who wishes to probe deeper.

Noll, Victor H., *Introduction to Educational Measurement* (2nd ed.), Houghton Mifflin, 1965.
   Chapter 7 presents a practical discussion of procedures for evaluating the teacher-made test.

Popham, James W. and T. R. Husek, "Implications of Criterion Referenced Measurement," *Journal of Educational Measurement* 6:1-9, Spring 1969.
   An excellent article for students wishing to learn more about this topic.

13

ASSIGNING MARKS AND
REPORTING STUDENT PROGRESS

Part of nearly every teacher's job is the assigning of marks or grades. Marks should be the result of accurate evaluations of the student's achievement toward the objectives of the course and nothing else. Marks are assigned for one basic reason: to report to the student, his parents, and other interested persons an evaluation of the student's achievement.

Marks and test scores are not the same. Test scores are the results of measurement. Marks are the end product of evaluation. Marks are the result of the teacher's interpretation of test and other scores. Marking is the evaluation phase of that very involved set of processes, often glibly referred to as measurement and evaluation. Collected evidence must be used if marks are to be assigned fairly.

The complete procedure for assigning marks may be logically divided into three steps: (1) determine objectives, (2) collect evidence of growth toward those objectives, (3) weigh the evidence and assign the mark. The determination of objectives has been discussed at length in Chapter 6. One of the major points which should be remembered from that discussion is that objectives, to be serviceable for evaluation, should be subdivided in terms of specific student behaviors. Various methods of collecting evidence of student achievement have been discussed in Chapters 7-10. Perhaps the most important point to be remembered from these discussions concerns the selection of the most effective technique. The teacher should know precisely the behavioral objectives he desires his students to accomplish, and he should select the most effective technique for measuring achievement toward these ends. This chapter is devoted to the third step: weighing the evidence and determining the mark. Perhaps the most important point which should be remembered from this chapter is that grades should be assigned fairly, but there is no "royal road" to fair marking. There is no convenient procedure that can be followed blindly. Evaluation, by its very nature, involves the use of judgment.

BASES FOR MARKING

Marks are usually assigned on the basis of one or more of the following considerations: (1) the performance of each student in relation to that of the rest of the class, (2) the performance of each student in relation to his capacity to perform, and (3) the performance of each student in relation to a predetermined standard of performance. You will notice that in each case the performance is evaluated by comparing it with something else. These bases are not mutually exclusive, and excessive dependence on any one can lead to ridiculous practices. A discussion of the strengths and weaknesses of each basis is presented next for the purpose of helping the teacher use them in *combination* to produce the fairest evaluations possible.

Curve grading

Marking on the basis of performance relative to that of the other class members is often referred to as grading on the curve. In this procedure, a certain percent of the class is assigned each mark. The large group of average scores around the middle of the distribution is assigned C, a smaller group just above average is assigned B, a similar group just below average is assigned D, and small groups at the extreme upper and lower ends of the distribution are assigned A and F, respectively. The exact proportion of the class which should be assigned each mark is often a troublesome problem. If it can be assumed that the class distribution approximates the normal curve, then proportions based on the standard deviation may be used. This process is discussed and illustrated in Chapter 3. You may wish to turn to that chapter to review the process before reading the following survey of advantages and disadvantages.

Advantages and disadvantages.   Curve grading has some distinct advantages. In the first place, grades assigned on this basis are more easily interpretable than grades assigned on other bases. On this basis, A means superior achievement, B means above average, C means average, D means below average, and F means inferior achievement. Many parents claim that they know where their children "stand" when grades are assigned on this basis. Also, teachers can be fairly certain of the achievement of a student when the achievement of his class is the basis of comparison.

One of the major disadvantages of curve grading occurs when the number of A's, B's, C's, D's, and F's is decided in advance of any measurement. Perhaps you have had a high school or college teacher who remarked on the first day of class, "Seven percent of you people will fail this course." If you have been in such a situation, no doubt you wondered how the teacher could judge the achievement of the students before he had collected any evidence. Obviously, he could not. You will notice that the above discussion of determining the number of grades on the basis of the normal curve was preceded by the statement, "If it can be assumed that the class distribution approximates the normal curve." In the average class of 20 to 30 students, the teacher should wait until evidence of achievement is collected before determining the distribution of marks.

Another disadvantage of exclusive application of curve grading is that it can place control of the quality of work in the hands of the class. In this situation, the better students may be pressured to "set the curve low." In college classes, weak students may be persuaded to stay in class and absorb the low grades.

In elementary and secondary school, a strict application of curve grading places the weak student in a frustrating position. No matter how hard he tries, he still receives D or F. This has caused some teachers to consider the capacity of the student when assigning marks.

Marking in relation to capacity to perform

No doubt there have always been teachers who considered student capacity when assigning marks. Widespread use of this practice, however, came about in the twentieth century, along with the emphasis on child study. Carried to an extreme, this was the "A for effort" idea. In this procedure, the child is given a high grade if he is performing at or above capacity and a low grade if he is performing below capacity, regardless of the amount of achievement.

The main disadvantage of this practice, of course, is the confusion which it creates. A student who is consistently given A's and B's in a subject, not because he does well in it but because his teachers consider that he is working to capacity, may be misled. He may enter high school or college believing he is sufficiently prepared, only to find out that he cannot compete. Furthermore, counselors, admission officers, and other teachers having no information on a student except his transcript of grades may be misled, also.

Another disadvantage of capacity grading is that the capacity of a student is sometimes difficult to determine. If a student dislikes a particular subject, his aversion to it can cause him to make low scores on tests used to determine his capacity, as well as on tests used to determine his achievement. It should also be remembered that measured capacity can change as the child grows and changes.

The advantages of capacity grading are that it encourages the weak student by positively reinforcing his efforts and it helps prevent "loafing" on the part of the strong students. Some teachers utilize these advantages by making minor adjustments of not more than one letter grade on a student's report card. If this is done, a note explaining the procedure should be permanently attached to the student's report card and transcript. A better practice, perhaps, is to assign the mark which indicates the actual achievement of each student and attach a note concerning effort of each student who is working very little or exceptionally hard.

Marking on the basis of a preset standard

One of the oldest and most widespread methods of determining marks has been percentage grading. This is the procedure often used by teachers who emphasize preset standards. Certainly, standards are necessary considerations in any system of evaluation. Percentage grading, however, presumes a degree of absoluteness that is just not present in educational measurement.

A "perfect" score on a teacher's test or even on a series of tests does not mean that a child has learned 100 percent of everything which could have been learned in a course, nor does a zero mean that the child has learned nothing at all. Tests are only samples. Furthermore, and most important, the difficulty of a test is determined by the teacher. He can make a test so difficult that no student makes above 50 percent. Is he justified, then, in giving F to everyone in the class? He can make a test so easy that no student makes below 90 percent. Is he then justified in giving all A's and B's?

The teacher who grades on percentage ends up being just as arbitrary as the teacher who grades on the curve. In this procedure, a test is scored directly as a percentage of the total number of points. On a test of 20 items, each item would be worth 5 points. Letter grades are also defined in terms of some percentage, such as: A = 95-100 percent; B = 90-94 percent; C = 80-89 percent; D = 75-79 percent; F = below 75 percent. If scores seem to be running too high, the teacher may begin to grade a little harder to bring them down. If they are running too low, he may grade a little easier. He can also make the *next test* more or less difficult in order to make the grades "come out right." It would appear to be much more sensible if he brought the arbitrary and relative nature of his grading out in the open by assigning grades on a visual inspection of scores. A description of that process follows.

ASSIGNING MARKS BY VISUAL INSPECTION OF SCORES

After experience with other methods, many teachers have come to utilize a simple inspection of scores as their basic method of assigning marks. This method allows the teacher to use the most concrete evidence of achievement which he possesses, that is, the performance of a student relative to that of others who have been taught and tested in the same manner. It also allows the teacher to use his best judgment and to give consideration to such factors as individual capacity and standards. The procedure may be used at any grade level and in any subject where evidence of achievement can be obtained in terms of a numerical score.

The procedure is quite simple to set up. Either lined notebook paper or graph paper may be used. After the scores have been obtained, determine the range, then set up the distribution horizontally along the bottom of the page. Assign a position near the right edge of the paper to the highest possible score, then write in other possible scores, proceeding across the page until the position for the lowest score is reached. Graphically record each score by placing an X in the appropriate position. The scores will fall in perfect rank order. In Figure 4, the total points possible was 80. The highest score made was 77 and the lowest was 42.

After the scores have been set in this type of distribution, they may be inspected to determine which scores are to be assigned which marks. Here again we are face to face with the exercise of good judgment. There are no strict rules to use in deciding where to draw the lines between the scores which are to receive the various marks. There are, however, a few rules of thumb that the teacher may consider. If C is used to designate average performance in your school, then the large group of scores around the median should be assigned C. The lines drawn at Q_1 and Q_3, which define the upper and lower quartiles, may suggest the limits of the C group. It appears logical, however, to assign the same mark to similar scores. The groups just above and just below the C group are assigned B and D respectively, indicating just-above and just-below average performance. The small group at the upper extreme is superior and is, therefore, assigned A. The small group at the lower extreme is assigned F or E, indicating inferior achievement.

Although groups may not be as well defined as those in Figure 4, you can expect similar groups to appear, if you have done a fairly reliable job of measuring. If your tests have been too easy or too difficult, the scores will pile up at the upper or lower end of the scale, and no differentiation between levels of achievement will be possible. The use of this method does not presume a definite percent of the scores to be assigned any mark. There may be a distribution in which everyone does sufficiently well, so that no F's are assigned. In other distributions, no one may do well enough to receive an A. In still other distributions, there may be large gaps just above or below average, and, therefore, no B's or D's.

Marks assigned by this procedure should be the result of the most judicious decisions it is possible for the teacher to make, and not the result of blind decisions which often occur with percent-

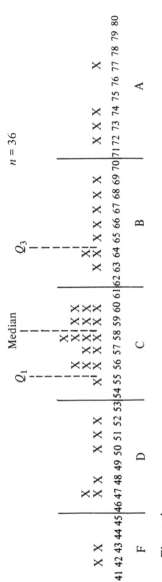

Figure 4
Grades assigned by visual inspection of scores.

```
    X          X                        X
    X X X    X X               X X    X X X
73 74 75 76 77 78 79 80 81 82 83 84 85 86 87 88 89 90 91 92 93 94 95 96 97 98 99 100
    C                    B                          A
       90% to 100% = A;   80% to 89% = B;   70% to 79% = C.
```

Figure 5
The fallacy of percentage grading.

age grading or predetermined curve grading. Figure 5 illustrates what can happen when a mark is defined as a certain percentage. It is obvious that scores 88 and 89 indicate achievement more similar to that of scores 90, 91 and 92 than that of scores 80 and 81. Scores 80 and 81 are, on the other hand, more similar to scores 77, 78 and 79 than to scores 88 and 89. Furthermore, neither teacher-made tests nor standardized tests are reliable enough to distinguish between an 89 and a 90, or a 79 and an 80. Differences as slight as one score are only chance differences and do not indicate "true" differences in achievement. If a similar test on the same material were administered to the same students, the ones who made 89 and 90 on the first test might easily reverse their scores on the second.

It was mentioned at the beginning of this discussion that the teacher could consider standards when assigning marks by this method. If a teacher has taught and tested in the same subject fairly consistently over a period of years, he has probably come to expect a certain standard of performance. He may wish to check the performance level of his current students by comparing their distribution of scores with distributions obtained in the past. If the current distribution appears shifted to the left, he may conclude that the class is not performing up to standard. If the distribution appears shifted to the right, he may conclude that the class is performing a little above standard. Such comparisons must, of course, be made tentatively and with caution. They are valid only if there have been no significant changes in the nature of the course or the tests.

Before leaving this discussion of marking by inspection of scores, a point needs to be made about combining evidences of achievement. Teachers often wish to combine evidence from several different sources when determining a mark for a grading period. Sources such as test scores, class work, homework, and special reports may all be used. The best way to combine such sources is on the basis of numerical points. Assign each student a certain number of points on each source, depending on the quality of his work. Each student's points may then be added to obtain a total score which may be placed in a distribution for inspection and marking. It is easier to weigh the relative importance of each source when points are used than it is when marks are assigned to each source before it is combined with the others. The more important sources should be assigned more total points. For example, if test scores are twice as important as homework, the total points possible on the tests should be twice those possible on homework.

You will notice that the discussion in the preceding paragraphs concerned combining evidences of achievement only. When only a letter grade is used on a report, it should indicate achievement only, and should not be influenced by such factors as class attitude and behavior. Desirable attitudes and proper classroom behavior may be important objectives, and a teacher may wish to report on them. If this is the case, he *should* report on them separately. He should not confuse the report by attempting to include several different factors in a single mark.

SPECIAL PROBLEMS IN MARKING

We can never arrive at a marking system that is equally usable in all situations. Changing goals, changing organizational structures, and endlessly changing instructional methodology preclude any "final solution" to the marking problem. Some of these special situations are discussed below.

Marking on the basis of gains

Since much of our instructional emphasis is on a student's individual *progress,* there are those who say that a marking system should reflect this progress, that is, it should be based upon gain. This, of course, is in contrast to the more common practice of marking on the basis of status.

There are several special problems involved in assigning marks on the basis of the individual's progress. Some of these are: (1) How can the teacher establish starting status and terminal status in order to arrive at gain? Should the student be tested with the same test on a before-and-after basis? (2) How much gain would be associated with a mark of A? B? C? (3) Could excellent gains result primarily from a starting base of total ignorance? Or could low gains result because the student was well versed in the material before it was studied? These and other questions of a similar nature will need answers before marking on the basis of gain receives wide acceptance.

Marking in the ungraded school

The assignment of students to grade levels is primarily a matter of administrative practice. However, it has in certain ways simplified the marking process, since such terms as "below grade level" and "above grade level" have figured in marking practices. However, in an ungraded elementary school, a different orientation is essential. A key question which faculties in ungraded schools must answer is: In view of our breaking away from grade-level "standards," how can we assign meaningful marks to our students? Certainly, this situation requires a much more descriptive type of report card than that which shows only a subject name followed by a grade; for example, "Arithmetic, *C.*" A widely used method of handling this problem is the report card (or dual report form) that shows the level at which the child is actually working in arithmetic and reading. His grades then reflect his performance at this level in a way that can be more accurately interpreted.

Marking in atypical groups

In recent years there has been a large increase in the number of special remedial and advanced classes in schools. Marking has been a persistent problem associated with these classes. The problem is especially acute in advanced classes. Many able students refuse to be placed in these classes, because, as they put it, "You do twice the work for a lower grade." This attitude is understandable. Although grades are not the end product of education, they are important, especially when a student is thinking about college admission policies. It does not seem fair for a student to receive a C for average performance in an advanced class, when such performance is above the A level in a regular class. If letter grades are the only designation of achievement it seems much more valid to assign a mark that reflects a student's level of performance in relation to what is usually expected of students at that grade level. If a student is performing at a level superior to the standard that is usually expected of students at that grade, then he should receive the mark that indicates superior performance. This does not mean that all the students in an advanced class would necessarily receive A's and B's. For various reasons, some may perform below the standard of expectancy for that grade level. They, too, should receive the marks that reflect their level of performance.

The same principle applies to students in remedial classes. If they are performing below the level expected of students at that stage of development, then they should receive marks that indicate below-average performance. The principle applies even though their performance may be near the top of the remedial class. Again, they need not *necessarily* receive below-average marks. Some may perform at or above the level expected and should, therefore, receive average or above-average grades.

Some school systems are beginning to report on achievement by methods that are more complete than letter grades alone—by such procedures as placing an "H" after each mark to designate an honors section or attaching notes to the report explaining the full meaning of the marks being used. In such cases, the teacher may

Name _____ Year _____

ACHIEVEMENT
A—superior
B—above average
C—average
D—below average
U—unsatisfactory

EFFORT
✓ indicates improvement needed

The child is graded at the level where he is receiving instruction. See Reading and Math Levels.

Personal and Social Growth

WORK HABITS	1.	2.	3.	4.
Follows directions				
Completes work satisfactorily				
Works independently				
Is self-confident				
Does neat work				
Thinks things through				

SOCIAL HABITS				
Cooperates with others				
Assumes his share of responsibility				
Listens attentively				
Shows emotional control				
Is courteous and friendly				
Respects personal and public property				
Respects hall and playground rules				

HEALTH HABITS				
Observes school health rules				
Practices good posture				
Shows evidence of adequate rest				

	Fall	Spring
Height		
Weight		

RECORD OF ATTENDANCE	1.	2.	3.	4.	Total
Days Present					
Days Absent					
Times Tardy					

Figure 6

Elementary report of progress, Sioux City Public Schools.
(Used by permission.)

Growth in Skills, Understandings, Appreciations

	1		2		3		4	
	Achievement	Effort	Achievement	Effort	Achievement	Effort	Achievement	Effort
READING								
LANGUAGE								
WRITING								
SPELLING								
MATHEMATICS								
SOCIAL STUDIES								
SCIENCE								
MUSIC								
PHYSICAL EDUCATION								

ART (see reverse side)

Primary Department				Intermediate Department			
Grade 1		Grade 2	Grade 3	Grade 4	Grade 5	Grade 6	
READING LEVELS							

Readiness	Pre. Primer	Primer	Book 1	Book 2^1	Book 2^2	Book 3^1	Book 3^2	Book 4^1	Book 4^2	Book 5^1	Book 5^2	Book 6^1	Book 6^2	Book 7^1	Book 7^2
L-1	L-2	L-3	L-4	L-5	L-6	L-7	L-8	L-9	L-10	L-11	L-12	L-13	L-14	L-15	L-16

MATHEMATICS LEVELS							
Primer	First	Second	Third	Fourth	Fifth	Sixth	Seventh

Each child has his own rate for learning. Your child is progressing through the elementary program at the rate shown above. An X indicates that the level has been completed satisfactorily. Your child is working in the next level.

assign marks in relation to performance within the section. Whatever method is used to report on student achievement, it should be easily understood by all who will use the report currently and in the future, and it should indicate as precisely as possible the performance level of each student.

METHODS OF REPORTING STUDENT PROGRESS

Specific reporting procedures vary from school to school, depending on local philosophy and tradition. It is generally agreed, however, that a report must be easily and clearly understood by all who will use it, and all reporting practices should be devoted to this end. Different local practices are usually slight modifications or combinations of five major methods: (1) letter or number grades, (2) satisfactory-unsatisfactory, (3) check lists, (4) written reports, and (5) parent-teacher conferences.

Letter or number grades have been widely used in the past, but recently there has been a trend to use them in combination with other methods or to replace them entirely. The reason for this trend is that a need has been expressed to report on achievement more specifically in terms of the major objectives of the course. Formerly the letters or numbers were defined in terms of an absolute percentage, but more often today they are defined in terms of relative standing in the class.

The use of S (satisfactory) and U (unsatisfactory) is an attempt to report a child's achievement in relation to his ability to achieve. If, in the teacher's judgment, a child is achieving at a rate commensurate with his ability, he is given an S, regardless of the level of his achievement in relation to that of his classmates. If the child is achieving at a rate below that of which he is capable, he is given a U. Sometimes three marks are used, such as O (outstanding), S (satisfactory), and U (unsatisfactory). The chief limitation of the system is the confusion that often results when it is used without further explanation. When the method is used by itself, one does not know whether an S means that a child is achieving normally for his age group, or whether he is achieving very little and the teacher thinks him incapable of doing better. This method is rarely used beyond the elementary grades. One can readily understand the puzzlement and anger of a parent whose child brings home D's and F's on his seventh-grade report card after making S's all through elementary school.

In order to overcome any confusion and to give consideration to capacity also, some schools have used what may be called a dual report form. This type of report, illustrated in Figure 6, is used in the public elementary schools of Sioux City, Iowa. You will notice that two marks are given in each subject, one for achievement and one for effort. Achievement is indicated by a letter defined in terms of class rank. If the teacher thinks a child is not trying, he checks the cell under effort. Notice also that the level at which the child is actually learning is indicated. In Sioux City, as in many elementary schools, personal and social growth of the child are also reported. Another feature of this part of the report which should be noticed is a breakdown of the major areas ("Work Habits," "Social Habits," and "Health Habits") into specific objectives. This is the distinguishing feature of the check list.

The *check list* is used to make the report more diagnostic. A subject like reading or arithmetic involves many different kinds of knowledge and skills. On a check list, these different objectives are listed, and a mark is given for each. Thus, parents (and teachers, too, we might add) can get a clearer understanding of the specific strengths and weaknesses of the child. The check list is one of the best methods of reporting, because it meets the criteria of clarity, completeness, and economy of time. It is unfortunate that it has not been adopted more widely in secondary schools. Learning, as well as reporting, would be enhanced if secondary teachers were more consciously aware of the specific objectives of their courses. A good example of this type of report is that used in the public elementary schools of Cameron Parish, Louisiana. The first-grade report is shown in Figure 7 and the report for grades 2 through 6 is shown in Figure 8. Each of these reports lists in fairly specific terms the specific elements of achievement in each subject area.

Report of _____ Your child's progress at school is reported as follows for the first semester since this is an adjustment period.

G - Good
A - Average
I - Improving
N - Needs Help

READINESS PERIOD — FIRST SEMESTER

	Period		
Growth Characteristic Abilities	1	2	3
Sits for short periods of time			
Follows teacher's instructions			
Makes new friends			
Works with others			
Does neat work			
Finishes work on time			

Language Arts

Reading

Learns progression of top to bottom			
Coordinates eye and hand movement from L. to R.			
Observes details and interprets meaning in pictures			
Sees likenesses and differences			
Hears beginning sounds			
Hears ending sounds			
Relates ideas or stories in sequence			
Speaks clearly and freely			
Listens attentively			
Learns a reading vocabulary			

Manuscript Writing

Makes original drawings using straight lines			
Makes original drawings using circles			
Learns name of letters			
Learns to write own name			
Writes neatly and correctly			

Mathematics

Recognizes and writes numerals			
Counts accurately			
Understands numbers			

	Periods					
Conduct	1	2	3	4	5	6
Classroom						
Playground						

	Periods					
Attendance	1	2	3	4	5	6
Number of days present						
Number of days absent						
I would like to have a conference with you						

Figure 7

First-grade report, Cameron Parish, Louisiana. (Used by permission.)

RECORD OF GROWTH IN SCHOOL WORK

SECOND SEMESTER

	Period			
	4	5	6	Final Avg.
Reading				
Your Child is reading on:				
Readiness				
Pre-Primer				
Primer				
First Reader				
Your Child				
Enjoys reading				
Reads silently				
Reads orally				
Understands what he reads				
Develops a reading vocabulary				
Manuscript Writing				
Learns name of letters				
Writes own name				
Writes neatly and spaces correctly				
Enjoys writing				
Mathematics				
Recognizes and writes numerals				
Counts accurately				
Understands numbers				
Works accurately				
Social Living - (Science, Health, Social Studies)				
Learns facts about people and things				
Takes an interest in nature				
Asks questions about facts				
Physical Education				
Participates				
Cooperates				
Enjoys				
Art				
Music				

Report of _____

PROGRESS IN SKILLS AND UNDERSTANDING

	1	2	3	SEM	4	5	6	SEM	Final
READING									
Understands what he reads									
Reads well orally									
Likes to read									
Word Recognition Skills									
Conduct									
HANDWRITING									
Neatness									
Legibility									
Conduct									
LANGUAGE									
Speaks clearly and correctly									
Expresses ideas well in written work									
Expresses ideas well orally									
Listens attentively									
Writes legibly									
Conduct									
SPELLING									
Applies skills correctly									
Masters words in lesson									
Conduct									
SOCIAL STUDIES									
Is learning necessary facts & concepts									
Uses reference materials, maps & charts									
Takes part in class discussion									
Conduct									
MATHEMATICS									
Knowledge of fundamental processes									
Solves problems accurately & neatly									
Conduct									
SCIENCE									
Shows interest in the world around him									
Learns important facts									
Shows initiative in experimentation									
Shows growth in understanding and observing health rules									
Conduct									
HEALTH & PHYSICAL EDUCATION									
Participation									
Attitude									
Cooperation									
Conduct									
FOREIGN LANGUAGE									
INDUSTRIAL ARTS									
HOME LIVING									

GRADING SCALE

A - Excellent   100 - 95   **D - Below Average**   75 - 70
B - Good   94 - 87   **F** - Unsatisfactory   (below 70)
C - Average   86 - 76

Figure 8

Elementary grades report, Cameron Parish, Louisiana. (Used by permission.)

	1	2	3	S E M	4	5	6	S E M	Final
ART									
MUSIC									
Vocal									
Band									

S - Satisfactory
U - Unsatisfactory

PROGRESS IN ATTITUDES AND APPRECIATION

	1	2	3	4	5	6
CONDUCT						
Obeys rules promptly						
Uses time well						
Is attentive in class						
Follows directions accurately						
Does work neatly and carefully						
Finishes assigned tasks						
Respects authority						
Accepts just criticism						
Respects property						
Is courteous and polite						
Exercises self control						
Works and plays well with others						
Practices good food habits						
Has good cafeteria manners						
Observes safety rules						

(X) Indicates need for improvement
( ) No mark indicates satisfactory progress

	1	2	3	4	5	6	Total
ATTENDANCE							
Days Present							
Days Absent							
Times Tardy							

The *written report* is usually used to supplement some other method of reporting. Sometimes space is provided on the regular report for additional comments at each reporting period. In some school systems, separate written reports are required at the end of each semester or term. The chief advantage of written reports is the freedom they allow in communication. The unique aspects of a particular student's progress, or lack of it, may be revealed in a written report. The disadvantage of a written report is the large amount of time and effort required in writing. If lengthy written reports are required on each pupil, four or five times a year, they are likely to degenerate into compilations of platitudes and generalizations which communicate nothing. Attempting to report student progress exclusively through written reports is a very difficult task. Problems of completeness, uniformity, specificity, and style—all combine to increase the difficulty. School systems that require written reports usually provide some form of outline for the report. By far the most widespread practice, however, is the provision of space on the regular report card for additional comments. Some report cards also provide space for the teacher or parent to request a conference when either feels the situation may justify it.

The *parent-teacher conference* is another excellent supplement to the regular report. In the conference, either party can raise questions for information and clarification, thereby promoting understanding between home and school. In some school systems, parent-teacher conferences may be arranged by either the parents or the teacher when it is felt that a conference would be beneficial to the child. In other systems, one or two conferences are planned during the year with parents of each child. Such conferences are often less beneficial than they might be because there is a lack of adequate preconference planning.

In the first place, no conference should be called unless there is some definite purpose to be accomplished. This does not mean that a conference should be called only when a student presents a problem. There are many positive reasons for calling a conference, such as simply getting better acquainted or providing specific positive information about a child's accomplishments in school.

Better rapport is maintained between school and home when conferences are called to report outstanding accomplishments as well as problems.

Many teachers are not skilled in conference technique. To overcome this problem, some schools organize workshops and other faculty training programs. Often, guidelines are developed to aid teachers in preparing for and conducting conferences. The following "Do's and Don'ts" were adapted from guidelines used in the public elementary schools of District 41, Glen Ellen, Illinois:

1. Do allow enough time (about 30 minutes), and start and terminate the conference promptly.

2. Do use a positive rather than a negative approach.

3. Do use specific examples of a child's behavior rather than vague generalities.

4. Do use open-ended questions to draw out the parent to discuss his child.

5. Do accept and consider carefully all the suggestions made by the parent.

6. Do not enter a conference with inadequate data about a child.

7. Do not monopolize the conference; give the parent time to react.

8. Do not compare a parent's child with others in the class.

9. Do not "talk down" to the parent.

10. Do not become defensive and argue with the parent.

Conferences, like most of the other innovations in reporting, are used almost exclusively in elementary schools. It is unfortunate that clearer and more comprehensive reporting practices are not also used in secondary schools. The situation at the secondary level is different, of course. The pupil-teacher ratio is greater, and no one teacher spends the large amount of time with secondary students that the elementary teacher spends with his students.

There is generally a guidance department that maintains some personal contact with student and home; however, the guidance counselor cannot be responsible for all home contacts. No doubt all concerned would benefit from more attention by secondary school personnel to precise and complete reporting practices.

RECOMMENDING PROMOTION AND NONPROMOTION

To promote or not to promote is a question that must be faced by every teacher. In the past, the practice of failing every child who did not come "up to standard" was widespread. More recently, new philosophies and purposes of education have changed this practice in many places. The view is now widely held that nonpromotion compounds, rather than eliminates, problems for many students. Certainly the student who continues to fail year after year is going to look upon school as a very dissatisfying place. The personal and social stigma of failure is, no doubt, psychologically damaging to some students. The comprehensive schools of today are attempting to promote the development of all students with wide ranges of ability. In these schools the emphasis is on individualized programs and instruction, rather than on the threat of failure for students of modest ability.

As a result of these new viewpoints and purposes, some schools have adopted the practice of "social promotion," wherein all students are automatically promoted. This practice, however, has created problems almost as serious as those it eliminated. The major problem created by social promotion is the development of a negative attitude toward school among many students and parents. If everyone is passed, regardless of his achievement or effort, many students will hold the school in contempt and put forth little or no effort at all. Therefore, neither the policy of failing all who do not come up to some arbitrarily fixed standard nor the policy of passing all, regardless of achievement or effort, seems wise.

The question of promotion or nonpromotion can be answered only in terms of what is best for each *individual student.* Many things must be considered in making this decision. Among the more important are the achievement, ability, effort, and maturity of the student; and the policies, programs, and philosophy of the school. All significant factors should be considered, but the decision should always be based on what will be best for the individual child.

QUESTIONS AND ACTIVITIES

1. What grading procedure will you use (or do you use) with your classes? Why do you prefer this one? Would you be willing to have your professor in measurement class use this procedure in determining *your* grade?

2. When a student makes an F, does this mean that the student has failed to learn or that the teacher has failed to teach? Support your position.

3. Would you lower a student's grade if he refused to develop a positive attitude toward your course but achieved well on your tests? Support your position.

4. If a student became confused and recorded his answers in a manner different from the procedure indicated in the test directions, would you count all his answers wrong? Support your position.

5. Assume that you use curve grading on two successive tests in your class. A student made a higher score on the second, but got a higher grade on the first. How could this happen? How could you explain it to his parents?

SUGGESTED READINGS

Ahmann, J. Stanley, and Marvin D. Glock, *Evaluating Pupil Growth* (3rd ed.), Allyn and Bacon, 1967.

A comprehensive and practical discussion of determining marks and reporting progress is presented in chapter 16.

Green, John A., Jr., *Teacher-Made Tests,* Harper & Row, 1963.
Chapter 8 has an informative and understandable treatment of basic marking procedures.

Karmel, Louis J., *Measurement and Evaluation in the Schools,* Macmillan, 1970.
Chapter 16 of this book discusses some of the purposes and procedures of marking and reporting.

National Education Association, Department of Classroom Teachers, *School Marks and Promotion,* Discussion Pamphlet No. 9, National Education Association, 1946.
Problems and procedures of marking and promoting are discussed in this pamphlet for the purpose of getting teachers to examine their own practices critically.

Remmers, H. H., N. L. Gage, and Francis Rummel, *A Practical Introduction to Measurement and Evaluation* (2nd ed.), Harper & Row, 1965.
A discussion of the major principles and practices of marking and reporting is found in chapter 9.

Smith, Fred M., "Go to the Head of the Class: Bases for Grading," *Louisiana Schools,* January, 1964.
This article presents the major strengths and weaknesses of the three bases for assigning marks.

Thorndike, Robert L., "Marks and Marking Systems," *Encyclopedia of Educational Research* (4th ed.), Robert L. Ebel (ed.), Macmillan, 1969.
A thorough, in-depth treatment of the topic. It should provide an excellent resource for faculty study.

USING STANDARDIZED TESTS

The use of standardized tests is a major feature of American education today. It has been estimated that approximately $25 million is spent annually on standardized tests in American schools. This represents something like 100 million tests administered at all levels of education from kindergarten through college.

During the past few years, there have been significant criticisms of the great amount of standardized testing in schools. These criticisms have more often concerned the misuse of standardized tests than the standardized tests themselves. Many of the criticisms are well founded. Too often, schools have established an extensive standardized testing program before the administration and faculty showed sufficient understanding of the proper uses and limitations of tests. One of the principal abuses of test scores is the tendency to regard them as precise quantifications of a student's innate ability or absolute achievement.

The extensive use of standardized tests and the possibilities for their misuse, as well as their potential value, make an understanding of their structure, proper uses, and limitations a necessity for all teachers. A standardized test may be described as a systematic task that has been "tried out." The group on which the test has been tried is known as the "norm" group. If you administer the test according to the standardized procedure, you may compare the performance of your group with the performance of the "norm" group, thereby adding meaning to the measurement. You may find that your group has done generally better or poorer or about the same as the norm group. It should be remembered that norm groups are not magical entities, indicating the level of performance all students *ought* to attain. The comparison is realistic only when the composition of the norm group is known. Students very often rank differently when compared with different groups.

CLASSIFICATION OF STANDARDIZED TESTS

Standardized tests are often classified according to what they measure. One such classification includes three categories: achievement tests, aptitude tests, and tests of personal-social characteristics.

Achievement tests are designed to indicate how much one has accomplished as a result of past training. We may wish to determine the present level of accomplishment or the amount of achievement over a given period of training. There are standardized achievement tests in almost every school subject; in most subjects, there are several. Your problem is to select the one that is most appropriate for you.

Aptitude tests are designed to indicate the rapidity and ease with which one may learn in the future. The difference between an aptitude and an achievement test in the same subject may be more apparent in their *use* than in their *content*. Intelligence tests are a type of aptitude test. They indicate which students are likely to learn more quickly and easily than others. Some aptitude tests that yield only one or two scores are referred to as general aptitude tests. Others are designed to measure specific abilities, such as mechanical aptitude or music aptitude.

Tests of personal-social characteristics are often referred to as *inventories* rather than *tests,* because there are no predetermined right or wrong answers to their questions. Interest and personality inventories are the major types included in this group. There is considerable controversy about their use in schoolwide testing programs. This is particularly true of personality inventories, which are considered by many educators and psychologists to be too technical and experimental for general school use.

Tests are also classified in several ways other than on the basis of what they measure. Several of the more common classifications are presented here.

Speed and power tests. A speed test is one in which speed is one of the important factors measured. Usually no one is expected to finish the test in the time given, and the amount and quality of work accomplished within the time limits is the criterion of success. A power test is one in which speed is not among the important factors measured. Some power tests have almost no time limits, but more often time limits are set. These time limits, however, are based on the amount of time it takes most people to finish and are used only to facilitate test administration.

Individual and group tests. An individual test is so called because it can be administered only to one person at a time. Two outstanding examples are the Stanford-Binet and the Wechsler intelligence tests. Group tests may be administered to many persons at the same time. This is the type used most frequently in schoolwide testing programs, because they are not only more economical but also easier to administer.

Verbal, nonverbal, and performance tests. Most tests used in schools are verbal tests. The directions and test items are presented in verbal or word form. In certain situations, however, such as among brain injured, illiterate, or very young children, nonverbal tests are necessary. These tests are composed of pictures, spatial symbols, or puzzles, but no words. A performance test usually implies some form of physical activity, such as designing patterns with small blocks of wood, screwing nuts onto bolts, or playing a musical instrument.

The same test may, of course, be classified in several ways at once. For example, the Wechsler Intelligence Scale for Children (WISC) is an individual aptitude test, part of which is verbal, part nonverbal, and part performance.

This introduction gives a general, if superficial, introduction to standardized tests. We now consider the use of standardized tests in the building of a schoolwide testing program.

14

A SCHOOLWIDE TESTING
PROGRAM

What is a *good* schoolwide testing program? How do you set up such a good program? Is our present testing program adequate? Are we testing too much? These are the types of questions to be discussed in this chapter.

A good standardized testing program, like any good school program, must grow out of the philosophy and needs peculiar to the school and its constituents. Although similarities exist, a good program for one school will not necessarily be a good program for another. The standardized testing program, like the teachers' testing program, must be developed according to certain logical steps, similar to those described in Chapter 5: Determine the purposes of the program, select the tests, administer the tests, score the tests, interpret the results, and evaluate the program.

PURPOSES OF THE PROGRAM

The first step in the building of a good standardized testing program is a determination of the purposes for which the test scores are to be used. The administration and faculty of a school must first ask itself, "What do we want to *do* with information that may be obtained through a standardized testing program?" Then the questions involving test selection, administration, and interpretation may be considered.

Each school will probably have reasons for using standardized tests that are peculiar to it alone. Several common uses of testing in general were given in Chapter 2. Some particular uses of standardized tests are presented here.

Standardized tests can provide a basis for assessing the ability level and the intellectual strengths and weaknesses of students. It should be noted that standardized tests *cannot* determine the absolute or total "intellectual power" of anyone. They can, however, indicate whether a child is developing at about the same rate as his agemates, or whether he is developing more slowly or faster than others. This type of information can aid the teacher in planning his teaching to fit the capabilities of his students.

Standardized achievement tests can provide a means of checking the validity of teacher-made tests. It is particularly difficult to construct tests that adequately measure achievement of intellectual skills, as described in Chapter 8. The teacher who is attempting this for the first time can check on the success of his efforts by using standardized tests constructed to measure this kind of achievement. Standardized tests often do a better job of measuring these complex outcomes of education than do teacher-made tests.

Standardized achievement tests can aid in diagnosing learning difficulties. The newer and better standardized achievement tests are very systematically organized. A complete *battery* of tests will measure achievement in all major subjects or in each of the basic learning skills. Furthermore, in some of the newer tests, such as the Sequential Tests of Educational Progress, each item has been classified according to specific objective and content area. The results of such tests can help the teacher determine the particular factors that may be contributing to a child's learning difficulties.

Standardized tests can provide evidence concerning an individual's pattern of growth over a period of years. The better standardized tests are integrated from one age level to the next. That is, they present standard or similar tasks at each age level, thus providing data for tracing an individual's growth pattern throughout his developmental years. By establishing the growth level at successive years, the *amount* of growth during given periods of time may be estimated also.

Standardized tests can provide information to aid in curriculum planning. How is an administrator to determine whether or not remedial or accelerated classes are needed in his school? After such classes are inaugurated, how are the students to be selected for these classes? How is the elementary teacher to accomplish appropriate grouping within his class? Such tasks and decisions as these must be based on a great deal of reliable information concerning the students who will be affected. Standardized tests are *one source* of such information. It cannot be emphasized too strongly that standardized test scores should never be used as the sole criterion for purposes of selection and grouping. Rather, they should be used in conjunction with all other information which is pertinent to the situation, such as past grades, teacher recommendations, and results of parent-teacher conferences.

Standardized tests can provide information for guidance. Two major objectives of all guidance programs are the promotion of self-understanding and wise decision making. Standardized tests are *one source* of information a counselor can use to promote these ends.

Standardized tests can aid in assessing the effectiveness of teaching methods and school programs. Here again is a procedure in which tests are too often misused. Evaluating teaching methods and schools is a very complex job. In the first place, standardized tests do not measure all the valuable benefits that students can receive. Second, the effectiveness of a school depends largely on the needs of and support from the community it serves. Standardized tests can aid in the assessment of teaching methods and school programs, but only when one is willing to consider all the other pertinent factors.

As was stated before, these are some of the common purposes for which standardized tests may be used. No doubt many schools will find other specific uses. Unless tests are to be used for some meaningful purpose that will promote the effectiveness of the school, there is no point in giving them at all. Too much time and money is already being spent accumulating test scores that are filed away in the principal's office and forgotten.

SELECTING THE APPROPRIATE TESTS

After the purposes for testing have been decided on, the faculty may consider the question, "What tests given at what levels will provide the information we need?" The process of selecting appropriate tests actually involves two steps. First, the *type* of tests to be given at the various grade levels must be determined. Second, the *particular* tests of each type must be selected.

Type and frequency

The type of tests and frequency of testing depend on several things, such as the purposes of the program, the amount of money available, the nature of the community, and the developmental patterns of children. Many schools give an achievement battery every year from grades 4 through 12. Others alternate with achievement tests and general aptitude tests. Various types of readiness tests are often administered in the first grade. During the junior high school years, a multiple-aptitude test is often administered to aid students in the selection of academic programs in high school and in tentative vocational planning. Two essential principles for a teacher to follow in determining the type and frequency of testing are consistency and repetition. An aptitude test should be given at least three times during a child's school career, and the number of years between testings should be approximately equal. Scores obtained at the fourth, seventh, and tenth grades provide a more reliable estimate of a student's ability than two scores obtained randomly. Achievement tests are usually given more frequently, and they too should be spaced evenly throughout elementary and secondary school. Furthermore, tests given at different levels should be part of the same articulated series. If you use the California or Metropolitan achievement tests in elementary school, you should use the higher levels of the same tests in secondary school. If you use the Otis Intelligence test in elementary school, you should use the higher levels of the Otis in secondary school. This provides a basis for comparing scores of an individual child throughout his various stages of development.

Which test?

Which particular test of a given type should be chosen? This question can be answered only by considering the three qualities by which a test is evaluated: reliability, validity, and usability. The reliability of a test may be estimated by checking the reliability studies reported in the test manual. Generally, reliability coefficients of .90 and above may be considered sufficiently high for tests that are to be used in a schoolwide testing program. The reliability of subscores that many tests yield should also be checked. Sometimes these scores are based on too few items to be sufficiently reliable.

You may remember that validity is determined in various ways, depending on the type of test being considered. The validity of an achievement test is determined by making a detailed inspection of the items of the test. There are numerous major achievement tests for every subject and grade level. No two of these measure achievement in a subject in exactly the same way. Test emphasis must parallel teaching emphasis. Your job is to determine which test measures achievement in a subject *as you teach it.* This can be done only by making a detailed inspection of each item of the test. The procedure for selecting achievement tests is discussed more completely in Chapter 15. The validity of an aptitude test is determined by checking studies of predictive and concurrent validity reported in the test manual. If an aptitude test is used to predict school performance, as it usually is, then some empirical evidence that it can be used for this purpose is necessary.

Who should be involved in the selection of tests? If tests are to be used effectively, those who will be expected to use them should be involved in their selection—teachers and guidance counselors as well as administrators. This is especially true of achievement tests, since teachers are in the best position to determine if a test measures achievement in a subject as they teach it. One of the chief reasons for the misuse of tests by teachers is that the entire program, from planning to test purchase, is often imposed by the administration of a school, with little or no faculty involvement.

ADMINISTERING STANDARDIZED TESTS

Any teacher who is willing to familiarize himself with the test and follow the directions given in the manual can administer any of the group tests designed for schoolwide use. Smooth test administration does take practice, however, and the teachers should be given time to read the manual and to practice giving the test to each other before they are to administer it to students. The necessity of adhering explicitly to directions and time limits cannot be stressed too strongly. If the directions specify a 4-minute time limit, that should be taken to mean *exactly* 4 minutes, not *about* 4 minutes. The directions should be read, not paraphrased.

If the standardized procedure is violated in any significant way, the results cannot be meaningfully compared with those of other groups; and the test has lost one of its most valuable characteristics.

Educators sometimes argue about the relative merits of fall versus spring testing. There are particular advantages of each, but generally one time is about as good as the other. The purposes of the program will often indicate which has more advantages for a given school. Whichever time is chosen, it is important that tests not be given near any important school event. Tests should be administered on as "normal" a day as possible, so that students will not be distracted. It need hardly be said that conditions of light, heat, noise, and space should be as conducive to concentration as possible.

SCORING STANDARDIZED TESTS

Most publishers of standardized tests provide easy and objective methods for scoring those tests that are designed for use in schoolwide testing programs. Any teacher can score the commonly used tests, but the task does require some practice and concentrated effort. This is especially true of the primary level, because very young students are not able to manipulate separate answer sheets and must indicate their answers in the test booklet. In higher grades, answer sheets should be used, because they are much easier to score than test booklets and also are more economical. Furthermore, teachers who are to score tests should be given time for this task during school hours, if at all possible. The value of the entire testing program will be destroyed unless the tests are scored carefully and accurately.

Many schools are using the machine scoring services offered by test publishers. The cost of these services runs from about 20 to 50 cents per student, depending on the number and types of scores reported. The older scoring machines required the use of a special electrographic pencil. Newer machines now in use require no special pencil, but the answer sheets for these machines are quite crowded and may cause difficulty for some students.

INTERPRETING STANDARDIZED TEST SCORES

Proper interpretation of standardized test scores is sufficiently complex to warrant treatment in a separate chapter. Accordingly, Chapter 18 is devoted entirely to score interpretation. At this point, we only caution against the overinterpretation of test scores. It should always be remembered that tests are only small samples of human behavior that allow you to compare the performance of different students on the same task. They are *not* absolute or precise measures of a student's ability or achievement.

EVALUATING THE STANDARDIZED TESTING PROGRAM

A standardized testing program is *good* if it supplies dependable information that allows teachers to do the things they need to do. To put it more succinctly, the program is good if the purposes are accomplished. This implies that a good program in one school will not necessarily be a good program in another school. The testing program must be evaluated in terms of the needs and purposes of the individual school. Nevertheless, there are elements common to all good testing programs. A few of the more important features are presented next.[1]

A good testing program takes its proper place in the total measurement program of the school. Standardized tests are only one source of information about students. Information from other

---

[1] These features were adapted from Frank B. Womer, "Characteristics of a Good Testing Program," *Guidance Services Newsletter,* Guidance Service Division, Department of Public Instruction, Lansing, Michigan, October, 1958.

sources, such as scholastic records, health records, and academic records, should also be compiled and used along with test scores.

A good testing program provides comprehensive coverage. It should provide information about special nonacademic aptitudes as well as general aptitude.

A good testing program is well organized: (1) It provides continuity of testing from grades 1 through 12 and sufficient repetition of testing to establish a reliable picture of the individual. Tests from the same series are used throughout the various grade levels. (2) Tests are used to serve multiple purposes where feasible. (3) The use of teachers and counselors for clerical tasks is minimized.

The program emphasizes proper use of test results by teachers, counselors, and administrators. Test results should be accessible to all who want them and who are able to use them properly. If test results are to be fully utilized, they must be reported to teachers, students, and parents. This does not mean that everyone should have access to all test scores, nor does it mean that scores which may be misinterpreted are given to students and parents without explanation. Test scores should be reported as simply and meaningfully as possible, preferably by counselors who have been trained in the task. In-service training programs should be utilized to develop and maintain competence of *teachers* in test-score interpretation and use.

QUESTIONS AND ACTIVITIES

1. As a class project, develop several objectives for a standardized testing program in a school having grades 1-12. Design a testing program to fulfill these objectives.

2. You are on a faculty committee to determine whether a limited amount of money should be used to add library books, improve teaching materials, or institute a program of standardized testing. What position would you take? Explain.

3. Why would such instruments as the Stanford-Binet, the Wechsler Intelligence Scale for Children, and the Rorschach Inkblot Test have limited use in a schoolwide testing program?

4. Why should the same achievement or aptitude test series be used throughout all grade levels?

5. An elementary teacher remarked that his school's program of standardized testing must be good, as it had been designed 20 years ago by an expert in the field. What are some changes that *should* have occurred in the program during this period?

SUGGESTED READINGS

Bauernfeind, Robert H., *Building A School Testing Program* (2nd ed.), Houghton Mifflin, 1970.
> This is a thorough discussion of the purposes, procedures, and uses of measurement devices in schools.

Chauncey, Henry, and John E. Dobbin, *Testing: Its Place in Education Today,* Harper & Row, 1964.
> An excellent discussion of the proper role of standardized tests is presented in terminology that the average teacher can understand.

Davis, Frederick, B., *Educational Measurements and Their Interpretation,* Wadsworth, 1964.
> A thorough discussion of the selection and administration of standardized tests is presented in chapter 3.

Mehrens, William A. and Irvin J. Lehmann, *Standardized Tests in Education,* Holt, Rinehart & Winston, 1969.
> Chapters 1 and 5 in this text present an excellent overview of the role of standardized tests in education. Trends, issues and principles of using tests are also discussed.

Stanley, Julian C., *Measurement in Today's Schools* (4th ed.), Prentice-Hall, 1964.
> Chapter 10 gives a comprehensive overview of the schoolwide testing program.

Thompson, Anton, "Tentative Guidelines for Proper and Improper Practices with Standardized Tests," *California Journal of Educational Research,* September, 1958, pp. 159-166.

This article presents some concise answers to common questions about the proper uses of standardized tests. Reprints are available from California Test Bureau.

Thorndike, Robert L., and Elizabeth Hagen, *Measurement and Evaluation in Psychology and Education* (3rd ed.), Wiley, 1969.

Chapter 16 contains a thorough discussion of important points to be considered in planning testing programs for all levels of education.

Womer, Frank B., "Characteristics of a Good Testing Program," *Guidance Services Newsletter,* Guidance Service Division, Department of Public Instruction, Lansing, Michigan, October, 1958.

Womer, Frank B., *Testing Programs in Michigan Schools,* University of Michigan, 1963.

This pamphlet is the report of a survey of standardized test programs in elementary and secondary schools in Michigan. The teacher can get an idea of the types of standardized tests given at various grade levels, and the methods of administration, scoring, and recording used.

15

MEASURING ACHIEVEMENT WITH STANDARDIZED TESTS

In the process of diagnosis and treatment, a doctor has a wide variety of tools at his disposal. A modern teacher also has many instruments to choose from. One of the most valuable instruments is tests, which take many forms; therefore, it is important for the teacher to understand the proper role of each in the educational process. In the area of achievement testing, many types of standardized tests are available. Further, the teacher can have as wide an assortment of teacher-made tests as his own ingenuity can devise—each with its own potential contribution to teaching.

STANDARDIZED VERSUS TEACHER-MADE ACHIEVEMENT TESTS

Although tests may not be fully comparable, the teacher has to balance one against the other when deciding which type to use. Many of the problems that teachers have had in using achievement tests have been based upon their attempts to use one type when another would have been better. To illustrate, could you compare the achievement of your class with national norms by using a test you prepared? On the other hand, how could you make effective use of a standardized test in assigning marks to your students at the end of a grading period? A characteristic of a good testing program is that a variety of tests is used, each in the situation where it can make its maximum contribution.

Standardized achievement tests

One of the most notable developments in the recent history of achievement testing is the speed with which new tests have been developed. The publication of such tests was essentially a sideline of certain textbook publishers a few decades ago. Now the preparation and publication of such tests has become the chief function of some large industrial concerns in America.   Indeed, one sometimes hears the criticism that we are so greatly involved with preparing and scoring tests that we seldom get around to the purpose of the whole thing—making intelligent use of the results. While there may be times when this criticism is valid, is it really the fault of a *test* if the results are not used?

Strengths and weaknesses of standardized achievement tests

A *major strength* of standardized achievement tests is that they are systematically planned to achieve a particular set of goals. Let us consider the steps that might be used by a test publisher in developing such a test.

Preliminary planning.   After a publisher has decided to prepare a test for a certain grade level in a specified subject area, he must do a great deal of advance planning. For example, if the test is to measure progress toward certain goals, it is necessary to find out what the goals are. This frequently involves examination of numerous textbooks, syllabi, and curricula. Following this development of a set of objectives, it is necessary to decide what content could be used in the test. A fairly detailed test plan is developed, then given a thorough examination by a panel of critics. This panel would probably include classroom teachers, subject-matter experts, and test technicians. On the basis of their comments, a final test plan would be developed.

Preparation of test items.   Regardless of the number of experts and consultants involved, someone has to write test questions. This individual or group uses the plan as a guide, then develops a large number of items that appear to conform to the pattern spelled out in the plan. In some cases, the actual writing of test items is done by a panel. More commonly, however, the panel simply reviews the work of one or more test technicians assigned to the project. However the mechanics may be handled, preliminary forms of the test are developed after a great deal of criticism and review.

Testing the test.   Even though a panelist may have had wide experience with tests, he cannot reliably predict the difficulty of an item. Further, an item that is perfectly clear to an adult might be not at all clear to a student. The only way to compile reliable information on the characteristics of a test item is to get the reaction of students to it. Hence, the preliminary forms of a test are administered to groups of students comparable to those for which the test is being designed. Its level of difficulty is computed, and its ability to discriminate is examined. For example, if high-ability students consistently answer incorrectly while low-ability students answer correctly, the item evidently requires further examination. If, in a multiple-choice item, a particular option is universally ignored, then it is not functioning properly.

As a result of the preliminary testing, each item is carefully studied. Some are discarded, while others undergo major revision. Ultimately, a list of the best items is prepared.

Preparing the final forms.   After the extensive amount of item analysis has been completed, it is a fairly simple task to put together the final forms of the test. The technician selects those items that offer a proper gradation of difficulty (from easy to difficult), places them in proper sequence, and selects enough of them to conform to time limitations. If several forms of the test are prepared simultaneously, an effort is made to achieve comparable gradation of difficulty in each. The tentative final form is subjected to analysis and criticism from many sources, with revisions as necessary.

Establishing norms.   The only way to set up a yardstick of achievement as measured by the new test is to administer the test. Frequently, an elaborate sampling procedure is used in arriving at norms. Efforts are made to select a sample, ranging from a few hundred to many thousands, that is representative of the entire population for which the test is designed. On the basis of the sample group's achievement on the test, it is possible to arrive at a set of standards by which future users of the test may *interpret* the results for their own students.

In addition to the systematic planning that goes into the preparation of a standardized achievement test, another strength is that these tests are statistically refined. It is beyond the scope of this book to point out in detail the many statistical procedures that are employed between preliminary planning and the final issue of a test. Every item as well as the entire test is subjected to an extensive examination by a variety of statistical operations, so that, by the time the test goes on the market, a tremendous amount of information has been compiled about it. Much of this is summarized in nontechnical or semitechnical terms in the teacher's manual. Such information adds greatly to the usefulness of the test as a measuring device. Further, statistical studies regarding the test usually continue after the test is issued commercially. This frequently results in major changes when the test is revised.

A *major weakness* of the standardized achievement test is inherent in the way it is designed. For example, let us consider a test that is being prepared for use in first-year algebra. How is it possible to produce a test that will function effectively in each of the thousands of first-year algebra classrooms in the nation? When one considers the wide diversity of text materials, teaching aims and procedures, and ability levels of students, he can begin to envision the tremendous difficulty in preparing an instrument that is valid in every class.

The problem is shared to some degree by publishers of textbooks aiming for a national market, but they generally assume that individual teachers will omit, supplement, make applications, and generally adapt text material to meet the needs of their classes. Such procedures, however, cannot be applied to a test. The test must be used as it is written, and under prescribed conditions, if it is to be a "standardized" test.

In summary, a major weakness of the standardized achievement test is that this test is designed to fit a composite set of objectives drawn from many sources. Hence, it is very unlikely that this test will completely fit the unique objectives of any individual teacher.

Strengths and weaknesses of teacher-made achievement tests

While the chief emphasis of this chapter is on the standardized achievement test, it is necessary to give some attention to certain features of teacher-made tests for purposes of comparison. Both types of tests are valuable tools for the teacher, though frequently he has to decide which type would be of more value in a particular situation. For this reason, it is important that we look at the strengths and weaknesses of each type.

Strengths.   A major strength of the teacher-made test is that it can be tailored to fit a particular, specific situation. For example, a teacher takes his general science class to visit a local museum of natural science. Clearly, the only type of test that would be useful at this point is one that the teacher makes. A history class has been studying about historical events in its own city, county, or state. Only a teacher-made test can fit the needs of this class.

One of the great strengths of the American public school system is that we do not have a nationwide set of procedures and goals, so that local conditions can figure prominently in teaching. For the same reason the only way many types of teaching-learning activities can be properly evaluated is with teacher-made tests.

Another strength of the teacher-made test is that it is well suited to frequent usage. Those who work with students know that frequent testing promotes efficient learning. Many teachers find that five to ten short tests over a unit of work are more effective in teaching than is a single, comprehensive unit test. The standardized tests are obviously unsuited for such use. Hence, a major strength of the teacher-made test is that it has flexibility in a variety of ways—length, frequency of usage, objectives tested, and many others.

Weaknesses.   Many of the features of teacher-made tests as commonly listed are in reality not characteristics of such tests in the abstract. Rather, they are characteristics of the tests as prepared under a particular set of. circumstances. Such is the case with the weaknesses of teacher-made tests discussed next.

One problem is that tests frequently do not relate to the particular objectives of the course. Many teachers unconsciously teach with a goal in mind but prepare tests that stress an entirely different goal. Consider, for example, the history teacher who stresses the major concepts in a unit but who tests primarily on memorization of dates—not because the dates are especially important, but because they fit readily into test questions. Such divergence is a violation of the basic principle that testing goals and teaching goals should be the same.

Another weakness that frequently appears is the lack of a critical attitude toward a test on the part of the teacher. The demands on a teacher's time are such that he may delay test preparation unduly. Thus, he may put together a test at the last possible moment, without any allowance for review and criticism. The likelihood of a good test resulting from such an effort is somewhat remote.

The test should be prepared far enough in advance so that the author or a colleague can give it critical evaluation before it is duplicated. Further, in case he maintains a file of back tests, the teacher should examine the test as a measuring instrument after it has been used in a class. Appropriate notes and revisions can frequently prevent repetition of certain types of errors. In short, if testing errors are to be minimized, the teacher should be constantly concerned about the quality of each item on his test.

USES OF STANDARDIZED ACHIEVEMENT TESTS

Uses of standardized tests in general were discussed in Chapter 14. We next review some of the specific uses a teacher may make of standardized achievement tests.

Many of the important uses of standardized achievement tests are administrative rather than instructional. For example, an elementary school principal whose school was located near a major military installation faced the task of assigning to appropriate grade levels students who had attended a wide diversity of schools. An effective aid in assigning students to grade levels in which they could function was a battery of standardized achievement tests.

Such administrative uses frequently do not involve the classroom teacher to an appreciable degree. Some of the uses of achievement tests that may be of interest to the classroom teacher follow:

Checking on the validity of teacher-made tests and grades.   It has been pointed out that standardized tests are not designed to serve as a basis for assigning marks; however, such tests can serve as a valuable aid in another way. If a teacher's testing and marking practices are valid, there should be relationships in the pattern of pupil achievement between teacher-made and standardized instruments. Specifically, if the rank-order listing of a class on the basis of standardized achievement tests is markedly different from such a listing based upon assigned marks, the teacher should re-examine his testing practices. While one should not automatically assume that the marking system is at fault in such a case, the careful planning that goes into the production of a standardized achievement test makes it unlikely that such a test would yield totally spurious results.

Determining individual growth rates over a period of years.   One of the most fascinating and frequently most useful aspects of a long-range testing program in a school is the way in which it mirrors individual growth. In many schools, all the results from the program of testing are kept in individual folders that follow the student through the progression of grades. Frequently, these results can serve very effectively as a basis for individual teacher-pupil conferences.

This same feature can be of help to a new teacher in learning about his class. For example, by scanning the individual cumulative records before school starts, a teacher can frequently observe probable areas of difficulty for certain students. The fact that Mary has trouble with spelling, John has not done well in arithmetic, that Billy will need extra help in English—these and many other such items can enable the teacher to launch an effective program of instruction with a minimum of wasted time and effort.

Comparing the effectiveness of two methods of instruction.   Experimental procedures in education frequently require the use of measuring devices that are more dependable than the teacher-made test. Consider, for example, a classroom teacher who is interested in comparing the effectiveness of Method A with that of Method B. The teacher might divide his class into two groups of approximately the same ability levels, or he might try Method A one year and Method B the following year. For his own purposes, it might be satisfactory to base his conclusions on his own observations. However, if he is to make any effort toward a real analysis, the teacher would need to devise a method for measuring the progress of each student. Probably no better method would be available than to administer a good achievement test at the beginning and end of the experiment. An examination of the test results for each student would indicate his progress during the period of the experiment. A comparison of the results for the two groups (one using Method A, the other using Method B) should be of value in comparing the effectiveness of the methods under study.

Sometimes test results from an achievement battery are used in comparing one teacher with another, or one school with another, though it is frequently asked what this really proves. These test results can, however, be of considerable value to a teacher in his self-analysis. If his students consistently compare favorably with test norms in some subject areas, but with equal consistency fall below grade level in others, it should tell the teacher that he needs to direct his efforts toward professional improvement in the latter areas.

Providing information about the students for guidance purposes.   An effective counselor needs to have a wide diversity of background information about each student, for which he can often draw on standardized achievement tests. For example, Joe is seriously considering mechanical engineering as a career choice. The counselor notes that Joe's test profiles have consistently indicated low achievement in mathematics. By making sure that Joe understands the type of training in mathematics required in an engineering curriculum, the counselor might spare Joe the painful experience of trying a program in which his chances of success are doubtful. While there are, of course, many aspects of guidance that are unrelated to careers, one can hardly imagine a guidance area in which achievement test results would not make a contribution.

Providing data for curricular changes.   The curriculum in the elementary and secondary schools never is stable. Parents frequently come to a realization of this fact when they try to help youngsters. It is not unusual for the parent to give up in frustration, since much of the new material is totally unfamiliar to students of an earlier generation.

Curricular changes are necessary, though it is important for teachers to avoid the attitude that something is "new, hence good" or "old, hence bad." All major curricular changes should be based upon valid research. For example, for years, arithmetic students were expected to achieve complete mastery of the multiplication facts in fourth grade. Is this realistic? Should they be able to complete these facts by the end of third grade? or second? Or would it be better to study them for 5 years? As experimental work is performed on such problems, it is obvious that some sort of standardized measuring instrument—generally an achievement test—is necessary.

Of course, curricular change occurs in many areas other than grade placement of topics. In any case, where one is proposing a way to improve a curriculum, the proposed system would be expected to prove its superiority over the existing one. In any such situation, research is needed, with standardized achievement tests frequently serving as a valuable tool.

TYPES OF STANDARDIZED ACHIEVEMENT TESTS

Standardized achievement tests are available in several different types. Some of the more common types are achievement batteries, survey tests in specific subjects, tests emphasizing basic understandings and skills, and diagnostic tests.

Achievement batteries consist of several separate tests designed to survey learning outcomes in the major academic areas. Because this design makes them more generally applicable, batteries are more widely used than single tests, especially in elementary and junior high schools. Batteries differ in the areas included at different age levels, usually adding more specific areas as the level of the test advances. For example, the Primary I battery (last half of grade 1) of the Metropolitan Achievement Tests includes four tests: Word Knowledge, Word Discrimination, Reading, and Arithmetic Concepts and Skills. Spelling is added to the Primary II (grade 2) Battery; Language and Arithmetic Computation are added to the Elementary Battery (grades 3 and 4); and Social Studies Information, Social Studies Skills, and Science are added to the Intermediate Battery (grades 5 and 6). The tests also increase in difficulty as level advances. Batteries published by different companies also differ slightly in the areas included. For example, the Science Research Associates Achievement Series for the lower grades uses two tests, Arithmetic and Reading. At the next higher level, a test in Language Arts is added. For the upper elementary grades, tests in Social Studies, Science, Language Arts, Reading and Arithmetic, along with a supplemental test on Work-Study Skills, are provided. A wide variety of subscores may be extracted from the tests in this series.

The fact that tests differ does not mean that one test is necessarily better than another, but it does mean that one test may be more or less valid for a particular school. The content of any achievement test should be examined in detail to determine whether it measures learning that is emphasized in the school.

At the secondary level particularly, it is often desirable to administer achievement tests in specific subjects. There are many tests designed to survey learning outcomes in almost every secondary school subject. Because these tests are specific, analysis of their content prior to use is even more important than it is in the more general achievement batteries. Different tests in the same subject often vary considerably in the amount of emphasis placed on various elements of the subjects. It is up to the teacher to select the test that most closely parallels the pattern of emphasis he uses in teaching the course. A teacher should be particularly careful if he is teaching a course like mathematics, which has recently undergone drastic changes. Tests published before the changes occurred are likely to be quite invalid when used in a class that has stressed newer topics.

Several tests published in recent years are primarily designed to measure broad educational outcomes that are not necessarily the result of one particular course. One of the first of these was the Iowa Tests of Basic Skills, designed to measure Vocabulary, Reading Comprehension, Language Skills, Work-Study Skills, and Arithmetic Skills in grades 1 through 9. A similar battery at the secondary level is the Iowa Tests of Educational Development (ITED). The ITED is designed to measure understanding and intellectual skills in nine basic areas: Social Studies Background, Natural Sciences Background, Correctness of Expression, Quantitative Thinking, Interpretation of Reading Materials in the Social Studies, Interpretation of Reading Materials in the Natural Sciences, Interpretation of Reading Materials in Literature, General Vocabulary, and Use of Sources of Information. Another battery designed for this purpose, which contains forms for all levels from grade 4 through college sophomores, is the Sequential Tests of Educational Progress (STEP). The seven tests in the STEP battery are Reading, Writing, Listening, Essay, Mathematics, Science, and Social Studies. It should be noted that these tests are not completely different from other test batteries; however, the degree of emphasis on understanding and intellectual skills is probably greatest in tests designed for that purpose.

Diagnostic tests are designed primarily to help a teacher determine areas of strength and weakness possessed by a student. These are most frequently used in basic areas involving complicated skills, such as reading and arithmetic. Diagnostic reading tests usually include such areas as vocabulary, reading speed, and reading comprehension. Arithmetic tests involve such skills as understanding of basic number concepts, arithmetic computation and arithmetic reasoning.

SELECTING STANDARDIZED ACHIEVEMENT TESTS

Standardized achievement tests are selected on the basis of those characteristics discussed in Chapter 4—reliability, validity, and usability.

The reliability of the major tests of the standard publishers is about the same. Coefficients of reliability on most single subject matter tests and on the tests included in achievement batteries usually vary from about .80 to .95. The teacher's major concern about the reliability of achievement tests lies in three situations. First, he should be wary of subtests that are small parts of some achievement tests. Sometimes these subtests are too short to yield sufficiently reliable scores. The teacher should check the reliability coefficients and standard errors of measurement of all subtest scores before using them separately. Second, he should be wary of the test that purports to measure achievement in a subject all the way from primary school through high school. The major batteries come in four or five different levels, each level spanning about three grades. The test that tries to span six or seven grades cannot provide a sample at any grade level that would be adequate to yield dependable scores. Third, he should not select a test on which no reliability or norming data are available. Good test publishers go to a great deal of expense and effort in norming and checking the reliability of their tests, and they are eager to provide information about it.

The major publishers expend considerable effort building tests that are valid. They check textbooks, courses of study, and school objectives, and often have committees of teachers aid them in selecting the content to be included. Naturally, they try to build a test that fits the objectives of the greatest number of teachers. This means that the test may include some elements of a subject you do not consider important and may leave out some elements you think are important, though you may still find the test useful. The only way you can tell if an achievement test is valid for you is to make a detailed analysis of its content. This procedure is best performed by a committee of teachers, since it involves far-reach-ing judgments. You should have a table of specifications or an outline of the major objectives of your course. As you read each item, classify it according to one of your objectives. If it does not fit any of your objectives, try to determine what it does measure. This is an involved and time-consuming task, but content validity is perhaps the most significant discriminating characteristic of standardized achievement tests. Furthermore, the intimate familiarity which will result from this procedure will place you in a much better position to understand and *use* the results of the test you do select.

Usability is particularly important in standardized achievement tests, because teachers are primarily the administrators and users of these tests. Long and complicated administrative and scoring procedures frustrate both teacher and students, and can adversely affect what might otherwise be a good program. Norm groups, with which students' scores are to be compared, should be clearly described, as should the tasks the tests represent. Individual report forms should be easy to complete and should provide for reporting in terms of the standard error of measurement. The time limits of the tests should fit the attention span of the children who are supposed to take them and should fit class time limits when possible. Finally, the cost of the test should be about the same as that of similar tests and in keeping with the school's test budget. In considering costs, you should distinguish between basic costs of test booklets and answer sheets, and costs for extras like special scoring and reporting services offered by some publishers. These extras are all right if you can afford them, but they add nothing to the reliability and validity of the tests. If your budget is limited, it is wiser to concentrate on the basics of a set of good tests and forget the extras and gimmicks.

QUESTIONS AND ACTIVITIES

1. In your educational experience, have you encountered situations in which the results obtained from a program of achievement testing were used in a particularly effective manner? Describe.

2. A parent insists that his child should have a higher mark in your course because of his high ranking on a standardized achievement test in the subject. How would you respond?

3. What are the advantages of having committees of teachers select standardized achievement tests? Would there be any disadvantages connected with this practice?

4. It has been said that a danger regarding the use of standardized achievement tests is that parents, teachers, or administrators might have too much faith in the exactness of the results. Do you see this as a valid statement? Explain.

SUGGESTED READINGS

Davis, Frederick B., *Educational Measurements and Their Interpretation,* Wadsworth, 1964.
> One of the few available discussions of the measurement of change is presented in chapter 10. Chapter 11 discusses the measurement of underachievement and overachievement.

Katz, Martin, *Selecting an Achievement Test: Principles and Procedures,* Evaluation and Advisory Service Series No. 3, Educational Testing Service, 1961.
> A very thorough and practical discussion of the principles and procedures of achievement test selection is presented in this booklet. It is currently available free of charge from the Evaluation and Advisory Service of ETS.

Mehrens, William A. and Irvin J. Lehmann, *Standardized Tests in Education,* Holt, Rinehart & Winston, 1969.
> A general discussion of standardized achievement tests and their uses in schools is presented in Chapter 3. The treatment is at a level which any teacher should be able to understand.

Noll, Victor H., *Introduction to Educational Measurement* (2nd ed.), Houghton Mifflin, 1955.
> Standardized achievement testing in the elementary school is discussed in chapter 8, and standardized achievement tests in the secondary school in chapter 9.

Sequential Tests of Educational Progress, Teachers Guide, Cooperative Test Division, Educational Testing Service, 1958.

Although designed specifically for use with the Sequential Tests of Educational Progress, this booklet presents an excellent procedure for making the most effective use of achievement tests in promoting learning.

Thorndike, Robert L., and Elizabeth Hagen, *Measurement and Evaluation in Psychology and Education* (3rd ed.), Wiley, 1969.

Chapter 9 presents an excellent discussion of the types of standardized achievement tests and their uses in education.

16

MEASURING INTELLIGENCE AND
APTITUDE WITH STANDARDIZED TESTS

SOME LEADERS IN THE DEVELOPMENT
OF INTELLIGENCE TESTING

Although educational movements usually come about because of social demands, there are invariably certain leaders who provide direction. Such has been the case in intelligence testing, where we should note the contributions of the following pioneers.

Sir Francis Galton, a British scholar, worked in many phases of testing. Many authorities believe that Galton's greatest contribution was in the area of statistical interpretation. He worked closely with his pupil Karl Pearson in developing a variety of mathematical procedures that have inestimable value in testing.

J. M. Cattell, an American psychologist, introduced the term *mental tests* and did a great deal of work in the development of such tests. A practical rather than theoretical worker, he was inclined to overemphasize the simple mental processes. As a writer and teacher, he was an outstanding contributor to the development of intelligence tests.

Alfred Binet, a French experimentalist, worked in several areas of science before settling on psychology. Sometimes referred to as the greatest single leader in the development of intelligence testing, Binet published the first scale for the measurement of intelligence in 1905.

Lewis Terman, of Stanford University, saw a great deal of merit in the work of Binet. He revised and expanded Binet's scale and in 1916 issued the Stanford-Binet test for use with American children. This test has long been a valuable instrument in American education.

A. S. Otis did the background work that developed into the Army Alpha test. His name is also associated with other tests, such as the Otis-Lennon Mental Ability Test, widely used in the schools of America.

L. L. Thurstone was one of the first American researchers to use factor analysis in the study of intelligence. He isolated what he termed the *primary mental abilities* and developed one of the first multifactor intelligence tests.

David Wechsler has developed two widely used individual instruments for intelligence testing: the Wechsler Intelligence Scale for Children and the Wechsler Adult Intelligence Scale.

O. K. Buros has, since 1938, provided the most convenient single reference in the area of mental measurements. His *Mental Measurements Yearbook,* kept current through frequent revision, provides a wealth of information about available tests.

THE NATURE OF INTELLIGENCE

In the past, those who have been interested in studying intelligence have not always agreed on its nature, nor is there complete agreement today. Binet conceived of intelligence as a very general trait, primarily the ability to profit from experience. E. L. Thorndike visualized intelligence as comprising many specific traits. In Thorndike's view, an intelligence test is essentially a task to be performed, and the number of specific "factors" of intelligence is limited only by the number of different tasks a test designer could devise.

During the 1930s, researchers began to utilize a statistical technique known as factor analysis in the study of intelligence. This technique is essentially a process of intercorrelating a large number of scores in an attempt to reduce the number of variables necessary to account for a phenomenon. Charles Spearman used this technique to formulate what has been called the "two-factor" theory of intelligence. According to this theory, intelligence consists of a general factor "g" underlying all intellectual tasks and various specific factors "s" associated with each different kind of task. L. L. Thurstone used factor analysis also, but formulated a slightly different theory of intelligence. In Thurstone's original formulation, he reported six factors that appeared to underlie the task contained in 56 different tests. These factors were Verbal (V), Number (N), Spatial (S), Word Fluency (W), Memory (M), and Reasoning (R). It was shown in later investigations that these were not necessarily the only factors or abilities comprising human intelligence. Other factors could be isolated by including different tasks in the original tests and by testing students with different cultural backgrounds. It was also shown that the factors correlated positively with each other, suggesting the existence of a general factor underlying them all.

More recent formulations of intelligence growing out of factor analysis studies are those presented by J. P. Guilford and Frederick B. Davis. Guilford has formulated a three-dimensional "structure of the intellect" (Figure 9). One dimension includes the types of test *content,* another deals with the *products* yielded, and the third dimension includes the types of *operations* involved. There are four different types of content, six types of products,

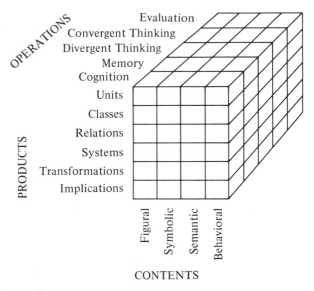

CONTENTS

Figure 9
Guilford's theoretical model for the complete structure of intellect.
(From J. P. Guilford, *Personality,* copyright © 1959 by McGraw-Hill
Book Company, p. 397. Used by permission of the publisher.)

and five different operations, yielding 120 (4 × 6 × 5) separate mental abilities. Guilford reports that about 50 of these abilities have actually been isolated.

Davis's model is less elaborate but more closely resembles the tasks included in most intelligence tests. This is a two-dimensional model including five types of activity in three major fields, yielding 15 separate abilities (Table 11). Davis states that this list by no means includes all human abilities or even all intellectual abilities. It does appear to include the major intellectual abilities, however, particularly those associated with learning. The three fields involve the three different types of symbols by which we think and communicate: verbal, numerical, and spatial. The five types of activity involve important ways in which we operate or work in each field: speed and accuracy of perception, memory, reasoning,

Table 11

Fifteen important abilities underlying intellectual activity

	Speed and Accuracy of Perception	Memory	Reasoning	Ideational Fluency	Visualization
Verbal	(1) Pv	(4) Mv	(7) Rv	(10) Iv	(13) Vv
Numerical	(2) Pn	(5) Mn	(8) Rn	(11) In	(14) Vn
Spatial	(3) Ps	(6) Ms	(9) Rs	(12) Is	(15) Vs

Source: From Frederick B. Davis, *Educational Measurements and Their Interpretation,* © 1964 by Wadsworth Publishing Company, Inc., Belmont, California, p. 120. Reprinted by permission of the publisher.

ideational fluency, and visualization. A few illustrations adapted from Davis will perhaps give a better understanding of the actual behavior involved in each operation and field.

Cell number 1 (Pv) involves perceptual speed and accuracy in verbal materials. This ability is tested with a speed test composed of items similar to the following:[1]

> *Directions:* If the two words on a line are spelled in exactly the same way, blacken the space under S; if they are spelled differently, blacken the space under D. Work as quickly as you can without making careless mistakes.

		S	D
1. Benghazi	Benghazi	......	......
2. Andaman	Andanan	......	......

[1] From Frederick B. Davis, *Educational Measurements and Their Interpretation,* © 1964 by Wadsworth Publishing Company, Inc., Belmont, California, pp. 121-125. Reprinted by permission of the publisher.

Perceptual speed and accuracy in numerical materials (Pn) and in spatial materials (Ps) are tested in a similar manner, with the exception that numbers and spatial symbols are used instead of words.

Ability number 4, memory for verbal materials (Mv) is measured by items involving knowledge of word meanings. For example:[2]

Odious most nearly means:

A. hateful
B. smelly
C. apparent
D. carefree
E. irreligious

Memory for numerical materials (Mn) is measured by items involving the speed and accuracy of basic arithmetical computations. Memory for spatial materials (Ms) is measured by items requiring a person to reproduce a spatial diagram after studying it for a short period of time, usually about ten seconds.

Reasoning in verbal materials (Rv) is measured by items requiring a person to make verbal analogies. Reasoning in numerical materials (Rn) is measured by requiring a person to solve mathematical problems. Reasoning in spatial materials is measured by requiring a person to determine the relationship between two objects, as in the following example:[3]

Directions: This is a test of your ability to recognize the relationship between figures. Look at the sample item below.

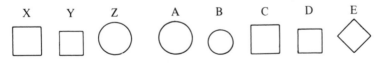

Notice the squares under the letters X and Y. Both are squares, but the one under the letter Y is smaller than the one

[2]Ibid.
[3]Ibid.

under the letter X. The figure under the letter Z is a circle. The figure that goes with it in the same way that figure Y goes with figure X is a small circle. This is the figure under the letter B. Therefore, B is the correct answer to the sample item. In each item in this part you are to locate the figure that goes with Z in the same way that Y goes with X. Then blacken the space on your separate answer sheet that has the same number and letter as your choice.

Ideational fluency is measured by determining how many words beginning with the same letter (Iv), how many combinations of positive numbers totaling another number (In), or how many objects having similar shapes (Is) one can name in a given period of time. The following item is an example of those designed to measure ideational fluency in numerical materials (In).[4]

Directions: Think of as many combinations of positive numbers as you can that will make 32. For example, you might think of $16 + 16$ or 2×16 or $15 + 15 + 2$. You will have 2 minutes. Write each combination on a separate line below.

$16 + 16$	_____	_____
2×16	_____	_____
$15 + 15 + 2$	_____	_____

Visualization of verbal materials (Vv) and numerical materials (Vn) may be measured by items that require a person to recognize mutilated words and numbers, as in the following example: [5]

Directions: On the line opposite each partially blotted number write what the number is.

A. ___4___   A. _____

B. ___6___   B. _____

Visualization of spatial materials (Vs) is measured by requiring persons to picture an object as it would look if seen at an angle different from that in which it is presented.

[4] Ibid.
[5] Ibid.

It should be evident from this discussion that the current view among most psychologists is that intelligence is *not* a single unitary ability. It consists of many abilities. Furthermore, it involves important qualities, such as *motivation,* which are uncontrolled in most intelligence tests. To borrow a phrase, intelligence is a "many-splendored thing." People generally tend to be stronger in some abilities than others, but rarely is a person found who is *extremely high* in one or two abilities and *extremely low* in others.

INTELLIGENCE VERSUS SCHOLASTIC APTITUDE

Ever since intelligence tests have been used in American schools, they have been criticized for not being "culturally fair." The charge has been that intelligence tests are composed of content and activities that are more characteristic of the middle-class cultural level of our society than of the lower level. It is generally true that upper- and middle-class children tend to score higher on intelligence tests than lower-class children, although there are exceptions at all levels. This has led some researchers to attempt to develop "culture-free" or "culture-fair" tests. These are tests that attempt to eliminate content and activities peculiar to any one cultural level, or to include content and activities equally from *all* cultural levels. The results of these efforts have not been consistently fruitful. In some studies, these tests yield results differing from the general pattern. In other studies, they yield results quite similar to those obtained with conventional intelligence tests. In the words of Henry Chauncey and John Dobbin, "These special tests of mental ability called 'culture-free tests of intelligence' or 'culture-fair tests' are still largely in an experimental state."[6]

An essential question in intelligence testing is this: "Do children from lower levels of our society who score low on intelli-

[6]Henry Chauncey and John E. Dobbin, *Testing: Its Place in Education Today,* Harper & Row, 1964, p. 22.

gence tests actually possess less innate intelligence than do middle-class children, or are their low scores primarily caused by their meager environment?" This is actually the old debate on the relative importance of heredity and environment, which raged during the 1920s and 1930s. The view accepted by most psychologists today is that intelligence is a composite of both innate capacity and environmental experience. Intelligence, as measured by today's intelligence tests, is the result of the *interaction* of heredity and environment; each contributes to intelligence test scores in unknown proportions.

What of the answer to our question? Can we justifiably conclude that children from lower levels of our society who score low on intelligence tests necessarily have low innate intelligence? No, we cannot; intelligence tests simply do not tell us this. Neither are we justified, however, in concluding that such children possess high innate intelligence. The only conclusion about innate intelligence we can justifiably reach at the present time is that we are not sure how much innate intelligence is possessed by anyone. No satisfactory measure of innate intelligence has yet been devised. If one is developed in the future, it may well grow out of physiological studies on the composition of the DNA molecule rather than out of purely psychological studies.

A realization of the present limitations of intelligence measurement has contributed to a recent trend toward the measurement of more operationally defined concepts. Few new "intelligence" tests have been developed since World War II. Several important new tests have been evolved since that time, but they have been called *aptitude* tests. The essential difference between an aptitude test and an intelligence test is not in the content of the test but in the way it is used. An aptitude is defined as the ability to learn easily and quickly, and to perform well in a field. In aptitude testing, we are not as concerned with what personal qualities the test measures as we are with how well the test predicts.

A *scholastic aptitude* test is designed to predict the ease and speed with which children can learn in school. It is not radically different from most group intelligence tests, but by utilizing the concept *scholastic aptitude* we avoid the implication of innateness associated with the concept *intelligence*. If a person from a culture different from that of middle- and upper-class America (let us suppose someone from another country who cannot read or write English) makes a low score on a commonly used group intelligence test, we certainly cannot conclude that he has little or no intelligence. If the test is a known predictor of scholastic aptitude, however, we can conclude that he had little scholastic aptitude *when he took the test.* That is, he could not learn quickly and easily in one of our schools where English is the primary medium of communication. This conclusion should in no way imply that the person cannot increase his scholastic aptitude by acquiring whatever knowledge or skill he lacked (in this case, knowledge of English).

Of course, we would still like to know which of those children from culturally deprived environments who make low scores on scholastic aptitude tests could appreciably improve their scholastic aptitude if their environment were enriched. There is little doubt that our society is losing the talents of a great many individuals because they are denied admission to certain schools and training programs on the basis of low aptitude test scores, which result from meager cultural environments. This has caused some educational leaders to advocate that standardized testing be banned in schools. Elimination of standardized testing does not appear to be the best answer, however. It would be "throwing out the baby with the bath water." If standardized tests are being misused, then misuse, rather than the entire testing program, should be eliminated. Scholastic aptitude tests *do* predict success in school (within the limits of their accuracy, of course). If a school or training program is so limited in funds and facilities that it must resort to selective admissions, then aptitude tests are *one* source of information on which selections may be made. The problem of enriching the environment of culturally deprived children in order that they may benefit from educational experiences is much larger than selection of persons for existing programs. It involves the efforts of society in general, rather than those of educators alone.

SELECTION OF INTELLIGENCE AND APTITUDE TESTS

Since "intelligence" tests given in a schoolwide testing program are used primarily as aptitude tests, that is, to predict who will learn quickly and easily, we will use the term *aptitude test* to refer to all tests designed and used for this purpose.

Aptitude tests are judged on the same basis as any other test—reliability, validity, and usability. The degree of reliability of all the major aptitude tests is similar. Coefficients of reliability usually range from about .80 to .95. As with other types of tests, the teacher should beware of the test that is too short and the test that purports to measure too wide a range of talent. Power tests requiring less than 10 minutes should be investigated thoroughly for evidence of reliability before being selected. In like manner, if a single level of a test purports to measure aptitude for more than three grades, one should demand evidence of reliability *for separated grade levels.* The better aptitude tests have different levels of a test for each two or three grades. The reliability of almost all tests is lower at the primary grade levels (1-3) than it is at elementary and secondary levels. Furthermore, averages often obscure large changes in individual scores over a period of time. One study with the Primary Mental Abilities Test found individual changes in total I.Q. of as much as 60 points from grade 3 to grade 6.[7] This lower dependability of aptitude test scores in primary grades should be remembered when such tests are used at this level, if, indeed, they are to be used here at all.

Since aptitude tests are used to predict future performance, one of the most important criteria of selection is *predictive validity.* You will remember that the chief type of validity for achievement tests was *content validity.* With aptitude tests, the primary concern is not with the *content* of the test but rather with its predictive qualities. Evidence of predictive validity should

---

[7]John A. R. Wilson, and Lealand D. Stier, "Instability of Sub-Sources on Forms of SRA Primary Mental Abilities Tests: Significance for Guidance," *Personnel and Guidance Journal,* April, 1962, pp. 708-711.

be found in the test manual or technical report in the form of correlations between test scores and other evidence of proficiency obtained at some time after the test was given. In the case of a scholastic aptitude test, this "other evidence" might be grade-point averages obtained in June and correlated with test scores obtained the preceding September. In the case of a secretarial aptitude test, the other evidence might be proficiency ratings by employers. Correlation coefficients between test scores and school grades usually range between .40 and .60. These coefficients indicate that only about 16 to 36 percent of the variance associated with future performance can be accounted for by test scores, so it should be evident that test scores do not provide us with sufficient evidence to tell a student, "On the basis of your test score, you will (or will not) succeed." Test scores do improve our ability to select people for special programs, however, especially when used with other information. Furthermore, the predictive validity of test scores is much greater at the upper and lower extremes than around the middle of the range, enabling us to be more certain about students with extreme scores. But, of course, we can never predict with complete accuracy what any individual may do in the future, regardless of the amount of information we collect about him. People are just too complicated for such preciseness.

Because aptitude tests in a schoolwide testing program will, in all probability, be administered, and, it is to be hoped, *used* by teachers, it is necessary to select tests with a fair degree of usability. The specific aspects of usability in aptitude tests are essentially the same as those discussed in Chapter 4 and Chapter 14. Teachers want a test with sufficiently simple administrative and scoring procedures for them to follow without a great deal of training in psychometrics. They also want a test that yields results that are relatively easy to interpret. Some tests provide for the construction of elaborate profiles composed of scores on many subtests, some of which are too short to be sufficiently reliable. Scores should be reported in terms of the standard error of measurement, which will be discussed in Chapter 18.

MAJOR TYPES OF INTELLIGENCE AND APTITUDE TESTS

In this section, brief descriptions of some of the more widely used intelligence and aptitude tests are presented to illustrate each type. The major source of information about specific tests is the *Mental Measurements Yearbooks,* edited by O. K. Buros, as well as the catalogues of major test publishers.

Individually administered intelligence tests

Individually administered intelligence tests are generally the most reliable of all tests of aptitude and intelligence. Probably the two most important reasons for this are that they are longer than most group tests, and that they are administered by a trained psychometrist (usually an individual holding one or more degrees in psychology with a specialty in psychological measurement) to one person at a time. These two factors that enhance the reliability of individual tests are also the ones that make the tests impractical for a schoolwide testing program. It takes from 1 to 1-1/2 hours to administer an individual test to a person, and the tests can be given only by a trained administrator with a strong background in psychology. The use of these tests in schools is limited, therefore, to special cases for which the time and expense can be justified.

Perhaps the most famous individually administered intelligence test is the Stanford-Binet. As stated at the beginning of this chapter, the Stanford-Binet is the forerunner of most present-day American intelligence tests. It is designed to measure general intelligence of children from ages 2 to 16. The test consists largely of vocabulary, verbal and nonverbal reasoning, rote memory, and spatial visualization.

Two individual intelligence tests that came into extensive use after World War II are the Wechsler Intelligence Scale for Children (WISC), and the Wechsler Adult Intelligence Scale (WAIS). The WISC is designed for children 5 to 15 years of age, while the WAIS is designed for subjects who are 16 and over. Both Wechsler scales consist of a verbal section and a performance section. Three scores are yielded: a verbal score, a performance score, and a total score. Eleven subtest scores are yielded also, but these are used with caution even by trained psychometrists.

Group intelligence tests

Group intelligence tests were developed during World War I in response to the need for screening large numbers of people for various training programs in a short time. This need, you will recognize, is quite similar to ours in education. It is easy to see, therefore, why such tests have been used widely in schools ever since their development for civilian use.

Group intelligence tests differ to some extent in the actual items presented, but they are all composed primarily of verbal, numerical, and spatial items, and usually yield a verbal, a non-verbal, and a total score. The California Test of Mental Maturity, for example, yields a language score based largely on verbal reasoning, memory, and vocabulary and a nonlanguage score based primarily on spatial reasoning and visualization, numerical reasoning and computation, and perceptual accuracy. A total score is obtained by combining the language and nonlanguage scores.

Scholastic aptitude tests

As stated previously, scholastic aptitude tests are not essentially different from group intelligence tests. They are designed, however, for the specific purpose of predicting learning success in schools—hence the name, *scholastic aptitude.*

One of the most widely used of this category is the School and College Ability Tests (SCAT). It was first published in 1955 by the Educational Testing Service and is designed to predict scholastic success from grade 4 through the second year of college. SCAT is convenient and easy to administer, and yields a verbal, a numerical, and total score. The predictive validity of SCAT scores has been found to be as high as, and, in some cases, higher than that of other tests used to predict scholastic success. An outstanding feature of SCAT is that scores are presented in terms of the standard error of measurement, rather than in single points. This feature emphasizes the degree of inaccuracy of such scores and presents a graphic method for identifying differences among the scores.

Multiple-aptitude batteries

At about the ninth or tenth grade, when it becomes necessary for students to begin career planning and to make specific curricular choices, it is often advantageous to include a multiple-aptitude test battery in a school's testing program. Multiple-aptitude batteries are designed to serve as guidance tools to aid students in learning about themselves. Although information is presented in most test manuals showing relationships between aptitude test scores and occupational success, they should never be interpreted as telling a student what he *ought* to be. Interpretation of these scores on an individual basis for purposes of career planning should be left to guidance counselors trained in counseling and test interpretation. Teachers should remember that specific aptitude test scores serve as one more source of information whereby a student may increase his understanding of himself. His choice of a career should be made on *all* the information he can gather about himself and his environment. Two of the most commonly used multiple-aptitude batteries are the Differential Aptitude Tests (DAT) and the Flanagan Aptitude Classification Tests (FACT). The DAT is composed of seven different tests: Verbal Reasoning, Numerical Ability, Abstract Reasoning, Space Relations, Mechanical Reasoning, Clerical Speed and Accuracy, and Language Usage. It is designed for use with boys and girls in grades 8 through 12. The FACT battery, designed for use in grades 9 through 12, is composed of 19 separate tests. A unique feature of this battery is what are called *occupational aptitude scores.* These are various combinations of different scores within the 19 areas, which are designed to predict success in 37 types of careers. Although it is a promising feature, additional data are needed before the predictive validity of these scores can be established.

In addition to multiple-aptitude batteries, numerous tests of special aptitudes are also available. There are tests of music aptitude, clerical aptitude, art judgment, color blindness, and manual dexterity, to name only a few. Some music and art teachers find it advantageous to use aptitude tests in these subjects for the purposes of identifying children with outstanding aptitude in these areas and to work more effectively with children with less than average aptitude. The major use of special aptitude tests in the schools, however, is made by guidance specialists in individual student counseling.

USING APTITUDE TEST RESULTS

Any test should be given only after the uses to be made of the results have been carefully considered. Hopefully, the day is past when aptitude or intelligence tests were given and scored, with the results then being filed away and forgotten because no one had really given any consideration as to how they might be used in the first place. Nearly everyone who has a professional or paternal interest in the child can improve his role in promoting the student's welfare when presented with *understandable* information concerning the youngster's aptitudes. School administrators can plan more adequately for the school curriculum and can select students for special classes in a more scientific manner when they have information in regard to the aptitudes of all their students.

Teachers are able to plan learning experiences to match the capabilities of a student only if they have information about those capabilities. Counselors are in a better position to help a student with his plans when they are aware of the student's aptitudes. The student is better able to plan his future and to understand himself, his actions, his feelings, and his relations with others when he is informed concerning his aptitudes. His parents are also in a better position to understand him and to know what to expect of his scholastic efforts if they are aware of his strengths and weaknesses.

The implication of these points is that all the persons mentioned have a need for information regarding the student's aptitudes. It cannot be emphasized too strongly, however, that the need is for *understandable information used wisely.* Many abuses of this kind of information have occurred simply because of a lack of knowledge concerning the nature of the information. Every school system in which standardized tests are used should conduct training sessions in the interpretation of those tests for all its personnel.

Intelligence and aptitude test results particularly have been misused since standardized tests were first developed. One of the most widespread problems has been the stereotyping of children on the basis of one or two intelligence test scores. If Suzie comes to us in grade *x* with an low I.Q. score, there is the tendency to seat her in a quiet corner, give her a box of crayons, and ignore her.   The information that "Suzie is dumb" goes with her from grade to grade, with the result that there are few who really try to teach her, and she makes very little progress. Such a situation is referred to in psychological circles as the "self-fulfilling prophecy." When we expect persons to perform in a given manner, we often react to them in such a way that they actually do perform as we anticipated. Make sure that you as a teacher do not fall into the trap of "branding" a student with a "scarlet I.Q." An intelligence or aptitude test does not measure an innate quality. Environment plays a large part in determining a person's performance on any test. On group tests, the child's ability to read is always a major factor influencing his performance. As a child grows, his environment can change; his reading ability can improve; his attitude toward tests can improve; and, most important, because of these changes his intelligence and aptitude test scores can improve. The particular problems concerned with interpreting all major types of test scores are discussed in Chapter 18.

QUESTIONS AND ACTIVITIES

1. What are the differences between intelligence and scholastic aptitude? Intelligence and creativity?

2. Read an article dating back to 1935 or earlier on the measurement of intelligence. Compare the concepts presented in the article with those currently dominant in this area.

3. The mother of an average-ability student in your class insists that you, the teacher, are not challenging her daughter, because an "intelligence test" given 7 years earlier indicated that the daughter had "a very high I.Q." How would you deal with this situation?

4. Compile a list of ways in which information in regard to a student's intelligence or ability would be helpful to a classroom teacher.

5. Can a person grow in intelligence?

6. A statement was made in this chapter that we do not know how much intelligence is possessed by anyone. What does this statement mean? What *do* we know about the intelligence of individuals?

SUGGESTED READINGS

Cronbach, Lee J., *Essentials of Psychological Testing* (3rd ed.), Harper & Row, 1970.
> This text, which has become a classic in the field, presents a comprehensive treatment of ability tests and their use in Part II. Seven chapters are devoted to this topic.

Davis, Frederick B., *Educational Measurements and Their Interpretation,* Wadsworth, 1964.
> Chapter 6 presents an excellent discussion of the most recent theory and research concerning the measurement of intelligence and aptitude.

Ilg, Frances L., and Louise Bates Ames, *School Readiness: Behavior Tests Used at the Gesell Institute,* Harper & Row, 1965.
> A thorough treatment of readiness and the readiness tests used at the Gesell Institute. One section of the text is written especially for teachers, administrators, and parents.

Mehrens, William A., and Irvin J. Lehmann, *Standardized Tests in Education,* Holt, Rinehart & Winston, 1969.

Chapter 2 presents a thorough perspective of aptitude tests and their use in schools.

Melville, S. D., *Using Test Results,* Educational Testing Service, 1960.
This leaflet was adapted from the script written for the film of the same title and is available free from ETS. It is a concise and understandable treatment of the construction and value of expectancy tables.

Seashore, Harold G., et al. (eds.), *What Is an Aptitude?* Test Service Bulletin, Number 36, issued by The Psychological Corporation.
This is a concise discussion that should improve the teacher's understanding of this concept.

Stanley, Julian C., *Measurement in Today's Schools* (4th ed.), Prentice-Hall, 1964.
Chapter 2 presents an excellent historical perspective of intelligence testing.

Thorndike, Robert L., and Elizabeth Hagen, *Measurement and Evaluation in Psychology and Education* (3rd ed.), Wiley, 1929.
Chapters 9 and 10 present an excellent discussion of the nature and measurement of intelligence and aptitudes.

17

PERSONALITY AND
INTEREST ASSESSMENT

The assessment of personality and interest is not one of the major activities of teachers but is usually left to the school psychologist or guidance counselor. As teachers become more sophisticated in measurement, however, they may be expected to have at least an acquaintance with the techniques and instruments employed in this area. This chapter is designed, therefore, to present a brief survey of techniques of personality and interest assessment, and to indicate certain limitations of their use in schoolwide testing programs.

PERSONALITY ASSESSMENT

Personality as a psychological concept

Personality is a very complex and sometimes nebulous concept. Psychologists themselves do not always agree on the nature of personality. One text on personality theory discusses twelve major theories along with numerous subtheories.[1]

Most theories of personality can be placed along a continuum of "outside-inside," that is, from an emphasis entirely on observable behavior to an emphasis entirely on the inner wellsprings of behavior. American psychology has traditionally tended to lean toward the behavioral end of the continuum, where personality may be defined simply as the sum total of one's behavior or as one's characteristic tendency to behave in a similar manner in similar situations. The European tradition has tended to emphasize the inside end of the continuum, which has its most elaborate manifestation in psychoanalytic theory originated by Sigmund Freud. Although placing their primary emphasis on behavior, contemporary American psychologists also recognize the existence of inner drives or needs that energize and give direction to behavior.

It is not within the scope or purpose of this text to go into a discussion of major personality theories but only to point out the fact that personality study is still in the experimental stage. Because of the rudimentary stage of personality assessment, there are no personality "tests" available at this time with the degree of reliability, validity, and usability sufficient for use in a school-wide testing program. The comments of Henry Chauncey and John Dobbin on this point are significant enough for quotation here.

> Measurement of personal qualities has not yet reached the level of validity and reliability needed to make it both safe and helpful in school use. Many of the instruments in the personality test category are highly respectable tools in the

[1]Calvin S. Hall and Gardner Lindzey, *Theories of Personality*, Wiley, 1957.

hands of clinical psychologists or psychiatrists; others are useful tools of research by experimental psychologists; still others are toe-holds on the edge of personality measurement and are published only so that other researchers can use them and improve on them. Most of them are the products of long effort by able and dedicated professionals. Some of them are perfectly innocuous in their practical usefulness; others are about as safe for general use as a do-it-yourself atomic energy kit. For the present then, the measurement of human personality characteristics is in the laboratory stage of development and not yet ready for general school use.[2]

Chauncey and Dobbin hasten to point out that a great deal of research is presently being conducted in the area of personality measurement and that we may expect instruments usable in school testing programs to become available in the near future. Let us now survey some of the techniques currently used in personality assessment.

Techniques of personality assessment

Personality inventories.   Personality inventories consist of long lists of questions or statements about one's actions and feelings, such as, "Do you usually sleep well?" and "Do you often feel alone in a crowd?" Although often referred to as "tests," they are not really tests, since there are no right or wrong answers. The person taking the inventory merely indicates whether or not the statement is true for him. There are many such inventories on the market, some of which have been developed for schools. The better inventories can be useful tools in the hands of a clinical psychologist, but as stated previously, they have not yet reached a degree of reliability, validity, and usability sufficient for use in a schoolwide testing program. Then, too, there is the ethical question of whether the school has a right to require this type of information of every student, especially when there are so few people in schools who can use it properly.

[2]Henry Chauncey and John E. Dobbin, *Testing: Its Place in Education Today,* Harper & Row, 1964, p. 165.

Aside from their lack of general usability, personality inventories also suffer from a significant difficulty in validity. Two people may read the same statement and interpret it quite differently. And more important than honest misinterpretation is the tendency of most people to answer the questions as they believe they *should* be answered rather than in terms of what is actually true. There is a natural tendency of people to put their best foot forward, and the tendency is greatly enhanced when the person realizes that he may be accepted or rejected for a training program or a position on the basis of his "test" score.

Projective techniques.   One attempt to overcome the problem of dishonesty associated with personality inventories has been through the development of projective techniques. In the projective technique, the person is presented with a stimulus (an ink blot, a picture, or perhaps an incomplete sentence) that creates a relatively unstructured situation. Since the examinee does not know what the desired response is, he can only make his true response. Perhaps the two most widely known projective techniques are the Rorschach Inkblot Test and the Murray Thematic Apperception Tests (TAT). The Rorschach consists of ten cards, each with a different shape of blot. The examinee is told simply to describe what he sees. The psychologist assesses certain personality characteristics of the examinee by analyzing the description. The procedure used with the TAT is similar to that used with the Rorschach: assessment is made by analyzing the responses of the examinee. The TAT is different from the Rorschach, however, in that it consists of a series of twenty pictures rather than ink blots. Projective techniques are actually clinical devices rather than objective tests, and as such, are useful only in the hands of a highly trained psychologist.

Situational tests.   In order to determine how a person will behave in anticipated situations, psychologists may create similar situations and place in them persons they are studying. This technique was employed in the selection and training of special types of troops during World War II. It is still employed in both industry and the armed services in screening men for top administrative positions. One situation that is sometimes used is to invite to a cocktail party the persons to be screened, and observe how much they drink and how they handle themselves under the influence of alcohol. To make observations in a situational test more objective, a rating scale may also be used.

Rating scales.   Rating scales may be used in a situational test or at any time a person is being observed. The rating scale lists the characteristics or actions to be observed and usually gives a 3-, 5-, or 7-point scale by which the characteristic may be rated. Psychologists using a rating scale will usually want to use it in collaboration with other psychologists, so that their judgments may be pooled. And, of course, it is desirable to observe a person several times before any conclusion about him is reached.

Sociograms.   Sociograms are actually devices for investigating the social structure of a group, rather than for analyzing the personality of an individual. They reveal such characteristics as cliques within the group, very popular individuals referred to as *stars,* and unpopular individuals referred to as *isolates.* They are constructed by first asking the group members to respond to questions such as "With which person in this class would you most like to study?" or "With which person in this class would you most like to play at recess?" Group members may be asked to name first, second, and third choices. After the responses have been collected, they are tabulated and the sociogram is constructed.[3] Table 12 illustrates the first and second choices of eight girls and seven boys which could possibly have been collected in response to the question, "With which person in the class would you most like to prepare a report?" Choosers are listed along the vertical axis and the chosen are listed along the horizontal axis.

[3]The intricacies of sociogram construction and interpretation are beyond the scope of this text. The interested teacher is referred to *How to Construct a Sociogram* by the Horace Mann–Lincoln Institute of School Experimentation, published by Teachers College, Columbia University, 1947.

Table 12

First and second choices of eight girls and seven boys

Choosers	Adam	Bob	Carl	Don	Joe	Jim	Sam	Ann	Betty	Carla	Fran	Jean	Sara	Sue	Norma
Adam				1			2								
Bob						1									2
Carl				1	2*										
Don						1*							2		
Joe			1*								2				
Jim				1*							2				
Sam			2	1											
Ann												2*		1*	
Betty											2		1		
Carla											1				2*
Fran				2									1*		
Jean								2*						1*	
Sara											2	1*			
Sue								2*				1*			
Norma											2*	1			
First Choice			1	4		2					3	1	2	2	
Second Choice			1	1	1		1	2			3	2	1	1		2

Asterisks indicate mutual choices. The number of times each student was chosen is at the bottom of the table.

Figure 10 is a sociogram based on the tabulated responses. The sociogram may reveal to a teacher situations he has already suspected. For instance, he probably already knows that Fran and Don are the most popular students in the class, but Betty, Adam, and Bob were chosen by no one. Carl, Joe, and Sam were named only once, and then all second choices. The teacher may also have realized that the girls are divided into two distinct groups or "cliques." The triangle of Jean, Sue, and Ann seems to be entirely isolated from the rest of the class.

Of course, constructing a sociogram is a beginning rather than an end. If no action is to be taken on the basis of the information, there is little use in collecting it. If the information is collected for the purpose of developing groups of mutually chosen individuals, then the groups should be formed in accordance with students' requests. The teacher may wish to alter the social structure of the class somewhat by forming groups composed of popular and unpopular students, in the hope that unpopular ones will be taken more wholeheartedly into the class structure. He should proceed slowly and cautiously, however, or more harm than good may be done. This kind of thing may be done best with the help of the school counselor or psychologist.

INTEREST ASSESSMENT

Nature of interests

The research on the nature and development of interests has not been as extensive as that on either aptitude or personality. We are not completely sure whether people are born with innate tendencies to like certain things and dislike others or whether our likes and dislikes are the result of environmental experiences. It seems likely that, as in the case of intelligence, both heredity and environment play a part. There is evidence that, in some cases,

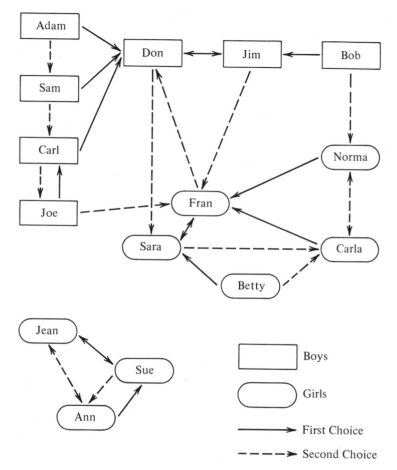

Figure 10
Sociogram based on data in Table 12.

interests follow aptitudes. That is, we grow to like certain activities because we can do them well and find satisfaction in their performance. There is also evidence, originally uncovered by E. K. Strong, Jr., that people engaged in similar occupations tend to have similar interests, and the interest patterns of an occupational group can be distinguished from those of people not engaged in that occupation. These findings concerning the similarity and dissimilarity of interest patterns among occupational groups are the basic principles on which interest inventories were developed.

Interest inventories

There are several different interest inventories available for use in schools, although the number is far less than the number of aptitude or achievement tests. Interest inventories, like personality inventories, are not actually "tests," because there are no right or wrong answers. An answer is correct only if it is a true expression of one's interest. The two most widely used interest inventories are the Strong Vocational Interest Blank and the Kuder Preference Record. Since these two instruments approach interest assessment in somewhat different ways, each is used as an illustration.

The Strong Vocational Interest Blank assesses interests by requiring a person to indicate a preference—"Like," "Indifferent," or "Dislike"—for long lists of such things as occupations, school subjects, amusements, and peculiarities of people. It also requires the subject to list his order of preference for certain activities, positions, and people, and to rate himself on personality characteristics. There are 400 items in all, and there are different forms for men and women. The Strong may be hand scored, but this is a very cumbersome and time-consuming process. It is usually best to send the completed answer sheet to one of the companies offering machine-scoring services for it. The scoring company also prepares a profile that compares a man's responses with those of men in 49 occupations. Women's responses are compared with those of women in 25 occupations. Thus, one is able to get an indication of the similarity or dissimilarity of the subject's interests to those of adults in various occupations.

The Kuder Preference Record requires one to make choices between triads of activities. On the most recent revision, Form E, there are 168 triads in which a choice must be made. In each triad, the subject is supposed to select the activity that he would like to do most and the one he would like to do least. For example, a given triad might include the following:

	Most	Least
Build a bird house	⋮ ⋮	⋮ ⋮
Read a book about birds	⋮ ⋮	⋮ ⋮
Classify birds	⋮ ⋮	⋮ ⋮

From these responses, a profile of interests in nine areas is constructed: outdoor, mechanical, computational, scientific, persuasive, artistic, literary, musical, social service, and clerical. Form E of the Kuder, published in 1964, was revised downward so that it could be used in grades 7 through 12.

The Kuder Preference Record differs from the Strong in several minor ways and in one very important way that is often overlooked by school counselors. The minor differences include such things as format, method of indicating responses, and method of scoring. Generally, the Kuder is easier to administer and to score than the Strong. The significant difference between the two involves the range of things for which one must indicate a preference. The Strong includes a very wide range of things for which a preference is indicated, such as work activities, hobbies, kinds of entertainment, music, art, and reading material. The Kuder includes only activities directly related to kinds of work. The Kuder gives a subject an indication of the kinds of jobs in which the work is similar to the kinds of activities he likes to perform. The Strong gives a subject an indication of the kinds of occupations engaged in by people whose interests are similar to his.

Interest inventories can be helpful instruments in the guidance of secondary school students by providing an opportunity for students to take an objective look at their interests. They may provide information of value in answer to such questions as the following: "In what areas do my interests lie?" "What occupational groups have interests similar to mine?" "Do I have a variety of interests or a few?" "Are my interests well developed in specific areas or are they quite general?" There are, however, serious limitations connected with the use of interest inventories which should always be observed.

Limitations of interest inventories.   Interest inventories do not tell a person what he *ought* to do or become. A high score on an interest inventory is no guarantee of success in any endeavor. Such things as aptitude and desire to excel are at least as important to success as interest. Interest inventories, properly used, open up areas for further investigation, rather than telling the subject what he *ought* to become.

A second limitation connected with the use of interest inventories is the lack of stability of interest of young people, especially below the senior high school level. It is not uncommon to find people who change their interests or discover new interests even after college. Any pattern of interests obtained before a person has reached maturity should be regarded as tentative. Generally, the younger the person, the less stable will be his interests.

A third limitation is the possible lack of validity associated with interest inventories. If a person has no conception or has a misconception of the nature of an activity, obviously he cannot make an intelligent choice about it. It is quite likely that some students will not have sufficient background to respond intelligently to some of the things included in interest inventories. This limitation is also a significant problem with younger children whose experiences are limited.

Considering these limitations, the teacher and counselor will want to approach the use of interest inventories with caution, especially with students below senior high school. Even with senior high students, interest patterns should be regarded as just one more, possibly tentative, piece in the puzzle that confronts most adolescents, "Who am I?"

1. What are the major limitations of interest and personality inventories in a schoolwide testing program?

2. Considering the different ways in which the term *personality* is used, what do you conceive it to be?

3. Are we born with certain interest patterns or are interests learned? Find some references pertinent to this question.

4. Could you devise an honesty inventory? How would you establish the validity of such an inventory?

SUGGESTED READINGS

Adams, Georgia S., *Measurement and Evaluation in Education, Psychology, and Guidance,* Holt, Rinehart & Winston, 1964.
    Chapters 7-9 present a thorough survey of the major techniques of personality and interest assessment.

Banney, Merl E., and Richard S. Hampleman, *Personal-Social Evaluation Techniques,* Center for Applied Research in Education, Washington, D.C., 1962.
    An excellent introduction to assessment of personal-social characteristics, written on a level that the teacher can understand.

Hall, Calvin S., and Gardner Lindzey, *Theories of Personality,* Wiley, 1957.
    A survey of the major schools of personality theory and a historical background of the major theories and theorists.

Horace Mann-Lincoln Institute of School Experimentation, *How to Construct a Sociogram,* Bureau of Publications, Teachers College, Columbia University, 1947.
    This booklet describes and illustrates the procedure for constructing a sociogram and also presents suggestions for interpretation and use.

Layton, Wilbur L., *Counseling Use of the Strong Vocational Interest Blank,* University of Minnesota, 1958.

This booklet is an excellent introduction to the interpretation and use of scores obtained with the Strong Vocational Interest Blank.

Karmel, Louis J., *Measurement and Evaluation in the Schools,* Macmillan, 1970.

Chapter 8 presents an overview of projective techniques, and Chapter 12 discusses personality and interest inventories. Both chapters are written in terms relevant to teachers.

18

ANALYZING AND INTERPRETING STANDARDIZED TEST SCORES

Let us begin this consideration of the meaning of standardized test scores by stating what is probably the most important fact to be realized about their interpretation: Test scores are *not* absolute, precise quantifications of innate human qualities. Tests are not keys that unlock the "psyche" of an individual and allow us to examine it. Tests are only *tasks* to be performed, and test scores indicate how well one person performs the task in relation to the performance of others. Let us hasten to add that test scores *can* be valuable sources of information *when they are properly used.* It is the purpose of this chapter to aid in their proper interpretation and use.

THE RELATIVE MEANING OF TEST SCORES

Raw test scores (the number of items answered correctly) have meaning for a teacher only when he has considered them in light of the tasks required of a student by the test and the performance of others on the test. For purposes of illustration, suppose that Johnny announced to his mother that he has made a raw score of 58 on an English achievement test. Johnny's mother may be ready to reprimand him; 58 doesn't appear to be very good. It probably isn't if the test consisted of 100 points; however, it is quite good if the test contained only 60 points. On the other hand, the 58 may be considered a good score even when the test consisted of 100 points, if it had been designed for the twelfth grade and Johnny is only in the fifth grade. Standardized test scores have only relative, not absolute, meanings. The relative nature of test scores makes knowledge of the groups to which an individual is compared of primary importance.

NORM GROUPS

As we have implied, an individual's test score is given meaning by comparing it with the scores of a known group. Such groups are usually referred to as *norm* groups. The test publisher administers the test to a group of students who are at the level for which the test was designed; then he prepares a *norms table* showing the performance of the group. The teacher uses the table to determine how Johnny's score compares with the scores of the norms group. If comparisons are to be meaningful, the norms group to which Johnny is compared should be appropriate. That is, the people comprising the norms group should be at the same level as Johnny and should have backgrounds similar to his. Major standardized test publishers try to obtain "national" norms. They select and test students from different geographical sections of the country and from different social levels; however, the teacher may sometimes be misled by a statement that reads, "The standardization sample included a national sample of 200,000 students." The 200,000 probably refers to all the students tested with all forms of the test at all levels. When you take fifth-grade Johnny's score obtained on Form A of the test to the norms table appropriate for that form and level, you are not comparing him with 200,000 *fifth graders*. The number of fifth graders who took Form A is more likely to be 1000 or 2000 or less. Teachers can interpret test scores much more meaningfully if they know the specific nature of the particular group to which a student is to be compared.

It is often desirable to compare a student's test performance with that of several norm groups. For example, Tom is a high school senior interested in attending the state university. Since Tom attends school in a rural, low socioeconomic area, it may be helpful to compare his test score with the publisher's national norms, local twelfth-grade norms accumulated over the past few years, and norms of students entering the state university. You might find that Tom compares quite favorably with the local norms, ranking at the 95th percentile, not quite so favorably with the national norms, ranking at the 75th percentile, and still less favorably with the college group, ranking at the 50th percentile.

One more point needs to be made about norms: They are not standards. They do not indicate what a student *ought* to score; that depends on his capacity, his background, the way he has been taught, and many other things. Norms merely provide information about how some persons have previously performed on the task.

PERCENTILES

We have just referred to percentile ranks, one of the most widely used expressions in standardized testing. A percentile rank simply indicates the percent of people in the norms group who scored below a given point. To continue with the preceding illustration, suppose that Tom had taken one of the commonly used scholastic aptitude tests and had made a raw score of 106. You will remember his percentile rankings were as follows: local norms, 95th percentile; national norms, 75th percentile; and college norms, 50th percentile. These percentile ranks mean that 95 percent of the students in the local group, 75 percent of the students in the national group, and 50 percent of the students in the college group made scores below 106.

Percentile ranks are widely used, because they can be easily understood by students, parents, and others whose statistical background may be limited. They have certain limitations, however, which should be understood by all teachers and others who plan to use standardized tests regularly. In the first place, percentile ranks are ordinal scales only. They only indicate relative position in a group. (You may find it helpful at this point to review the meaning of nominal, ordinal, interval, and ratio scales in Chapter 1.) Secondly, percentile ranks are unequal units. The difference between adjacent percentile ranks at the extremes is greater than the difference at the mean. Consider the following illustration.

If we were to select 100 adults at random and measure their heights, we would be likely to get the distribution shown in Figure 11. If you will consider the distribution briefly, it should become obvious that the 50 people between 5½ and 6 feet are much closer together in terms of height than the five people between 4½ and 5 feet, or those between 6½ and 7 feet. This phenomenon is associated with all normal distributions. The difference between people near the mean on whatever they are being measured is smaller than the difference between those at the extremes. Therefore, if one child's achievement test score ranks him at the 10th percentile in the fall, and in the spring, when we test him again, he ranks at the 20th percentile, we may say that he has made a greater raw gain than a child who moved from the 40th to the 50th percentile between fall and spring. The inequality of percentile units may also be seen by studying percentile tables in test manuals. A study of any percentile table will reveal a greater raw score distance

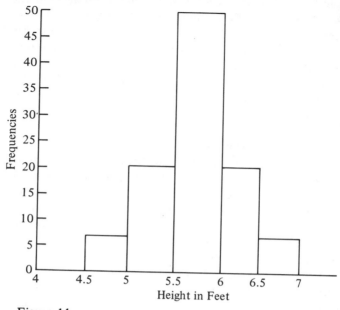

Figure 11
Distribution of 100 people according to height.

between percentile ranks at the extremes than between similar percentile ranks near the mean. In order to overcome the inequality in size associated with percentiles, some test makers use standard scores.

STANDARD SCORES

Test scores expressed in terms of the standard deviation of the distribution are called standard scores. Their chief advantage over percentiles is that they represent equal numbers of raw scores regardless of their position in the distribution.

The basic type of standard score is the z score. A z score tells directly the number of standard deviation units a raw score is from the mean (see Figure 12). For example, if Joe made a raw score of 46 in a distribution with a mean of 40 and a standard deviation of 4, his z score would be +1.5. He is 6 raw-score points or 1½ standard deviations above the mean. Expressed as a mathematical formula, we have

$$z = \frac{X - \overline{X}}{\sigma} = \frac{46 - 40}{4} = \frac{6}{4} = 1.5$$

where X = the raw score
$\overline{X}$ = the raw score mean
σ = the standard deviation

An inspection of Figure 12 will show that Joe's z score of 1.5 places him at about the 93rd percentile, assuming the distribution is normal. You will also note in Figure 12 that half the z scores are negative numbers and that they frequently involve one or two decimal places. In order to eliminate these two difficulties associated with z scores, other standard score scales were developed. In each type of standard score scale, the raw score mean and the standard deviation are equated to a number so that the resulting calibrations will be easy to handle. Look at Figure 12 again. On it are found all the major standard score scales including deviation I.Q. You will notice that on the T score scale, the mean is equated to 50 and the standard deviation is equated to 10. Joe's z score of 1.5 would give him a T score of 65. For the Army General Classifications Test (AGCT), a scale was developed with an arbitrary mean of 100 and a standard deviation of 20. Joe's z score of 1.5 gives him an AGCT score of 130. The College Entrance Examination Board (CEEB) uses a scale with a mean of 500 and a standard deviation of 100; thus, Joe's 1.5 z score gives him a CEEB score of 650. In all cases, Joe's percentile rank is approximately 93, assuming a normal distribution.

A slightly different type of standard score from those discussed above is also shown in Figure 12. This is the stanine. The stanine is different in that it refers to an area or range rather than

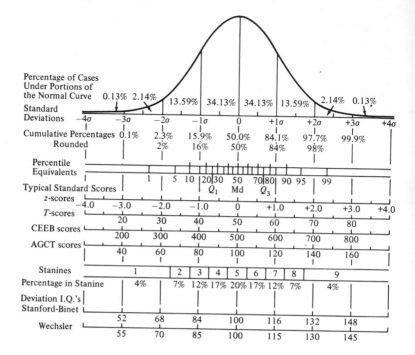

Figure 12

Relationships of scores in a normal distribution. Note: This chart cannot be used to equate scores on one test with scores on another test. For example, both 600 on the CEEB and 120 on the AGCT are one standard deviation above their respective means, but they do not represent "equal" standings because the scores were obtained from different groups. (Adapted from Harold G. Seashore et al., *Test Service Bulletin,* no. 54, Psychological Corporation, January, 1956.)

a single point. The term *stanine* comes from "standard nine." It may be noted from Figure 12 that, with the exception of the 1st and 9th stanines, the total distribution is divided into equal areas. Each of these areas covers an equal number of raw score units. Stanine 5 lies across the mean; Stanine 1 includes the lowest scores; and Stanine 9 includes the highest scores. One advantage of the stanine over the other type of scores is that by defining an area of the distribution rather than a single point, the lack of complete test preciseness is emphasized. However, the amount of error in a test does not usually equal the range of a stanine. The amount of error in a given test score is better indicated by using the standard error of measurement which is discussed later in this chapter.

THE INTELLIGENCE QUOTIENT

Because the intelligence quotient is one of the most widely known forms of test score, and probably the most misinterpreted, it needs to be given special consideration. The original concept of the I.Q. was first proposed by a German psychologist named Wilhelm Stern. It was popularized by Terman in the first editions of the Stanford-Binet. This original I.Q. was simply an expression of the ratio between one's mental age and his chronological age, multiplied by 100. The formula for its determination is:

$$I.Q. = \frac{\text{mental age}}{\text{chronological age}} \times 100$$

If Johnny's mental age is 12 and his chronological age is 9, we have:

$$\frac{12}{9} \times 100 = 133$$

If Johnny's mental age is the same as his chronological age, we have:

$$\frac{9}{9} \times 100 = 100$$

This form of intelligence quotient is referred to as the *ratio* I.Q. to distinguish it from the *deviation* I.Q., which is now the more widely used, because it overcomes some of the weaknesses of the original concept. Let us explore some of these weaknesses.

In the first place, the mental age which forms the basis for computation of the ratio is nothing more than a converted test score. Johnny's mental age (MA) of 12 means that his raw score on the test was equal to the mean raw score of the 12-year-old children in the norms group. Being a converted test score, the MA is subject to all the unreliability associated with test scores. We have already established the fact that tests are only estimates of a person's performance in relation to that of others. We should also remember that, although Johnny's score was equal to that of average 12-year-olds, he is still a 9-year-old boy. The test is only a small sample of behavior, and we cannot assume that Johnny is identical in all respects to the average 12-year-old.

Another weakness of the ratio I.Q. is its practical uselessness with adults. Although some aspects of intelligence may tend to continue developing on into middle age, general mental development begins to level off in the early twenties, just as physical development does. Between the ages of about 5 and 16, the mental age scale works fairly well, but is not feasible much beyond that. On tests that use ratio I.Q.'s with adults, everyone beyond about 15 is given a chronological age of about 16 years.

A third weakness of the ratio I.Q. stems from the shrinkage of mental age units with advancing age, and the relationship of this phenomenon to the standard deviation. Remembering the formula for the ratio, I.Q. = MA/CA $\times$ 100, consider the following example:

$$\frac{4}{3} \times 100 = 133 \qquad \frac{8}{6} \times 100 = 133 \qquad \frac{12}{9} \times 100 = 133$$

Notice that at age 3, an MA only one year in advance of the CA will give an I.Q. of 133, while at age 6, an MA advance of two years is necessary to yield the same I.Q., and at age 9, a *three*-year advance is necessary to yield the I.Q. of 133. If the 133 is to mean the same at all ages, the standard deviation must increase with each succeeding year. For example, if the standard deviation is 1 MA unit at age 3, then an I.Q. of 133 obtained by a 3-year-old will place him one standard deviation above the mean or at the 84th percentile. If an I.Q. of 133 is to have the same meaning at age 6, then the standard deviation must be 2 MA units, and at age 9, it must be 3 MA units. Unfortunately, this is not always the case. On some intelligence tests, the standard deviation varies considerably, and an I.Q. of 133 may place a child at the 84th percentile at one age, the 90th percentile at another age, and at the 70th percentile at yet another age.

Because of these weaknesses associated with the ratio I.Q., most test makers have abandoned it in favor of the deviation I.Q. Deviation I.Q.'s are actually standard scores with an assumed mean and standard deviation equated to the raw mean and standard deviation at each age level. On the Wechsler scales (WAIS and WISC), the mean is equated to 100 and the standard deviation to 15 (Figure 12). Therefore, a Wechsler I.Q. of 130 always places the person two standard deviations above the mean or at the 98th percentile. Until its revision in 1960, the Stanford-Binet used the ratio I.Q. With the 1960 revision, its authors also decided to use deviation I.Q. The Stanford-Binet used a mean of 100 and a standard deviation of 16, because this scale was close to former Stanford-Binet scales.

THE GRADE-EQUIVALENT SCORE

Another score almost as widely used and misused as the I.Q. is the grade-equivalent score. This type of score is expressed in grade-placement terms. For example, a score of 4.8 means fourth grade and eighth month of school; a score of 6.5 means sixth grade, fifth month; and so on. Grade-equivalent scores are obtained by averaging the raw scores of samples of pupils at the different grade levels in the publisher's norm groups. If a child has a grade-equivalent score of 7.5, this means that his raw score on the test was equal to the average raw score of the children in the publisher's norm who were in the fifth month of the seventh grade when they took the test.

An error often made in interpreting the grade-equivalent score is the mistaken notion that this score indicates the school level at which the pupil is or should be performing. If a fifth-grade child obtains a grade-equivalent score of 7.5, this does not mean that he should be promoted to the seventh grade. Neither does it mean that the child should be given seventh-grade work. What it really means is that the child is an above average fifth-grade student. The child made his high rank by marking more correct answers on the test than did the average fifth grader. A consideration of the grade-equivalency scale reveals that, because the grade level is equated to the average score of a group, one-half would be expected to be above that level and one-half below it. Furthermore, a standardized test is only a small sample of behavior and does not measure all the qualities necessary for school performance. Also, the content of different tests, even called by the same name, may differ. Therefore, a child might not attain the same results when administered tests from two different batteries. There *are* special types of tests, particularly in the areas of reading, which do indicate the functional level of the child. However, these tests are different from the *usual standardized* tests and do not yield grade-equivalent scores of the classical type discussed here.

Another serious error connected with interpreting grade equivalent scores occurs when a pupil's standing on one test is compared with his standing on another test. The problem here is similar to that associated with the ratio I.Q. The standard deviation may differ markedly from test to test, even within the same battery. For example, a child in the fourth month of the fourth grade (4.4) takes the XYZ Achievement Battery containing, among others, a Mathematics Principles Test and a Reading Comprehension Test. Suppose also that his grade equivalent score on each of the two tests is 5.4. It might be expected, on the basis of this information, that his standing on the two tests would be equal. It would be if the standard deviation of the two tests were equal. Suppose, however, that the standard deviation is 1 grade equivalency on the mathematics test and 2 on the reading test. This would mean that his 5.4 places him at the *84th* percentile on the mathematics test, and at the *98th* percentile on the reading test. Unless one knows the standard deviation for each age group on each test in the battery, he cannot know how far above or below the mean a grade equivalent score places a pupil. Hence, he could not use this score to make meaningful comparisons of standings on different tests. Perhaps the greatest weakness of the grade equivalent score is that it appears to be so easy to use, when actually it is rather complicated.

USE OF A BAND OF SCORES—THE STANDARD ERROR OF MEASUREMENT

Throughout this text, we have repeated the fact that test scores are not precise measurements of a student's ability or achievement. In order to keep ourselves consciously aware of this point, it is desirable to record test scores as bands or intervals, rather than as single points.

You will remember that the reliability coefficient of a test indicates the degree of test accuracy. The higher the reliability coefficient, the more accurate the test. Knowing the reliability coefficient, we can determine the degree of *inaccuracy* of the test. This is reported in test manuals as the standard error of measurement, and it works in this way. Suppose Johnny makes a raw score of 36 on a test. We look in the test manual and find that the standard error for this test is 4 raw score points. We then add 4 to 36 and subtract 4 from 36 to obtain a score interval of 32-40. This tells us that if it were possible to give Johnny the test an infinite number of times, about 2/3 of his scores would fall between 32 and 40. You will remember from Chapter 3 that plus and minus one standard deviation from the mean includes about 2/3 of the cases. If we wish to be more confident in our estimate of Johnny's actual ability, we can increase the size of our interval to include 2 standard errors of measurement on either side of the score. In this case, we would have 36 plus and minus 8, giving us a score interval of 28-44. In an infinite number of testings, 95 percent of the measures of Johnny's ability would be within this range. (Two standard deviations on either side of the mean include about 95 percent of the cases.)

Besides keeping us consciously aware of the inaccuracy of test scores, the use of score bands facilitates making comparisons between students and between scores obtained by the same student on two different tests. Let us suppose that Jim's and Mary's scores on a verbal aptitude test were 53 and 49, respectively. Can we confidently say that Jim possesses more verbal aptitude than Mary? Let us see. We look in the test manual and find that the standard error of the test is 5 points. When we add 5 points to Jim's score (53) and subtract 5 points from it, we get an interval of 48-58. When we add 5 points to and subtract 5 points from Mary's score, we get an interval of 44-54. As you can see, these intervals overlap considerably. Jim's true score might be 48 and Mary's might be 54. Therefore, we have little justification for assuming that Jim possesses any more verbal aptitude than Mary.

Now let us compare Jim's verbal aptitude score to his numerical aptitude score. We have already said that his verbal aptitude score was 53 and that the standard error of the verbal aptitude test was 5. Let us assume that his numerical aptitude score was 65 and that the standard error of measurement of the numerical aptitude test is 4. This would give Jim a numerical aptitude band of 61-69. Notice that this does not overlap his verbal aptitude band of 48-58. Therefore, we may say with reasonable certainty that Jim's numerical aptitude is greater than his verbal aptitude, as measured by those tests. Intervals should always be used when recording and reporting test scores to individuals, which is our next topic.

RECORDING AND REPORTING TEST SCORES

Recording test scores is not an extremely complex process, but the record should be complete and reasonably easy to understand. An entry such as

Jim Simpson	Arithmetic Achievement	43
Name	Test	Score

may be understandable to the person who administered the test, but it will not mean much to anyone else. Did the test stress understanding of basic arithmetical concepts or ability to compute? When was the test given? Is the 43 a raw score, a percentile rank, or some form of standard score? If the score is a comparison of Jim's with some norms group, what was the composition of the group? All of these questions are left unanswered in the above entry. To be meaningful and complete, a test record should include:

1. Name of the test
2. Nature of the task involved
3. Raw score
4. Type of converted score (percentile rank, or standard score)
5. Size and nature of the publisher's norm group
6. Relation of the score to local norms, if these are available.

This information requires the preparation of a record form that may be completed for each student. Such forms may be prepared and duplicated by the school, or they may be obtained from test publishers. An excellent example of a form that combines simplicity and completeness is the one issued by the Educational Testing Service (Figure 13). Notice that all the information essential to proper interpretation is included on this form. Notice also that scores are recorded on the form as *bands,* which enables interscore comparisons to be made. Space is provided for recording scores from two test batteries published by ETS, the Sequential Tests of Educational Progress (STEP), and the School and College Ability Tests (SCAT). This form is a convenient instrument for reporting scores to students and parents, also.

Figure 13.

SCAT-STEP student report. (Used by permission of the Co-operative Test Division, Educational Testing Service, Princeton, New Jersey.)

STEP
Mathematics . . . measures your ability to understand numbers and ways of working with them (for example, addition and division), such sumbols as $+$, $\sqrt{}$, and $<$, relationships between objects in space, how two changing things can depend on each other (for example, distance and speed), how to draw conclusions from facts, and how to make estimations and predictions when you do not have all the information. Mathematics teachers call these concepts *number and operation, symbolism, measurement and geometry, function and relation, deduction and inference,*

STEP   and *probability and statistics.*
Science . . . measures your ability to recognize and state problems relating to science, to select ways of getting information about the problems, to understand and judge the information you get, to predict what the solutions to these problems may be, and to work with symbols and numbers used in science problems. Some of the questions are about biology materials; some are about chemistry, physics, meteorology, astronomy, and geology. All of the questions present science in practical situations (for example, in the home, on the farm, and at work.)

STEP
Social Studies . . . measures your ability to understand the kinds of social studies materials which a citizen in a democracy should be able to deal with. These include maps, graphs, cartoons, editorials, debates, and historical documents. There are questions about history, geography, economics, government, and sociology.

STEP
Reading . . . measures your ability to read materials and then answer questions about what you have read. These questions ask you to remember specific things the author said, to understand what he meant and why he might have said what he did, and to criticize his ideas. The reading materials include directions, announcements, newspaper and magazine articles, letters, stories, poetry, and plays.

STEP
Listening . . . measures your ability to listen to materials and then answer questions about what you have heard. The Listening test is very much like the Reading test except, of course, you *hear* instead of *see* the things you are asked to remember, understand, or criticize.

STEP
Writing . . . measures your ability to criticize materials written by other students in terms of the ways they are organized or written. The questions ask you to pick out errors or weaknesses in the writing and choose revisions which best correct the errors or weaknesses. The materials were written by students in schools and colleges in various parts of the United States; they include letters, answers to test questions, school newspaper articles, announcements, essays, outlines, directions, and stories.

SCAT
Verbal . . . measures your ability to understand sentences and give the meanings of words. This ability is most important in such school courses as English, foreign languages, and social studies (history, civics, etc.).

SCAT
Quantitive . . . measures your ability to perform operations with numbers and to solve mathematics problems stated in words. This ability is most important in such school courses as mathematics and science.

SCAT
Total . . . combines your scores on SCAT Verbal and SCAT Quantitative to provide the *single* best measure of your general capacity to do the work of the next higher level of schooling.

When standardized tests were first used in schools, the scores were locked in the principal's office, and hardly anyone was allowed access to them. It was felt that this type of information should not be placed in the hands of people who might misuse it. Certainly, persons who cannot understand and properly use test scores should not have access to them. It was soon apparent to many school administrators, however, that if test scores were to be locked away and not used, a great deal of the value of the testing program would not be realized. Efforts were then made to help teachers understand test scores, so that they could fully utilize the information in their teaching. Teachers today generally are acquiring sufficient background in educational measurement to enable them to use test scores properly, and the current emphasis is on getting teachers to make greater use of them.

There is still reluctance among some school administrators to report test scores to students and parents. The reason given for this reluctance is that parents and students cannot interpret them properly. This is probably true, but if parents and students are to make wise decisions about the student's future, they need the information that standardized tests can provide, as well as the information provided by grades. Precautions certainly should be taken to prevent misinterpretations, but test scores should be reported to parents and to students also, when they are old enough to make some use of them. In junior and senior high school, students must begin to make decisions about the future, and test scores are one source of information they can use.

A form similar to that in Figure 13 is not too difficult for many parents to understand, especially if a guidance counselor is available to go over it with them. Individual interpretation of test results by a trained guidance counselor is far superior to any form that is passed out in class, discussed generally, and taken home. In either case, simple concrete statements of all the information listed on the page should be used.

QUESTIONS AND ACTIVITIES

1. Suppose that, in your capacity as a ninth-grade homeroom teacher, you are confronted with the following situation:

Jim and his parents have requested a conference with you about his low grades. After checking into the situation, you find that Jim's aptitude and achievement test scores have been consistently around the 5th percentile. You find also that Jim's father is exerting tremendous pressure on him to make high grades so that he will be admitted to the prestige college from which his father graduated.

How would you handle the conference?

2. How would you explain the meaning of an I.Q. to a parent who insisted that it was an absolute measure of a person's innate intelligence?

3. What conclusions might you draw if one of your students, who had been doing very poorly on your teacher-made achievement tests, scored at the 98th percentile on a standardized achievement test in that subject?

4. It has been said that test scores discriminate among individuals only to the degree of above average, average, and below average. What is the basis of this statement?

SUGGESTED READINGS

Anderson, Scarvia B., *Interpreting Test Results Realistically,* Educational Testing Service, 1960.

This leaflet is a summary of the script written for the film of the same title. The teacher's understanding of test scores can be considerably improved by viewing the film and reading the leaflet. Both the film and leaflet are available free from ETS.

Clark, Robert, "The Intelligence Quotient," *Test Service Bulletin,* No. 77, Harcourt Brace Jovanovich, 1957.

This article is in the form of a question-and-answer interview. The questions are of great concern to teachers, and the answers are as direct and simple as the topic permits.

Davis, Frederick B., *Educational Measurements and Their Interpretation,* Wadsworth, 1964.
Chapters 2, 8, and 9 deal specifically with the meaning and interpretation of test scores.

Dion, Robert, "Norms Are Not Goals," *The Newsletter of the Elementary School Principals Association of Connecticut,* October, 1958.
This is an excellent discussion of the meaning of norms and the process of drawing samples.

Lenon, Roger T., "Scores and Norms," *Encyclopedia of Educational Research,* (4th ed.), Robert L. Ebel (ed.), Macmillan, 1969.
This article should be an excellent resource for the student wishing to pursue the topic in greater depth.

Lien, Arnold J. *Measurement and Evaluation of Learning: A Handbook for Teachers,* Brown, 1967.
Procedures and issues in reporting test information to pupils and parents are discussed in chapter 10. This is a treatment which any teacher should easily comprehend.

Lyman, Howard, *Test Scores and What They Mean* (2nd ed.) Prentice-Hall, 1971.
This is one of the most complete treatments of standardized test scores available.

McLaughlin, Kenneth, *Interpretation of Test Results,* U.S. Department of Health, Education, and Welfare, 1964.
This bulletin describes several procedures a teacher can use in analyzing a set of test scores. Concisely written on a level the average teacher can understand, it may be obtained from the Superintendent of Documents, Washington.

Seashore, Harold G., et al. (eds.), "On Telling Parents About Test Results," *Test Service Bulletin,* No. 54, Psychological Corporation, 1956.
An excellent discussion of the propriety and procedure of reporting test scores to parents.

APPENDIXES

A CONDENSED VERSION OF THE COGNITIVE DOMAIN OF THE TAXONOMY OF EDUCATIONAL OBJECTIVES

KNOWLEDGE

1.00 Knowledge

Knowledge, as defined here, involves the recall of specifics and universals, the recall of methods and processes, or the recall of a

From Benjamin S. Bloom (editor), Max D. Engelhart, Edward J. Furst, Walker H. Hill, and David R. Krathwohl, *Taxonomy of Educational Objectives, Handbook I: Cognitive Domain*, McKay, 1956, pp. 201-207.

pattern, structure, or setting. For measurement purposes, the recall situation involves little more than bringing to mind the appropriate material. Although some alteration of the material may be required, this is a relatively minor part of the task. The knowledge objectives emphasize most the psychological processes of remembering. The process of relating is also involved in that a knowledge test situation requires the organization and reorganization of a problem such that it will furnish the appropriate signals and cues for the information and knowledge the individual possesses. To use an analogy, if one thinks of the mind as a file, the problem in a knowledge test situation is that of finding in the problem or task the appropriate signals, cues, and clues which will most effectively bring out whatever knowledge is filed or stored.

1.10   Knowledge of specifics.

The recall of specific and isolable bits of information. The emphasis is on symbols with concrete referents. This material, which is at a very low level of abstraction, may be thought of as the elements from which more complex and abstract forms of knowledge are built.

1.11   *Knowledge of terminology.*   Knowledge of the referents for specific symbols (verbal and nonverbal). This may include knowledge of the most generally accepted symbol referent, knowledge of the variety of symbols which may be used for a single referent, or knowledge of the referent most appropriate to a given use of a symbol.

To define technical terms by giving their attributes, properties, or relations.

Familiarity with a large number of words in their common range of meanings.[1]

1.12   *Knowledge of specific facts.*   Knowledge of dates, events, persons, places, etc. This may include very precise and

---

[1]Each subcategory is followed by illustrative educational objectives selected from the literature.

specific information such as the specific date or exact magnitude of a phenomenon. It may also include approximate or relative information such as an approximate time period or the general order of magnitude of a phenomenon.

The recall of major facts about particular cultures.

The possession of a minimum knowledge about the organisms studied in the laboratory.

1.20 Knowledge of ways and means of dealing with specifics.

Knowledge of the ways of organizing, studying, judging, and criticizing. This includes the methods of inquiry, the chronological sequences, and the standards of judgment within a field as well as the patterns of organization through which the areas of the fields themselves are determined and internally organized. This knowledge is at an intermediate level of abstraction between specific knowledge on the one hand and knowledge of universals on the other. It does not so much demand the activity of the student in using the materials as it does a more passive awareness of their nature.

1.21 *Knowledge of conventions.*

Knowledge of characteristic ways of treating and presenting ideas and phenomena. For purposes of communication and consistency, workers in a field employ usages, styles, practices, and forms which best suit their purposes and/or which appear to suit best the phenomena with which they deal. It should be recognized that although these forms and conventions are likely to be set up on arbitrary, accidental, or authoritative bases, they are retained because of the general agreement or concurrence of individuals concerned with the subject, phenomena, or problem.

Familiarity with the forms and conventions of the major types of works; e.g., verse, plays, scientific papers, etc.

To make pupils conscious of correct form and usage in speech and writing.

1.22 *Knowledge of trends and sequences.*   Knowledge of the processes, directions, and movements of phenomena with respect to time.

Understanding of the continuity and development of American culture as exemplified in American life.

Knowledge of the basic trends underlying the development of public assistance programs.

1.23 *Knowledge of classifications and categories.*   Knowledge of the classes, sets, divisions, and arrangements that are regarded as fundamental for a given subject field, purpose, argument, or problem.

To recognize the area encompassed by various kinds of problems or materials.

Becoming familiar with a range of types of literature.

1.24 *Knowledge of criteria.*   Knowledge of the criteria by which facts, principles, opinions, and conduct are tested or judged.

Familiarity with criteria for judgment appropriate to the type of work and the purpose for which it is read.

Knowledge of criteria for the evaluation of recreational activities.

1.25 *Knowledge of methodology.*   Knowledge of the methods of inquiry, techniques, and procedures employed in a particular subject field as well as those employed in investigating particular problems and phenomena. The emphasis here is on the individual's knowledge of the method rather than his ability to use the method.

Knowledge of scientific methods for evaluating health concepts.

The student shall know the methods of attack relevant to the kinds of problems of concern to the social sciences.

1.30   Knowledge of the universals and
abstractions in a field

Knowledge of the major schemes and patterns by which phenomena and ideas are organized. These are the large structures, theories, and generalizations which dominate a subject field or which are quite generally used in studying phenomena or solving problems. These are at the highest levels of abstraction and complexity.

1.31   *Knowledge of principles and generalizations.*   Knowledge of particular abstractions which summarize observations of phenomena. These are the abstractions which are of value in explaining, describing, predicting, or in determining the most appropriate and relevant action or direction to be taken.

Knowledge of the important principles by which our experience with biological phenomena is summarized.

The recall of major generalizations about particular cultures.

1.32   *Knowledge of theories and structures.*   Knowledge of the *body* of principles and generalizations together with their interrelations which present a clear, rounded, and systematic view of a complex phenomenon, problem, or field. These are the most abstract formulations, and they can be used to show the interrelation and organization of a great range of specifics.

The recall of major theories about particular cultures.

Knowledge of a relatively complete formulation of the theory of evolution.

INTELLECTUAL ABILITIES AND SKILLS

Abilities and skills refer to organized modes of operation and generalized techniques for dealing with materials and problems.

The materials and problems may be of such a nature that little or no specialized and technical information is required. Such information as is required can be assumed to be part of the individual's general fund of knowledge. Other problems may require specialized and technical information at a rather high level such that specific knowledge and skill in dealing with the problem and the materials are required. The abilities and skills objectives emphasize the mental processes of organizing and reorganizing material to achieve a particular purpose. The materials may be given or remembered.

2.00   Comprehension

This represents the lowest level of understanding. It refers to a type of understanding or apprehension such that the individual knows what is being communicated and can make use of the material or idea being communicated without necessarily relating it to other material or seeing its fullest implications.

2.10   Translation.

Comprehension as evidenced by the care and accuracy with which the communication is paraphrased or rendered from one language or form of communication to another. Translation is judged on the basis of faithfulness and accuracy; that is, on the extent to which the material in the original communication is preserved although the form of the communication has been altered.

The ability to understand nonliteral statements (metaphor, symbolism, irony, exaggeration).

Skill in translating mathematical verbal material into symbolic statements are vice versa.

2.20   Interpretation.

The explanation or summarization of a communication. Whereas translation involves an objective part-for-part rendering of a communication, interpretation involves a reordering, rearrangement, or new view of the material.

The ability to grasp the thought of the work as a whole at any desired level of generality.

The ability to interpret various types of social data.

2.30   Extrapolation.

The extension of trends or tendencies beyond the given data to determine implications, consequences, corollaries, effects, etc., which are in accordance with the conditions described in the original communication.

The ability to deal with the conclusions of a work in terms of the immediate inference made from the explicit statements.

Skill in predicting continuation of trends.

3.00   Application

The use of abstractions in particular and concrete situations. The abstractions may be in the form of general ideas, rules of procedures, or generalized methods. The abstractions may also be technical principles, ideas, and theories which must be remembered and applied.

Application to the phenomena discussed in one paper of the scientific terms or concepts used in other papers.

The ability to predict the probable effect of a change in a factor on a biological situation previously at equilibrium.

4.00   Analysis

The breakdown of a communication into its constituent elements or parts such that the relative hierarchy of ideas is made clear and/or the relations between the ideas expressed are made explicit. Such analyses are intended to clarify the communication, to indicate how the communication is organized, and the way in which it manages to convey its effects, as well as its basis and arrangement.

4.10   Analysis of elements.

Identification of the elements included in a communication.
    The ability to recognize unstated assumptions.
    Skill in distinguishing facts from hypotheses.

4.20   Analysis of relationships.

The connections and interactions between elements and parts of a communication.
    Ability to check the consistency of hypotheses with given information and assumptions.
    Skill in comprehending the interrelationships among the ideas in a passage.

4.30   Analysis of organizational principles.

The organization, systematic arrangement, and structure which hold the communication together. This includes the "explicit" as well as "implicit" structure. It includes the bases, necessary arrangement, and mechanics which make the communication a unit.
    The ability to recognize form and pattern in literary or artistic works as a means of understanding their meaning.
    Ability to recognize the general techniques used in persuasive materials, such as advertising, propaganda, etc.

5.00   Synthesis

The putting together of elements and parts so as to form a whole. This involves the process of working with pieces, parts, elements, etc., and arranging and combining them in such a way as to constitute a pattern or structure not clearly there before.

5.10   Production of a unique communication.

The development of a communication in which the writer or speaker attempts to convey ideas, feelings, and/or experiences to others.

Skill in writing, using an excellent organization of ideas and statements.

Ability to tell a personal experience effectively.

5.20   Production of a plan, or proposed set of operations.

The development of a plan of work or the proposal of a plan of operations. The plan should satisfy requirements of the task which may be given to the student or which he may develop for himself.

Ability to propose ways of testing hypotheses.

Ability to plan a unit of instruction for a particular teaching situation.

5.30   Derivation of a set of abstract relations.

The development of a set of abstract relations either to classify or explain particular data or phenomena, or the deduction of propositions and relations from a set of basic propositions or symbolic representations.

Ability to formulate appropriate hypotheses based upon an analysis of factors involved, and to modify such hypotheses in the light of new factors and considerations.

Ability to make mathematical discoveries and generalizations.

6.00   Evaluation

Judgments about the value of material and methods for given purposes. Quantitative and qualitative judgments about the extent to which material and methods satisfy criteria. Use of a standard of appraisal. The criteria may be those determined by the student or those which are given to him.

6.10   Judgments in terms of internal evidence.

Evaluation of the accuracy of a communication from such evidence as logical accuracy, consistency, and other internal criteria.

Judging by internal standards, the ability to assess general probability of accuracy in reporting facts from the care given to exactness of statement, documentation, proof, etc.

The ability to indicate logical fallacies in arguments.

6.20   Judgments in terms of external criteria.

Evaluation of material with reference to selected or remembered criteria.

The comparison of major theories, generalizations, and facts about particular cultures.

Judging by external standards, the ability to compare a work with the highest known standards in its field—especially with other works of recognized excellence.

B

A CONDENSED VERSION OF THE AFFECTIVE DOMAIN OF THE TAXONOMY OF EDUCATIONAL OBJECTIVES

1.0 Receiving (Attending)

At this level we are concerned that the learner be sensitized to the existence of certain phenomena and stimuli; that is, that he be willing to receive or to attend to them. This is clearly the first and crucial step if the learner is to be properly oriented to learn what

From David R. Krathwohl, Benjamin S. Bloom, and Bertram B. Masia, *Taxonomy of Educational Objectives, Handbook II: Affective Domain,* McKay, 1964, pp. 176-185.

the teacher intends that he will. To indicate that this is the bottom rung of the ladder, however, is not at all to imply that the teacher is starting *de novo*. Because of previous experience (formal or informal), the student brings to each situation a point of view or set which may facilitate or hinder his recognition of the phenomena to which the teacher is trying to sensitize him.

The category of *Receiving* has been divided into three subcategories to indicate three different levels of attending to phenomena. While the division points between the subcategories are arbitrary, the subcategories do represent a continuum. From an extremely passive position or role on the part of the learner, where the sole responsibility for the evocation of the behavior rests with the teacher—that is, the responsibility rests with him for "capturing" the student's attention—the continuum extends to a point at which the learner directs his attention, at least at a semiconscious level, toward the preferred stimuli.

1.1 Awareness

Awareness is almost a cognitive behavior. But unlike *Knowledge,* the lowest level of the cognitive domain, we are not so much concerned with a memory of, or ability to recall, an item or fact as we are that, given appropriate opportunity, the learner will merely be conscious of something—that he take into account a situation, phenomenon, object, or state of affairs. Like *Knowledge* it does not imply an assessment of the qualities or nature of the stimulus, but unlike *Knowledge* it does not necessarily imply attention. There can be simple awareness without specific discrimination or recognition of the objective characteristics of the object, even though these characteristics must be deemed to have an effect. The individual may not be able to verbalize the aspects of the stimulus which cause the awareness.

Develops awareness of aesthetic factors in dress, furnishings, architecture, city design, good art, and the like.

Develops some consciousness of color, form, arrangement, and design in the objects and structures around him and in descriptive or symbolic representations of people, things, and situations.[1]

1.2   Willingness to receive

In this category we have come a step up the ladder but are still dealing with what appears to be cognitive behavior. At a minimum level, we are here describing the behavior of being willing to tolerate a given stimulus, not to avoid it. Like *Awareness,* it involves a neutrality or suspended judgment toward the stimulus. At this level of the continuum the teacher is not concerned that the student seek it out, nor even, perhaps, that in an environment crowded with many other stimuli the learner will necessarily attend to the stimulus. Rather, at worst, given the opportunity to attend in a field with relatively few competing stimuli, the learner is not actively seeking to avoid it. At best, he is willing to take notice of the phenomenon and give it his attention.

Attends (carefully) when others speak—in direct conversation, on the telephone, in audiences.

Appreciation (tolerance) of cultural patterns exhibited by individuals from other groups—religious, social, political, economic, national, etc.

Increase in sensitivity to human need and pressing social problems.

1.3 Controlled or selected attention

At a somewhat higher level we are concerned with a new phenomenon, the differentiation of a given stimulus into figure and

---

[1]Illustrative objectives selected from the literature follow the description of each subcategory.

ground at a conscious or perhaps semiconscious level—the differentiation of aspects of a stimulus which is perceived as clearly marked off from adjacent impressions. The perception is still without tension or assessment, and the student may not know the technical terms or symbols with which to describe it correctly or precisely to others. In some instances it may refer not so much to the selectivity of attention as to the control of attention, so that when certain stimuli are present they will be attended to. There is an element of the learner's controlling the attention here, so that the favored stimulus is selected and attended to despite competing and distracting stimuli.

Listens to music with some discrimination as to its mood and meaning and with some recognition of the contributions of various musical elements and instruments to the total effect.

Alertness toward human values and judgments on life as they are recorded in literature.

2.0   Responding

At this level we are concerned with responses which go beyond merely attending to the phenomenon. The student is sufficiently motivated that he is not just *1.2 Willing to attend,* but perhaps it is correct to say that he is actively attending. As a first stage in a "learning by doing" process the student is committing himself in some small measure to the phenomena involved. This is a very low level of commitment, and we would not say at this level that this was "a value of his" or that he had "such and such an attitude." These terms belong to the next higher level that we describe. But we could say that he is doing something with or about the phenomenon besides merely perceiving it, as would be true at the next level below this of *1.3 Controlled or selected attention.*

This is the category that many teachers will find best describes their "interest" objectives. Most commonly we use the term to indicate the desire that a child become sufficiently involved in or committed to a subject, phenomenon, or activity that he will seek it out and gain satisfaction from working with it or engaging in it.

2.1 Acquiescence in responding

We might use the word "obedience" or "compliance" to describe this behavior. As both of these terms indicate, there is a passiveness so far as the initiation of the behavior is concerned, and the stimulus calling for this behavior is not subtle. Compliance is perhaps a better term than obedience, since there is more of the element of reaction to a suggestion and less of the implication of resistance or yielding unwillingly. The student makes the response, but he has not fully accepted the necessity for doing so.

Willingness to comply with health regulations.

Obeys playground regulations.

2.2 Willingness to respond

The key to this level is in the term "willingness," with its implication of capacity for voluntary activity. There is the implication that the learner is sufficiently committed to exhibiting the behavior that he does so not just because of a fear of punishment, but "on his own" or voluntarily. It may help to note that the element of resistance or of yielding unwillingly, which is possibly present at the previous level, is here replaced with consent or proceeding from one's own choice.

Acquaints himself with significant current issues in international, political, social, and economic affairs through voluntary reading and discussion.

Acceptance of responsibility for his own health and for the protection of the health of others.

2.3 Satisfaction in response

The additional element in the step beyond the *Willingness to respond* level, the consent, the assent to responding, or the voluntary response, is that the behavior is accompanied by a feeling of satisfaction, an emotional response, generally of pleasure, zest, or enjoyment. The location of this category in the hierarchy has given us a great deal of difficulty. Just where in the process of internalization the attachment of an emotional response, kick, or thrill to a behavior occurs has been hard to determine. For that matter there is some uncertainty as to whether the level of internalization at which it occurs may not depend on the particular behavior. We have even questioned whether it should be a category. If our structure is to be a hierarchy, then each category should include the behavior in the next level below it. The emotional component appears gradually through the range of internalization categories. The attempt to specify a given position in the hierarchy as *the* one at which the emotional component is added is doomed to failure.

The category is arbitrarily placed at this point in the hierarchy where it seems to appear most frequently and where it is cited as or appears to be an important component of the objectives at this level on the continuum. The category's inclusion at this point serves the pragmatic purpose of reminding us of the presence of the emotional component and its value in the building of affective behaviors. But it should not be thought of as appearing and occurring at this one point in the continuum and thus destroying the hierarchy which we are attempting to build.

Enjoyment of self-expression in music and in arts and crafts as another means of personal enrichment.

Finds pleasure in reading for recreation.

Takes pleasure in conversing with many different kinds of people.

3.0   Valuing

This is the only category headed by a term which is in common use in the expression of objectives by teachers. Further, it is employed in its usual sense: that a thing, phenomenon, or behavior has worth. This abstract concept of worth is in part a result of the individual's own valuing or assessment, but it is much more a social product that has been slowly internalized or accepted and has come to be used by the student as his own criterion of worth.

Behavior categorized at this level is sufficiently consistent and stable to have taken on the characteristics of a belief or an attitude. The learner displays this behavior with sufficient consistency in appropriate situations that he comes to be perceived as holding a value. At this level, we are not concerned with the relationships among values but rather with the internalization of a set of specified, ideal, values. Viewed from another standpoint, the objectives classified here are the prime stuff from which the conscience of the individual is developed into active control of behavior.

This category will be found appropriate for many objectives that use the term "attitude" (as well as, of course, "value").

An important element of behavior characterized by *Valuing* is that it is motivated, not by the desire to comply or obey, but by the individual's commitment to the underlying value guiding the behavior.

3.1 Acceptance of a value

At this level we are concerned with the ascribing of worth to a phenomenon, behavior, object, etc. The term "belief," which is defined as "the emotional acceptance of a proposition or doctrine upon what one implicitly considers adequate ground" (English and English, 1958, p. 64), describes quite well what may be thought of as the dominant characteristic here. Beliefs have varying degrees of certitude. At this lowest level of *Valuing* we are concerned with the lowest levels of certainty; that is, there is more of a readiness to re-evaluate one's position than at the higher levels. It is a position that is somewhat tentative.

One of the distinguishing characteristics of this behavior is consistency of response to the class of objects, phenomena, etc. with which the belief or attitude is identified. It is consistent enough so that the person is perceived by others as holding the belief or value. At the level we are describing here, he is both sufficiently consistent that others can identify the value, and sufficiently committed that he is willing to be so identified.

Continuing desire to develop the ability to speak and write effectively.

Grows in his sense of kinship with human beings of all nations.

3.2 Preference for a value

The provision for this subdivision arose out of a feeling that there were objectives that expressed a level of internalization between the mere acceptance of a value and commitment or conviction in the usual connotation of deep involvement in an area. Behavior at this level implies not just the acceptance of a value to the point of being willing to be identified with it, but the individual is sufficiently committed to the value to pursue it, to seek it out, to want it.

Assumes responsibility for drawing reticent members of a group into conversation.

Deliberately examines a variety of viewpoints on controversial issues with a view to forming opinions about them.

Actively participates in arranging for the showing of contemporary artistic efforts.

3.3 Commitment

Belief at this level involves a high degree of certainty. The ideas of "conviction" and "certainty beyond a shadow of a doubt" help to convey further the level of behavior intended. In some instances this may border on faith, in the sense of it being a firm emotional acceptance of a belief upon admittedly nonrational grounds. Loyalty to a position, group, or cause would also be classified here.

The person who displays behavior at this level is clearly perceived as holding the value. He acts to further the thing valued in some way, to extend the possibility of his developing it, to deepen his involvement with it and with the things representing it. He tries to convince others and seeks converts to his cause. There is a tension here which needs to be satisfied; action is the result of an aroused need or drive. There is a real motivation to act out the behavior.

Devotion to those ideas and ideals which are the foundations of democracy.

Faith in the power of reason and in methods of experiment and discussion.

4.0   Organization

As the learner successively internalizes values, he encounters situations for which more than one value is relevant. Thus, necessity arises for (a) the organization of the values into a system, (b) the determination of the interrelationships among them, and (c) the establishment of the dominant and pervasive ones. Such a system is built gradually, subject to change as new values are incorporated. This category is intended as the proper classification for objectives which describe the beginnings of the building of a value system. It is subdivided into two levels, since a prerequisite to interrelating is the conceptualization of the value in a form which permits organization. *Conceptualization* forms the first subdivision in the organization process, *Organization of a value system* the second.

While the order of the two subcategories seems appropriate enough with reference to one another, it is not so certain that *4.1 Conceptualization of a value* is properly placed as the next level above *3.3 Commitment.* Conceptualization undoubtedly begins at an earlier level for some objectives. Like *2.3 Satisfaction in response,* it is doubtful that a single completely satisfactory location for this category can be found. Positioning it before *4.2 Organization of a value system* appropriately indicates a prerequisite of such a system. It also calls attention to a component of affective growth that occurs at least by this point on the continuum but may begin earlier.

4.1 Conceptualization of a value

In the previous category, *3.0 Valuing,* we noted that consistency and stability are integral characteristics of the particular value or belief. At this level (*4.1*) the quality of abstraction or conceptualization is added. This permits the individual to see how the value relates to those that he already holds or to new ones that he is coming to hold.

Conceptualization will be abstract, and in this sense it will be symbolic. But the symbols need not be verbal symbols. Whether conceptualization first appears at this point on the affective continuum is a moot point, as noted above.

Attempts to identify the characteristics of an art object which he admires.

Forms judgments as to the responsibility of society for conserving human and material resources.

4.2 Organization of a value system

Objectives properly classified here are those which require the learner to bring together a complex of values, possibly disparate values, and to bring these into an ordered relationship with one another. Ideally, the ordered relationship will be one which is harmonious and internally consistent. This is, of course, the goal of such objectives, which seek to have the student formulate a philosophy of life. In actuality, the integration may be something less than entirely harmonious. More likely the relationship is better described as a kind of dynamic equilibrium which is, in part, dependent upon those portions of the environment which are salient at any point in time. In many instances the organization of values may result in their synthesis into a new value or value complex of a higher order.

Weighs alternative social policies and practices against the standards of the public welfare rather than the advantage of specialized and narrow interest groups.

Develops a plan for regulating his rest in accordance with the demands of his activities.

5.0   Characterization by a value or value complex

At this level of internalization the values already have a place in the individual's value hierarchy, are organized into some kind of internally consistent system, have controlled the behavior of the individual for a sufficient time that he has adapted to behaving this way; and an evocation of the behavior no longer arouses emotion or affect except when the individual is threatened or challenged.

The individual acts consistently in accordance with the values he has internalized at this level, and our concern is to indicate two things: (a) the generalization of this control to so much of the individual's behavior that he is described and characterized as a person by these pervasive controlling tendencies and (b) the integration of these beliefs, ideas, and attitudes into a total philosophy or world view. These two aspects constitute the subcategories.

5.1 Generalized set

The generalized set is that which gives an internal consistency to the system of attitudes and values at any particular moment. It is selective responding at a very high level. It is sometimes spoken of as a determining tendency, an orientation toward phenomena, or a predisposition to act in a certain way. The generalized set is a response to highly generalized phenomena. It is a persistent and consistent response to a family of related situations or objects. It may often be an unconscious set which guides action without conscious forethought. The generalized set may be thought of as closely related to the idea of an attitude cluster, where the commonality is based on behavioral characteristics rather than the subject or object of the attitude. A generalized set is a basic orientation which enables the individual to reduce and order the complex world about him and to act consistently and effectively in it.

Readiness to revise judgments and to change behavior in the light of evidence.

Judges problems and issues in terms of situations, issues, purposes, and consequences involved rather than in terms of fixed, dogmatic precepts of emotionally wishful thinking.

5.2 Characterization

This, the peak of the internalization process, includes those objectives which are broadest with respect both to the phenomena covered and to the range of behavior which they comprise. Thus, here are found those objectives which concern one's view of the universe, one's philosophy of life, one's *Weltanschauung*—a value system having as its object the whole of what is known or knowable.

Objectives categorized here are more than generalized sets in the sense that they involve a greater inclusiveness and, within the group of attitudes, behaviors, beliefs, or ideas, an emphasis on internal consistency. Though this internal consistency may not always be exhibited behaviorally by the students toward whom the objective is directed, since we are categorizing teachers' objectives, this consistency feature will always be a component of *Characterization* objectives.

As the title of the category implies, these objectives are so encompassing that they tend to characterize the individual almost completely.

Develops for regulation of one's personal and civic life a code of behavior based on ethical principles consistent with democratic ideals.

Develops a consistent philosophy of life.

INDEX

72 73 74 75 76   9 8 7 6 5 4 3 2 1

LIBRARY
L.S.U. IN SHREVEPORT